NATIONAL INSTITUTE SOCIAL SERVICES LIBRARY
NO. 47

PROBLEMS, TASKS AND OUTCOMES

National Institute Social Services Library

PROBLEMS, TASKS AND OUTCOMES

The evaluation of task-centered casework in three settings

E. Matilda Goldberg
Jane Gibbons
Ian Sinclair

London
GEORGE ALLEN & UNWIN
Boston   Sydney

George Allen & Unwin (Publishers) Ltd,
40 Museum Street, London WC1A 1LU, UK

George Allen & Unwin (Publishers) Ltd,
Park Lane, Hemel Hempstead, Herts HP2 4TE, UK

Allen & Unwin, Inc.,
Fifty Cross Street, Winchester, Mass. 01890, USA

George Allen & Unwin Australia Pty Ltd,
8 Napier Street, North Sydney, NSW 2060, Australia

First published in 1985.

British Library Cataloguing in Publication Data

Goldberg, Matilda E.
    Problems, tasks and outcomes.—(National Institute social services library; no.47)
1. Social case work
I. Title   II. Gibbons, Jane
III. Sinclair, Ian,   IV. Series
361.3'2   HV43
ISBN 0-04-361053-6

Library of Congress Cataloging in Publication Data

Goldberg, E. Matilda (Elsa Matilda)
    Problems, tasks, and outcomes.
(National Institute social services library; no. 47)
Includes index.
1. Social case work—Case studies.   2. Social service—Great Britain—Case studies.   I. Gibbons, Jane.   II. Sinclair, Ian, 1938-
III. Title.   IV. Series.
HV43.G59 1984   361.6'2'0941   84-12361
ISBN 0-04-361053-6 (alk. paper)

Set in 10 on 11 point Times by Setrite
and printed in Great Britain
by Billing and Sons Ltd, London and Worcester

1985

CONTENTS

INTRODUCTION

This book presents three studies of a specific type of focused casework, which has been termed 'task-centred'. Why bother to produce yet another book on casework at a time when 'community social work' holds the centre of attention and there is a general disillusionment with casework? This is the question with which our introduction is primarily concerned.

Throughout the past decade or more there has been a growing uncertainty about what social workers do, how effective they are, what they ought to do and the training they need. These doubts culminated in the setting up of the Barclay Committee on 'The social worker's role and tasks' (Barclay, 1982). This report roughly divides the functions of social workers into 'counselling' and 'social care planning'. Like the earlier Seebohm Report, it makes a strong case for community-based social work, seeing the social worker as supporting other formal and informal groups and as a co-ordinator of services, rather than primarily as a direct case worker. Many recent studies of social work come to similar conclusions (Goldberg and Warburton, 1979; Challis and Davies, 1980; Hadley and McGrath, 1984; Black *et al.*, 1983). These studies took place in both urban and rural areas, and some show clearly that social workers in local authority social services departments spend a great deal of their time on social-care planning in the Barclay sense, namely, on assessment, on providing information, advice and advocacy and on mobilising practical help. The discovery that 'social care planning' occupies such a central place in the duties of social workers may have come as a surprise to many people, since until recently social work was considered to be almost synonymous with casework.

However, the studies quoted above also indicate that social services departments are still involved in counselling and casework, particularly with children and families. Moreover, many of their activities which have not been traditionally regarded as casework (for example, providing advice) can be informed by an understanding of how the client feels and by other skills and attitudes associated with counselling. In other settings, such as voluntary casework agencies, probation or primary health care, appreciably more time is taken up by casework or counselling. Hence casework is still a significant component of social work and research into its nature and effects is still required.

THE EFFECTIVENESS OF SOCIAL CASEWORK

Until well into the 1970s most of the literature on social work was concerned with unravelling the mysteries of a form of casework which was greatly influenced by often half-digested psychoanalytic theory and practice. The main emphasis of this type of casework was on the exploration of motives and of the early life experiences which were held to be responsible for the clients' current problems in living. The main aim was the achievement of insight into these chains of causative events and eventual recognition of how they were affecting current behaviour and relationships.

It is well known that the results of a number of research studies have thrown doubts on the efficacy of such counselling with its dominant concern with individual psychopathology. Many reasons have been advanced for the failure to show that it has any demonstrable effects on the behaviour and attitudes of clients. The vagueness of the goals pursued made the establishment of criteria for success or failure almost impossible. It was very difficult to describe precisely what actually went on in the encounter between clients and workers; casework often proved to be an inappropriate method of treatment in situations where environmental influences needed tackling. In any case, the achievement of insight or self-understanding did not necessarily lead to knowledge of how to bring about change. In these circumstances measurement of changes in behaviour, inter-personal relationships, or in environmental conditions did not seem appropriate.

The methodology of these studies endeavouring to measure the outcomes of casework has also been criticised: they often relied on group comparisons which masked individual variations; criteria used in measuring differences were irrelevant to the finer qualitative nuances of the interaction between worker and client and their impact on the clients' feelings, attitudes and behaviour. These criticisms were aptly summarised in a radio talk by Clifford Yorke (1982): 'They attempted to measure what is immeasurable.' The debate continues.

As we have seen, despite its failure to show any appreciable measurable effect, casework with individuals and families continues to occupy a place in social work in both statutory and voluntary agencies. This is readily understandable since many people experience crises in their personal and family relationships, have to learn to cope with disabilities either in themselves or in a member of their family, or through their deviant behaviour offend law-abiding people. The challenge, as we see it, is not to retreat from the practice of casework altogether and to attempt to transform the whole of the social work effort into community social work (the Barclay Report does not suggest this either), but:

(1) to become more specific about the elements that constitute so-called community social work and about the situations in which such an approach is appropriate; and
(2) to tackle afresh the role of social casework within this wider spectrum of social work and to tease out its properties, possibilities and limits.

This second step will almost certainly mean that claims about the effectiveness of casework, which in the past have been rather vague, speculative and ambitious, will need to be scaled down to more modest propositions. In order to arrive at testable propositions we shall need more clarity about the aims of casework, the problems it tackles and the methods it uses.

In more recent studies of the effectiveness of social casework there is already a detectable tendency for greater specificity about problems, objectives and methods. Reid and Hanrahan (1981) reviewed eighteen controlled experimental studies of direct social work intervention carried out in the United States and Canada between 1973 and 1979. They found that practice usually consisted of 'well-organised procedures usually carried out in a stepwise manner and designed to achieve relatively specific goals' (p. 12). Targets were more circum-scribed than in earlier studies and the researchers had more control over the experimental variables since they usually planned the inter-ventions and took responsibility for their implementation, although they did not carry them out themselves. The researchers usually looked for outcome data on observations of client behaviour, and did not attempt to measure such concepts as ego strength and improved social functioning. The most striking difference from earlier evaluative research was that the outcomes of most of these eighteen studies were positive to some degree. Although the interventions were often unambitious and their practical effect limited, Reid and his colleague suggest that 'these small successes of the present are better than the grand failures of the past' (p. 17). The authors conclude that behavioural contracting and task-centred methods in which the practitioner secures from clients commitments to undertake specific problem-solving actions as a voluntary collaborator are particularly promising.

ORIGINS OF TASK-CENTRED CASEWORK

The ideas put forward by Reid and Hanrahan had already been

exemplified in the development of task-centred casework. This method is intended to make a significant contribution to casework and group work and, in principle, also to community work through an insistence on specification of the target problems considered relevant by both client and helper, and through an emphasis on the formulation of feasible objectives and tasks to be carried out by the client and helper to achieve these objectives. This striving towards explicitness by both actors about problem, ends and means makes the method accessible to measurement of input and outcome from the point of view of the client, the practitioner and, in a research context, an independent assessor or observer.

The development of task-centred casework sprang from Reid and Shyne's experiment entitled *Brief and Extended Casework* (1969) which aimed at assessing the relative effectiveness of two different patterns of casework in alleviating family problems: planned short-term service limited to eight interviews and open-ended long-term service lasting up to eighteen months. To the surprise of everybody (including the workers themselves) the families receiving planned short-term service progressed on the researchers' measures more than similar families who had long-term treatment; these results held for the follow-up period as well as for the assessment carried out at the end of the treatment. The differences occurred mainly in the slightly improved categories, but remarkably in most of the comparisons a consistently higher proportion of continued service cases showed deterioration. These suggestions of a law of diminishing returns have been echoed in other studies of treatment, including probation. For example, in the IMPACT experiment reconviction rates were lower than expected in one-year orders and significantly higher than expected in three-year orders (Folkard *et al.*, 1976).

The analysis of the tape-recorded interviews in the Reid and Shyne study showed that in short-term treatment social workers used more techniques directed towards promoting change, less passive exploration and more active intervention than in long-term treatment. The clients preferred the active style and expressed more positive feelings about the social workers. Reid and Shyne suggested that the immediacy, sharpness and urgency of short-term work lead, in comparison with long-term help, to less improvisation and drift and more selectivity in treatment objectives, more focus on realisable goals and less concentration on unalterable underlying causes. Furthermore, the 'set' was different from the very beginning: clients accepted that change would occur within a brief period.

Following this experiment Reid and his colleague Laura Epstein went on to develop the elements that seemed to be responsible for the success of planned, brief casework into a more systematic and goal-oriented framework which they called 'task-centred' (Reid and Epstein, 1972).

WHAT IS TASK-CENTRED CASEWORK?

In essence, task-centred casework is a method of social work in which clients are helped to carry out problem-alleviating tasks within agreed periods of time. The approach concentrates on limited achievable goals and pays more attention than is customary in traditional social work to the clients' conceptions of their problems and their possible solutions.

The underlying theory of this practice model is akin to crisis theory, namely that the temporary breakdown in problem-coping triggers off corrective change forces. These forces, it is postulated, operate quickly to reduce problems to a tolerable level, after which the client's motivation for further change lessens. Setting limits in advance may increase and quicken these processes of change in two ways: by providing a deadline against which both client and practitioner must work, and by heightening expectations that certain changes can occur within the time limit.

EIGHT PROBLEM AREAS

Since the problem the client identifies and wishes to work on is the centrepiece of task-centred method, a problem typology was developed by Reid which summarises eight situations commonly presented by clients to social workers:

(1) Inter-personal conflict
(2) Dissatisfaction in social relations
(3) Problems with formal organisations
(4) Difficulties in role performance
(5) Problems of social transition
(6) Reactive emotional distress
(7) Inadequate resources
(8) Behavioural problems

These categories describe problem situations rather than client types.

FIVE PHASES

The social worker's role in task-centred casework is to help the client to identify the problems he is most anxious to resolve, formulate to a modest achievable goal or task, and to help him to achieve it. The method has approximately five phases.

The *initial* phase is that of problem exploration, in which the problems of concern to the client are elicited and clarified, if possible defined in explicit behavioural terms, and ranked in order of importance to the client. This problem exploration can be extensive, and the target area chosen is not usually the first problem presented.

At the *second* stage an agreement is reached with the client on the target problem to be tackled, which is then classified by the worker under one of the eight headings.

In the *third* phase the client and social worker decide what is to be done to alleviate the problem; and tasks – representing an immediate objective to be pursued – are formulated. Agreement is then reached on the amount and duration of the social worker's involvement. This duration does not usually exceed three months, with interviews generally occurring on a weekly basis.

Thereafter, during the *fourth* phase, the techniques and strategies of the social worker are directed towards facilitating the achievement of the tasks. There is no prescribed method for doing this, and the worker is free to be imaginative and spontaneous, although the need to maintain a focus on the task inevitably entails less exploration and more direction than is usual in traditional casework.

The setting of time limits at the beginning implies an agreement about termination, which is the *fifth* phase. In the last interview the worker explores once more, with the client, the original nature of his problem; they review what has been done about it, and how much has been achieved. The contributions of both client and worker are examined, and the client's ability to cope in the future assessed.

As will be discussed later, certain aspects of the model had to be adapted to the judicial requirements of a probation setting.

THE BACKGROUND OF THE THREE STUDIES

One of us, after carrying out an experiment in social work with elderly people about the same time as Reid and Shyne were engaged in their experimental study, came to somewhat similar and complementary conclusions; for example, in testing the relative effectiveness of social work carried out by trained and untrained workers the findings suggested that the trained workers (whose supervision was strongly focused on definition of aims and problems to be tackled) were more able to deploy their skills and methods of intervention differentially in relation to different problems than the workers without formal training. The results also showed that a combination of practical help and casework can lead – even among very elderly people – not only to a reduction of practical needs, but also to improvement in social and psychological functioning (Goldberg *et al.*, 1970). This focus on concrete practical problems as well as feelings and attitudes is also found in the task-centred method which, while concentrating on the achievement of specific concrete tasks, seeks to be alert to, and deal with, feelings and attitudes which appear to hinder progress. Stimulated by Reid and Shyne's and Reid and Epstein's work and the results of her study Tilda Goldberg began to explore the task-centred method with an area team in Buckinghamshire (Goldberg *et al.*, 1977).

The small Buckinghamshire study produced some hypotheses which are confirmed by the projects reported in this volume: for instance, the method was found to be only applicable to a minority of social work clients. There were clients who did not acknowledge the existence of problems or, if they did, expected others to change or who were victims of a destructive environment. Further, the social services departments, like the probation service, carried surveillance and protective functions, for example, on behalf of children at risk of being neglected or abused, or for delinquents. In these situations a target problem could be clearly perceived by the referrer or the neighbours, but was not necessarily acknowledged by the clients or their families and hence was not amenable to task-centred casework. The method – in common with other casework methods – also proved unsuccessful with clients who had deeply ingrained and complex chronic problems in living. However, the study also pointed to positive gains of the method which too became apparent in the projects reported in this book: for example, more clarity of thinking and forward planning for individual cases on the part of social workers, greater independence and participation by clients, discouragement of aimless 'visiting', an increase of self-confidence experienced by clients through the achievements of small, recognisable objectives and a lessening of feelings of unease by social workers about their inability to resolve the whole multitude of problems that beset their clients.

The pilot study seemed promising enough to warrant further systematic testing of the task-centred model in social services departments as well as other settings. The intention was to introduce and evaluate the method in a probation setting, in intake teams of social services departments, in a general hospital setting, and in a voluntary casework agency. As in the pilot study, it was necessary to induct social workers into the aims and techniques of task-centred casework in order to research the method itself.

In all these settings the work was to be experimental, in the sense that a new method was being applied and tested rather than in the sense of an experimental research design which allocates cases randomly to similar experimental and control groups and then compares outcomes. Such designs are usually only worthwhile when the treatment to be evaluated is understood in some detail and fairly precise hypotheses can be formulated about its method of operation and expected outcomes. The projects in the four settings therefore used simple before and after designs, in which an attempt was made to compare the state of the clients' problems before and after casework as seen by the clients themselves, the social workers and an outside observer. In the probation setting it was also possible to use the independent outcome measure of reconviction. The overall aim was to see what happened when the task-centred method was applied in different settings which served different types of clients and operated under different time pressures. It was also hoped to establish more firmly the type of clients for whom the method seemed suitable, the type of workers who seemed comfortable and successful in applying the method and the types of problems that could reasonably be tackled by this form of intervention. From such a base it was intended to develop more sharply focused experimental studies.

An early discovery was that the task-centred method was difficult to apply in a busy general hospital setting and – somewhat surprisingly in view of the American experience – in a voluntary casework agency. In the hospital, social workers were mainly concerned with practical arrangements and emergency work which did not lend itself to deliberate planning. The clients' movements were determined by their medical rather than their social needs. Although the hospital workers were interested in the method and reported some success with it, it proved impossible to assemble an adequate sample of cases for research. The workers in the voluntary agency appeared to be deeply committed to the exploratory, insight-seeking method of casework and were not basically prepared to limit themselves to a specific problem area and to mutually agreed specific tasks. They found the more business-like approach of the task-centred method hard to adopt. Here, too, it proved impossible to acquire an adequate sample of cases.

Thus, the programme of research sponsored by the National Institute for Social Work divided into two main streams: one concerned with probation and one with social work in social services departments. Both sets of studies were exploratory and they were well complemented by a study which was undertaken at approximately the same time in a medical setting and which used an experimental design. This project focused on a special group of hospital patients who had deliberately poisoned themselves by taking an overdose of drugs. It was located in the Department of Psychiatry of the Southampton University Medical School and was directed by Professor Gibbons. It adopted a random allocation controlled experimental design in which self-poisoning patients receiving task-centred casework were compared with a similar comparison group who received the customary general practitioner or psychiatric after-care services.

It was decided to bring together the results of the National Institute for Social Work studies in social services and probation with those of the Southampton study of parasuicide. In this way, readers would have easy access to all the systematic attempts at evaluating the task-centred model in this country so far. The progress and results of these three projects which used similar methods of assessment and evaluation form the content of this book. As will be seen, despite the differences in settings, types of clients dealt with and in study designs, the findings and conclusions of the three studies were not dissimilar. Taken together, they begin to provide a rounded picture of the limitations and possibilities of the task-centred method and of the skills it requires.

REFERENCES: INTRODUCTION

Barclay, Peter (chairman) (1982), *Social Workers: Their Role and Tasks. Report of the Working Party* (London: Bedford Square Press).

Black, J., Brown, R., Burns, D., Critcher, C., Grant, G., and Stockford, R. (1983), *Social Work in Context: A Comparative Study of Three Social Services Teams* (London: Tavistock).

Challis, David, and Davies, Bleddyn (1980), 'A new approach to community care for the elderly', *British Journal of Social Work*, vol. 10, no. 1, pp. 1–18.

Folkard, M. S., Smith, D. E., and Smith, D. D. (1976), *IMPACT. Intensive Matched Probation and After-Care Treatment. Volume II: The Results of the Experiment*, Home Office Research Studies, No. 36 (London: HMSO).

Goldberg, E. M., Mortimer, A., and Williams, B. T. (1970), *Helping the Aged: A Field Experiment in Social Work* (London: Allen & Unwin).

Goldberg, E. M., Walker, D., and Robinson, J. (1977), 'Exploring the task centred casework method', *Social Work Today*, vol. 9, no. 2, pp. 9–14.

Goldberg, E. M., and Warburton, R. W. (1979), *Ends and Means in Social Work* (London: Allen & Unwin).

Hadley, R., and McGrath, M. (1984), *When Social Services Are Local: The Normanton Experience* (London: Allen & Unwin).

Reid, W. J., and Epstein, L. (1972), *Task-Centered Casework* (New York: Columbia University Press).

Reid, W. J., and Hanrahan, P. (1981), 'The effectiveness of social work: recent evidence', in E. M. Goldberg, and N. Connolly (eds), *Evaluative Research in Social Care* (London: Heinemann) pp. 9–20.

Reid, W. J., and Shyne, A. W. (1969), *Brief and Extended Casework* (New York: Columbia University Press).

Yorke, Clifford (1982), 'Freud rediscovered'. Broadcast, BBC, 24 October 1982. Published as, 'Freud rediscovered: self-awareness in the study of the mind', *Listener*, 28 October 1982, p. 10.

PART I

TASK-CENTRED CASEWORK IN TWO INTAKE TEAMS

by Ian Sinclair and David Walker

ACKNOWLEDGEMENTS: PART I

The work on which this report was based was carried out by David Walker as part of a programme set up by Tilda Goldberg. Further credit should be given to the social workers and their managers with whom the National Institute for Social Work collaborated on the project, and without whom it would not have been possible, and to the two assessors, Ms Blunt and Ms Moffatt, who carried out the follow-up interviews. Both assessors were trained social workers, and with their fieldwork colleagues they added much to the insights gained in the research.

Ian Sinclair was responsible for the analysis and write-up of the research and is indebted to Brendan McGuinness and Peter Gorbach for help with statistical advice and computing. Ann Mackenzie typed the report, and Raj Seegoolam provided most of the tables, both performing their tasks with a rare patience and courtesy.

Above all, thanks are due to the anonymous clients whose co-operation made the research possible.

Chapter 1

INTRODUCTION TO PART ONE

BACKGROUND TO THE PROJECT

The widespread doubts about the place of social work in social services departments arise in part from its lack of an agreed theoretical basis. Most social workers in these departments organise their time and describe their activities in terms of cases, and at one time they could readily have justified this framework by an appeal to their expertise in social casework. Unfortunately, as we have described in the Introduction, there is now a common disbelief in the efficacy of casework, with the result that social workers lack generally accepted tools for the job they appear to be doing. In response to this dilemma, social workers could retreat from the practice of casework altogether, or alternatively they could become clearer about what it is and why it is important.

In keeping with the first of these responses, there has been a growth of interest in group work, community work, the use of volunteers, 'community social work' and various forms of radical action which focus on general issues rather than individuals. Clearly, there is much that is attractive in such solutions. Social work with individuals may patch up the wounds, but can do little about the war, or even the battle: there is a moral as well as a financial appeal in the idea that the community might care for its own. Yet while it is pleasant to look forward to the millenium of good neighbours, reliable volunteers and robust self-help, there are certain things which these resources cannot of their nature achieve. Social workers are alone in being able to exercise certain statutory functions (for example, those related to the reception of children into care), have access to resources in a way which community groups do not, and have a legitimacy as advocates for other resources which is again not generally shared. To judge from research studies of local authority practice (for example, Goldberg and Warburton, 1979) social services departments have given a focus to their efforts by concentrating on those individuals and families in respect of whom they might have to exercise statutory powers or for whom they have particular resources. The use of these powers and resources involves decisions about individuals in which social workers are usually crucially involved. In so far as this continues to be true, it is unlikely that social casework in social services departments will ever wither away.

The second solution to the dilemma posed by the attacks on casework, and the one shared by the editors of this book, is to develop and test more effective methods. The attempt to do this has led directly to task-centred casework, and an understanding of the merits of this method in social services departments requires a brief description of the criticisms themselves.

One of the first and most influential criticisms of casework was made by Barbara Wootton (Wootton, 1960). Her view propounded before the Seebohm Report was that most social work theory was pretentious and foolish:

> Modern definitions of social casework, if taken at face value, involve claims to powers which verge on omniscience and omnipotence: one can only suppose that those who perpetrate the claims in cold print must, for some as yet unexplained reason, have been totally deserted by their sense of humour. (Wootton, 1960, p. 271)

Barbara Wootton reserved her censure for the literature rather than the practice of social work, remarking that the 'arrogance of the language in which social workers described their activities is not generally matched by the work they do'. Otherwise she thought it would be 'hardly credible that they would not constantly get their faces slapped' (p. 279). Unfortunately, a later study (Mayer and Timms, 1970) suggested that many clients were as bemused as Professor Wootton by their workers' activities. The researchers found that some clients 'assumed that their workers would share their views concerning problem solving, and when this did not turn out to be the case, they imputed erroneous meanings to their workers' activities' (p. 138). Mayer and Timms's research was carried out in a voluntary agency and later studies of clients in social services departments (MacKay et al., 1973; Glampson and Goldberg, 1976) suggested that clients were generally very satisfied with what they got from social workers. The criticism is nevertheless still made that clients want something more practical and less verbal than they receive.

The picture of casework as a rather purposeless and unplanned activity has been reinforced by a number of pieces of research which have examined the work of social workers since the Seebohm Report. The reorganisation following that report resulted in considerable movement among experienced field social workers and their replacement by others with less experience and a much wider area of work to cover. Not surprisingly, the new workers seem to have found it at least as difficult as their predecessors to give a coherent account of their activities. Much social work in the new departments seems to be focused on a small group of clients who receive intermittent long-term support or monitoring, punctuated by hectic activity in times of crisis (Goldberg and Warburton, 1979; Mattinson and Sinclair, 1979). One study found that much casework was 'from the perspective of the participants...aimless, muddled, and deleterious for morale' (Sainsbury, 1980), and another that the workers could give no coherent rationale for many of their activities (Parsloe, 1978). None of the researchers who have described such practice expects much good to come from it.

These criticisms would, of course, matter less if it could be shown that, in some instances at least, casework was effective. Unfortunately, as pointed out in the Introduction, a large number of field experiments have now found that casework, even in favourable circumstances, apparently has very little impact on the behaviour or fate of its clients (Fischer, 1976; Wood, 1978). Despite occasional experiments which go against this trend (for example, Goldberg *et al.*, 1970; Shaw, 1974; Sinclair *et al.*, 1974; Jones *et al.*, 1976; Stein and Gambrill, 1977), it is clear that the long-term impact of casework is usually small and its effective ingredients elusive, if not non-existent.

The characteristics of task-centred casework have been described in the Introduction, and its development can be seen as a logical response to some of the attacks on long-term social work. On the one hand, social work has been criticised as vague, endless, aimless and over-ambitious; there is evidence that clients may not understand the type of help that is being offered, and researchers have, by and large, failed to find much difference in outcome between clients who have received social work and similar people who have not. On the other hand, task-centred casework stresses clarity, brevity, purpose, agreement between client and worker on what they are about, and the achievement of feasible goals. It seems a particularly appropriate technique for use in social services departments where workers complain of shortage of time and a variety of pressures upon them, and of the difficulty of defining for themselves a feasible task.

THE PROJECT

In 1977 Goldberg *et al.* summarised the unsatisfactory situation in relation to casework in social services departments and posed some of the questions which needed to be answered:

What then constitutes social work in a social services department? Has casework any place within it? One thing is clear: if social work is to survive as a viable discipline, its aims and content will have to be more clearly specified, and the skills involved examined afresh. (Goldberg *et al.*, 1977, p. 9)

At the time of posing these questions, Tilda Goldberg had already begun a programme of research into task-centred casework in the hope of arriving at some of the answers. As we have outlined, this programme involved projects in a hospital, a voluntary agency, a probation department and a social services department.

The social services project which is the subject of this part of the book took place in an Inner London social services department, and involved two teams of social workers. Both of these teams were 'intake teams' and concerned with new referrals, but in one team two social workers withdrew from the project on the grounds that it 'wouldn't work', and their places were taken by two members of a long-term team.

In contrast to many such experiments which use workers specifically recruited for the project, the teams were given no extra resources to facilitate the research. However, each social worker taking part in the project agreed to devote to it a period of one and a half hours per week. Since most of them were unfamiliar with the method, they initially spent this time in learning about the model and gaining practice in its use. At the same time, the research instruments for classifying target problems and tasks and for measuring progress on task achievement were introduced and tried out.

The teaching was carried out by the research social worker (David Walker), and involved the giving of information, role plays, and discussions about the model and its use with cases. Each project member tried the method on at least one case. The training phase lasted approximately three months, and was completed when the research worker was confident that each participating social worker had an adequate grasp of the model and was able to complete the research instruments satisfactorily.

The main phase of the project involved the selection of a sample of cases with whom the method would be tried. At any one time, each participating social worker was expected to carry two project cases with whom they were trying the method, and were said to have a vacancy if they were carrying less than this. It was agreed that whenever a project member had a vacancy, the next case allocated to him or her would be included in the sample. Such cases would include those whom he or she picked up when on duty. The agreed exceptions to this were those cases which involved straightforward advice or the provision of a service, and cases requiring social enquiry reports.

The social workers with project cases completed their usual records on them and these were made available to the researchers. They also filled in a number of forms which described the clients' progress through the model and which included a task achievement scale. This scale was rated by the social worker in consultation with the client, and covered the degree to which the tasks agreed had been successfully completed at the end of the contact. At the final interview, the social workers also asked the client to agree to a visit by an independent assessor. Given this agreement, she visited soon after and asked the clients for their view of the casework they had received. She also asked them to complete a five-point 'problem reduction scale'. This scale sought information on the problem with which the client had most wanted help and the degree to which it seemed to have improved or deteriorated since the client first contacted the social worker. The research instruments were, with very minor modifications, the same as those used in the probation study.

The chapters which follow will use the data gathered through these instruments to tackle a number of important questions:

(1) What kinds of client entered the project, and what sort of problems did they have?

(2) What were the apparent outcomes of the work with them – for example, how many of them were able to agree with their worker on a problem to be tackled, and how many thought that their problems had been substantially reduced?

(3) What reasons for these outcomes are suggested by the social workers' and their clients' accounts of the processes of case-work – for example, what do the 'successful' clients have to say about the particular things that helped them?

(4) What are the associations between outcome, the characteristics of the clients, the different offices they attended, and the different social workers to whom they were allocated?

The conclusion will suggest that although, as always intended, the project produced limited results, it did provide important evidence on the potentialities of task-centred casework, as well as on the dilemmas of social casework in general and the steps which might help to resolve them.

Chapter 2

CLIENTS AND OUTCOMES

THE CLIENTS

The 133 project referrals reflected the end-result of a process which is as yet little understood. The composition of the sample must have been influenced by the social problems of the project areas, the expectations of social services commonly held in them, and the availability of alternative sources of help. Equally, it must have depended on the priorities of the social services and the way they channelled different requests to social workers, social work assistants, or home helps. The importance of these various factors cannot be estimated, and it is thus unsafe to assume that the sample is representative of cases in inner city areas, let alone in social services as a whole. The first step is therefore to describe the clients, so that they can be compared with others found in different locations.

In one respect, the sample reflected a selection process that is almost certainly very common. Examination of 100 referrals in each area showed that although a third of these involved elderly clients, only 14 per cent of such elderly clients saw a social worker or were allocated to one. By contrast, slightly more than three out of four of the remaining cases were at least offered a chance of seeing a social worker. This fact was reflected in the age distribution of the principal clients in the sample, as set out in Table 2.1. As can be seen, about 60 per cent of the project cases were young adults aged between 20 and 40, with teenagers and those in their forties the next largest groups.

A second characteristic of these clients was that they were very largely women. Seventy-three per cent of those classified as principal clients were female, 20 per cent male and in a further 7 per cent the case was classified as a 'family' one. As most of the social workers were also women, social work was, in this instance, very largely a service by women for women. This formulation, however, neglects the degree to which the women were representative of their families. In the great majority (83 per cent) of cases the principal client was responsible for dependent children. Thus although the social worker

Table 2.1   *Ages of Principal Clients*

Age group	N	%
Less than 20	15	11
20–29	34	26
30–39	43	32
40–49	15	11
50–59	9	7
60–69	5	4
70 or over	11	8
Not known	1	1
Total	133	100

Note: In family cases the age of the mother (or, if she was client, the father) was recorded as that of the principal client.

Table 2.2   *Referral Source of Cases*

Referral source	N	%
Self	60	45
Relative/neighbour	15	11
Non-local authority agency	9	7
Court	1	1
School/education welfare	7	5
Other local authority department	16	12
Hospital	7	5
Councillor	2	2
GP or health visitor	13	10
Social security	3	2
Total	133	100

Table 2.3   *Living Group of Principal Client*

Living group	N	%
Elderly living alone	8	6
2 elderly people together	4	3
Adult(s) and children	104	78
Three generations	7	5
Adult alone	8	6
2 adults together	2	2
Total	133	100

might be dealing with the principal client, the problem considered almost always had a bearing on the family as a whole.

Nevertheless, despite this qualification (and also the hopes of the 1960s), the records support the idea that social workers were primarily relating to individual clients rather than to families as such. In some respects this practice may have simplified the workers' task, in so far as they could negotiate with the client without necessarily having to consider the priorities and wishes of other members of the family. However, despite their absence from the contact between worker and client, other actors could still influence its content and outcome. Among the most important of these actors were those who were living with the clients or who referred them. Data on these two groups are given in Tables 2.2 and 2.3.

These two tables provide a reminder that social services are heavily involved with individuals who are normally considered dependent. Over 90 per cent of the cases were associated with a child or an old person, and in over half the clients either were, or were considered, unwilling or unable to refer themselves. Not surprisingly, the problems which these clients brought to the department seemed to reflect the situations of people coping with dependency in themselves or others, not particularly well off in terms of money, housing, or other resources, and hence vulnerable to withdrawals of support from spouse, children, or families of origin.

Table 2.4 sets out a rough classification of the clients' problem situations at referral, as inferred from the social workers' records. A number of clients could have been put in more than one category (for example, a client leaving her husband is likely to have housing, marital and financial problems), and when this occurred the client was allocated to the first group listed. The classification reflects the views of the social workers recording the application, and the way the clients chose to present themselves (in contrast, for example, to broken legs, problems can only exist in the eyes of some beholder). Nevertheless, the problem groups reflect real distinctions in terms of the content of the work the social worker might be called upon to perform, the origin and statutory basis of the request, and some of the constraints which might affect the action to be taken. For these reasons it is worth considering the groups in a little more detail.

Twelve cases involved elderly clients. Six of these were considered in some sense at risk, in that they were referred by someone else who was worried that they might fall or wander off, or in some other way fail to cope. A further six were referred primarily with a view to services such as a home help or telephone or, in one case, to see if relief could be given to a daughter who was over-burdened by the care of her elderly mother.

Table 2.4 *Problem Groups of Principal Clients*

Problem group	N	%
Elderly at risk	6	5
Elderly other problem	6	5
Social control problem	17	13
Transition to one-parent family	16	12
Marital discord	15	11
Parent/child discord	11	8
Requires care for child	13	10
Finance	20	15
Housing	9	7
Other emotional distress	16	12
Other	4	3
Total	133	100

Note: Where more than one problem could have been coded, the first category mentioned was used.

Seventeen cases could be classified under the heading of 'social control'. These were a rather miscellaneous group. They included, for example, a young man referred from homeless families' accommodation because of complaints over his behaviour, requests to investigate alleged child abuse, truancy and behaviour problems at school, a short-term care order connected with teenage drug abuse, and a compulsory admission under the 1959 Mental Health Act following a suicide attempt. What these cases had in common, and what makes them interesting from the point of view of task-centred casework, is that none of them involved clients who had come voluntarily to the social services.

The largest group of clients (almost exactly a third of the total) were involved with problems of family relationships. Roughly three-quarters of these concerned difficulties between husband and wife, and from the point of view of the social worker these cases split into two groups which could not always be distinguished at referral. In one group the spouse (almost invariably the wife) was leaving home and the social worker was taken up with the consequences of this (for example, with encouraging the woman to seek legal advice, arranging temporary accommodation, negotiating changes in tenancy, and providing support over problems of finance and child care as the woman settled down to her new existence). In the second group the marital problem was not resolved by separation and the social worker's role seemed much less clear. The final group of family-relationship cases involved disputes between parents and children. In some of these cases, the parents were complaining that their children were out of hand, while in others it was the children who came to the office complaining that they had been thrown out of home or wished to leave in any case.

A recognisable group of cases arose from requests by women for day care or short-term reception into care for their children. Some of these women were going into hospital, others were wishing to go out to work and wanted a referral to a baby minder or a day nursery, others were desperate and depressed and wanted a break from their children – sometimes even to the extent of fearing that they might injure them. Despite their variety, these thirteen requests seemed to evoke similar attitudes and responses in the social workers, and can usefully be grouped together.

A further twenty-nine cases involved financial or accommodation problems which did not obviously stem from family difficulties. These problems were often far from straightforward. A number of clients had accumulated spectacular combinations of rent arrears, hire-purchase and fuel debts, and these problems, apart from being daunting in themselves, were sometimes compounded by the distraught, despairing, or overtly feckless responses of the debtors. In the same way, accommodation problems, which were probably difficult enough in the context of the housing shortage, were sometimes presented together with family tension and personal distress.

Apart from four cases which fitted no obvious classification, the only remaining group involved sixteen clients who were referred (usually by others) because they were felt to be in distress and failing in some way to cope. These cases included clients who were seen as depressed or mentally ill and whose problems were felt to have a social component, but not one for which the social services had an obvious remedy. Some of these cases appeared to have been mentally ill over a long period, whereas others seemed to be responding to a recent event such as the departure of a boyfriend or the adoption of a child.

Taken as a whole, this list illustrates a number of points, of which the first is the variety of problems to which task-centred casework was to be applied. On first principles there is no reason to assume that a social worker who is skilled in sorting out financial problems will necessarily be equally skilled in laying on effective support for the elderly at risk, sorting out confrontations between parents and children, noting the warning signals of non-accidental injury, or even in giving good advice on how to sort out a housing difficulty. It follows that success in task-centred work may depend on skill in dealing with a particular problem raised by the particular case, as well as on skill in applying the model itself. The respective importance of these different types of skill can only be determined by empirical research.

A second point arising from these data is that in social services it may be the exception rather than the rule to find that a problem can be resolved through the co-operation of social worker and client alone. In problems of family relationships the social worker may have ethical obligations to more than one party, for example, to the child as well as to the mother, and may feel, in any case, that from a practical point of view both need to be involved. The problems of the elderly and of the emotionally distressed who are referred by others concern not only the apparent client but also the referrer who was worried enough about the situation to ask for something to be done about it, who may well have considerable power in the situation, and who may not agree with the client about what should happen. In financial, housing and social control cases, the social worker has to take account of statutory obligations and of the policies and resources of his or her own and other agencies, and so may not be able to do what the client wants however much it may seem desirable to do so. Thus social workers are dealing with groups of clients who are commonly regarded as either dependent or incapable, who are often referred for help without seeking it themselves, and who may be ineligible for the help they seek. Task-centred casework relies heavily on the client's motivation and capacity to resolve his or her own problems, given an appropriate structure in which to do so. It will be interesting to see how far it can be successfully applied in this situation.

OUTPUT: STAGES REACHED

The applicability of task-centred casework to the project clients can be described in terms of the numbers of them who completed the different stages in the model. This can be done, since the project social workers routinely recorded the important stages, that is, of problem formulation, task agreement, setting of time limits, and the completion of the final assessment. The records can also be used to examine other formal aspects of the model and, in particular, the importance or otherwise of reaching early agreement with the clients and of being specific about what is to be tackled and achieved. This section is concerned with describing the clients' progress through the model, as conceived in this rather abstract way, and relating their progress to outcome.

Figure 2.1 gives the basic data on the degree to which it proved possible to apply the task-centred model. Forty-seven cases (35 per cent of the sample) passed through all the stages of the model and were considered 'fully task-centred'. Of these forty-seven, forty were followed up and interviewed by an independent assessor, and of these twenty-two (17 per cent of the sample) considered that the most important problem that they had at the time of their approach to

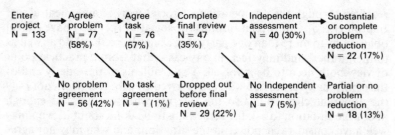

Figure 2.1   *Clients' progress through the model*

social services was completely or substantially reduced, and a further eight (6 per cent of the sample) that it was 'a little better'. It is possible that these figures should be slightly adjusted to allow for the seven task-centred clients who were not followed up. These seven, however, provided five of the twelve clients whose task achievement was rated by their social workers as partial or non-existent, but only two of the thirty-five whose task achievement was rated as complete or substantial. It is, therefore, very unlikely that the addition of these seven would have done much for the overall 'success rate'.

These figures seem to confirm the suggestion that task-centred casework would be difficult to apply in a social services department setting. In about two-thirds of the cases, the method was not fully applied, and this proportion would be much greater if allowance was made for those who were seen as needing services only; only about one in four of the clients reported any amelioration of their problem that could be connected with the full application of the method, and only about one in six reported any substantial improvement. It should be remembered, however, that 70 per cent of the clients were not followed up, and these may have included a high proportion whose problems spontaneously improved, who only had need of services, or who were helped by a chance to review their problems in a structured way. A doctor might well be delighted with any treatment that benefited as many as one in four of his or her patients; in the current state of knowledge about social work it is essential to follow up any leads that may identify successful practice with any group of clients, however small.

A further reason for paying serious attention to task-centred casework is that, as can be seen from Table 2.5, it does not require a heavy investment of resources. The long-term cases described by Goldberg and Warburton (1979) consumed social work time and other services over periods of years without, in many instances, any apparent change for the better. In contrast, contact with the project cases was typically brief. None of the task-centred cases took more

Table 2.5 *Number of Interviews by Task-Centredness*

No. of interviews	0–1	2–3	4–5	6–7	8–9	10–12	Not known	Total
Task-centred clients	0	11	21	4	8	3	0	47
Not task-centred	22	29	11	5	1	1	17	86
Total N	22	40	32	9	9	4	17	133

than twelve interviews, and more than two-thirds were completed within five. Even less time was spent on the eighty-six cases with whom the method was tried but not fully carried out. Only seven of these were known to have received more than five interviews. Task-centred casework is not necessarily more economical than traditional ways of working – contact at intake is, in any case, known to be brief (Goldberg and Warburton, 1979) – but it is clearly a major advantage of the method that, in contrast to some others, it could be applied to suitable cases without a major increase in resources.

A further implication of these figures is that the initial stage of contact between worker and client must be very important. More than six out of ten of the cases which do not become task-centred 'drop out' at this stage before a problem is agreed. Furthermore, given that those who complete all stages in the model will probably do so within five interviews, it would seem essential that worker and client settle down to business as quickly as possible. This conclusion is in keeping with those of the American developers of the model, who have urged the value of reaching agreement with the client on at least one problem at the beginning of task-centred casework and, if possible, by the end of the first interview. They recognise, however, that clients may be uncertain about the nature of the problem, and that in some cases other people may need to be seen before the problem can be agreed. For these reasons, the stage of problem definition may need to be spread out for up to four interviews (Reid, 1978).

The data suggest that the British workers followed this advice. In 50 per cent of the cases where agreement was reached, it was achieved in the first interview, in 35 per cent in the second interview, and in only 14 per cent in the third or fourth. Agreement on the problem was never delayed for five or more interviews. The majority of clients who reached agreement on the problem in the first two interviews continued to see the social worker, whereas the majority of those who did not discontinued contact.

A further reason for stressing the importance of this stage in the model is that it was associated not only with continuance but also with reports of successful completion of the next stage. As was seen in

Figure 2.1, only one of the clients who were said to have agreed on the problem to be tackled failed to agree on the tasks necessary to do this. This striking finding could be interpreted in two ways. It may be that the motivation of the clients who reached the stage of problem formulation and agreement was so strong that they more or less inevitably agreed on the tasks. Alternatively, and much more plausibly, it may be that the formulation of a problem was so intertwined with the formulation of a task that the success of one depended on the success of the other. In other words, not only were tasks formulated in the light of the problems, problems were also formulated in the light of the tasks that might be undertaken.

Having achieved agreement on tasks and problems, the workers recorded them using as far as possible the client's own words. This made it possible to see how far the problems and tasks were 'specific' as recommended by Reid and Epstein (1972), and how much specificity related to outcome. In practice, problems and tasks were very variously described, and were not always easy to classify as specific or otherwise. Some statements covered a variety of problems together with information on the background to them – for example, 'In homeless families' accommodation. Financial problems. Poor relationship between mother and daughter'. Others covered only one problem: 'She wants to have a better relationship with her son.' Other statements contained an implicit analysis of the situation, or a prediction of how things would turn out, or a justification or explanation for a request – for example, 'the family cooped up in a one-bedroomed flat, and this is causing depression in the wife and marital problems'. This last statement includes both an explanation of the depression and perhaps a justification for asking the social worker to do something about rehousing. Other clients were more direct: 'I have nowhere to go when I get my baby. Can you help me to get a place?'

A similar variety was found in the specification of tasks. Some statements focused on the processes whereby help was to be given – for example, the client was to set up arrangements whereby all debts were to be gradually paid off. Other statements were more specific – for example, the client was to investigate whether she was eligible for Family Income Supplement; others more general – for example, the client was to carry out those activities necessary to establish herself as an 'independent unit'.

These examples suggest that it may be helpful to conceive of 'specificity' not as varying along only one dimension, but rather as including a number of different components, such as the number of problems or tasks proposed, the clarity with which they are formulated, and the degree to which they are concrete or abstract. Despite this difficulty, the research social worker, David Walker, was able to develop a rating of specificity on a four-point scale, and felt that he had achieved adequate agreement between two independent raters who used it to classify twenty project cases.

One reason for considering that these specificity ratings may be valid is that, as can be seen from Tables 2.6 and 2.7, they showed an interesting association with outcome. The more specific the problem, the less likely was the case to become fully task-centred (an association which just reaches significance). On the other hand, among those clients who received a follow-up interview specificity was associated with a 'good outcome' (an association which just fails to reach significance). The relationships between task specificity and these two forms

Table 2.6 *Task-Centredness by Target Problem Specificity*

			Specificity						
	Specific		Fairly specific		Minimally specific		Global		Total	
Task-centredness	N	%	N	%	N	%	N	%	N	%
Task-centred	17	50	12	71	11	65	7	78	47	61
Not task-centred	17	50	5	29	6	35	2	22	30	39
Total	34	100	17	100	17	100	9	100	77	100

$\tau C = \cdot 2$; $p < \cdot 05$.

Note: Cases with no agreed problem omitted.

Table 2.7 *Target Problem Specificity by Problem Reduction*

Problem specificity	No. of cases	Average problem reduction score
Specific	14	3·9
Fairly specific	11	3·3
Minimally specific	10	3·6
Global	5	2·8
Total	40	3·5

On the 4×5 Table, $\tau C = \cdot 19$; $\cdot 10 > p > \cdot 05$.

Note: In this and subsequent tables, problem reduction score is based on a rating running from 1 (worse) to 5 (complete problem reduction). This table is restricted to those with a problem reduction score.

of outcome were similar but not significant. If these trends are confirmed in other research, a possible explanation is that the main virtue of specificity is that it saves time. Where a problem is clearly specified, social worker and client can see whether they are getting anywhere and can cease contact if they are not.

If this interpretation is correct, social workers who wish to maintain contact with their clients may sometimes avoid specificity. In cases in which a child is at risk, for example, a social worker may wish to stay in touch irrespective of the parents' wishes, and for this reason may be tempted to disguise the true purposes of his or her visits. An examination of task and problem specificity by problem group gave some suggestion that this process may have occurred. In only three out of the ten social control cases where problem formulation was achieved was there apparently much specificity about what the problem was.

Not surprisingly, 'financial' cases were more likely to receive high ratings for problem and task specificity. By contrast, although the numbers were small, the data suggested that specificity was also difficult to achieve in cases where the client was generally distressed or depressed, and in social transition cases where the social worker agreed to tide the client over a difficult patch. Thus while there was no reason to doubt the importance of specificity, there were grounds for thinking that more work should be done on what it means, its consequences, and its desirability in different kinds of case.

The last aspect of the task-centred model to be discussed in this section is the setting of time limits. At the beginning of the project, most of the workers agreed with the idea of setting these limits but, in general, it was not an explicit feature of their work. To set a time limit is to suggest a possibility of success, and this is precisely its purpose. However, the workers were not used to predicting success – or even perhaps to expecting it – and the research social worker felt that a number of them had unrealistic expectations of the magnitude of the success a social worker should achieve. As a result they were anxious that by setting a time limit for achieving a specific objective they would seem uncaring, and they were particularly concerned about being too structured or practical with clients who were in distress or felt unable to see any solution to their problems. In such cases they had a tendency to suggest 'working together for a short while' or 'seeing how things developed'. More generally, they tended to link a time limit to an external event such as a committee meeting or hearing, or would explain it on the ground that the intake team only held cases for three months.

As a result perhaps of these uncertainties, there appeared to be no correlation between the workers' notes of the numbers of weeks or interviews agreed as a time limit (where these were available) and the actual number of weeks or interviews the case took. Moreover, while, as can be seen from Tables 2.8 and 2.9, time limits were set in most of the cases where a problem was agreed, they were not associated with task-centredness or with problem reduction in the cases which were followed up. Again, it would be rash to assume that these limits are of no value – the workers certainly felt that they could be – but, as with specificity, more thought needs to be given as to whether they are equally helpful in all situations.

Thus a general issue raised by this chapter is what elements in the task-centred model are appropriate for which cases. There was a considerable variety in the cases dealt with by the intake teams in the two areas. Time limits and specificity may be essential in arranging short-term care for the children of a mother who has to go into hospital for a minor operation, but inappropriate in cases of extreme depression after bereavement (what would one wish the bereaved client to do – snap out of it by a certain date?). Other principles of task-centred casework for example, that it is important to get early agreement on the nature of the work, may apply more generally. The evidence certainly supports the view that early agreement is crucial if the client is to continue, and the rather low proportion of cases who

Table 2.8   *Task-Centredness by Time Limits*

	Time limit set		No time limit set		Total	
	N	%	N	%	N	%
Task-centred	38	61	9	60	47	61
Not task-centred	24	39	6	40	30	39
Total	62	100	15	100	77	100

Note: Cases with no agreed problem omitted.

Table 2.9   *Time Limits by Problem Reduction*

	No. of cases	Average problem reduction score
Time limits set	33	3·6
No time limits set	7	3·1
Total	40	3·5

On the 2×5 table, $\tau C = \cdot 11$; $p > \cdot 10$.

made successful use of all the steps in the model may be explained by the potential conflicts of interest between the client and worker, or others whose resources or co-operation may be essential for success.

These issues are taken up again in the following chapters, but it is important to see that the model provides not only a set of principles for governing workers' practice but also a framework against which other methods of work can be appraised. In certain cases it may be necessary for social workers to go forward without the client's agreement, or with an agreement so imprecise as to be almost meaningless, or without specific time limits. In such cases the task-centred model encourages the worker to be clear that this is happening and to ask whether the outcome is likely to justify the effort. In this way the model may make more likely the clarity of thought, respect for the client's wishes, and economy in the use of time which are among its virtues.

Chapter 3

PROCESS AND OUTCOME

The clients took varied courses through the different stages of the task-centred model. Some 'dropped out', breaking contact with the social worker either before or after agreement had been reached on the problem to be tackled; others who received a follow-up interview felt that their problems were worse, or changed little if at all for the better; yet others felt that their main problem had been completely or substantially resolved. This chapter is concerned with the possible reasons for these divergencies, with the kind of social work which seemed successful, and with the kinds of success that could be achieved.

The present section considers the clients who dropped out of the project without completing the full task-centred sequence. Since these clients were not followed up, the only data available on them came from the special records kept by the social workers for the project and the unstandardised notes which they kept on all clients as part of their everyday work. Read together, these records can sometimes give a convincing picture of the transactions between worker and client – there is a feeling that 'this is what is happening, and this is why'. At other times the records give a catalogue of events with little evidence of why things had turned out as they did. Nevertheless, no one could read these social work accounts without feeling that their understanding of the processes of task-centred casework had been enhanced, and it seems important to try and convey some of this understanding to the reader. Inevitably, the research methodology used to do this must be clinical and impressionistic, so that the conclusions should be considered as in need of further testing.

Using this clinical method, a rough classification was made of the apparent reasons for which clients dropped out before agreeing on the problem to be tackled. The classification was based on all the information available on the clients (and in a number of cases this was insufficient to allow them to be put in any group), and the results are set out in Table 3.1.

Table 3.1   *Reasons for Drop-Out before Problem Agreement*

Reason	No. of clients
Client failed to contact	6
Client withdrew after first contact	5
Client acknowledged no problem	3
Client and worker disagreed over problem	13
Client had resolved own problem	6
Client judged ineligible	5
Client 'needed service only'	8
Client 'incapable of response'	3
Not classified	7
Total N	56

As can be seen from table, the majority of clients who dropped out appeared not to want what the social worker had to offer. Thus six clients failed to make contact at all after the initial inquiry (in one case the client died), and five more signified that task-centred casework was not for them by withdrawing after one interview and before a target problem had been established. One of these five cases involved a family who were in continuous financial difficulties, while the other four all had problems with relationships. For example:

> Miss Hargreaves,* aged 16, came into the office having recently discovered that she was pregnant. Her family had been very angry about this, and she wanted somewhere to live away from them. At the initial interview, the social worker got permission to invite Miss Hargreaves's mother to the office, and then held lengthy interviews with mother and daughter, both separately and together. The interviews were strained and emotional, and it became clear that there was a great deal of tension in the family. The social worker emphasised that before any relevant help could be offered, there was a need for further discussion and that it would be important to involve Mr Hargreaves. The clients agreed to this, but made no further contact.

This example illustrates a negotiation between client and social worker about the nature of the problem and the type of help which might be appropriate to it. Clearly such negotiations were likely to be more difficult when there was more than one party involved. These 'third-party difficulties' also emerged in the three cases in which the clients were referred by other people and did not acknowledge that

---

* In this report all names have been changed to prevent identification.

they needed help, and to a certain extent in those cases where the client and agency did not agree on the nature of the problem. The first of these groups included two elderly people who had been referred by anxious relatives and who did not want to alter their situation. The second category included the thirteen cases where the client thought there was no problem while the social worker did, or where the client defined his or her problem in a way the social worker found unacceptable. For example:

Mrs Elsworthy was offered help on the suggestion of the worker involved with another member of the family. After a lengthy discussion Mrs Elsworthy did not feel she wanted further help, and although later events confirmed the accuracy of the worker's assessment, Mrs Elsworthy sought help elsewhere.

In a further six cases (all self-referred and concerned with either practical difficulties or relationship problems) the clients resolved the problem themselves, although they may well have been helped by the information they were given or by the opportunity to talk about their situation.

Mrs Godfrey requested help at a time of crisis, and when this was not immediately available (an appointment had been offered) managed to 'sort things out' sufficiently on her own. The situation that had led to the crisis had not changed, and would quite possibly recur. However, Mrs Godfrey did not want social work help at the time of the interview.

In sixteen cases the judgement that task-centred casework was inappropriate seems to have been made by the social worker. In five of these this was for 'administrative reasons' – the client either moved or was found to be in contact with other agencies, and was therefore deemed ineligible for service. In eleven more cases, the social worker seems to have decided that the case was not suitable, almost always because the client was seen as needing a service (for example, home help) only, but in three cases because the client was thought unable to respond.

Mrs Mansa was married to a diagnosed schizophrenic who refused help. She was finding it increasingly difficult to cope with his unpredictable behaviour, but would not consider separation because of the needs of their children and of her own feelings of guilt. Instead, she wanted to talk to someone without necessarily arriving at any decision.

The task-centred model requires that the practitioner's activity should have focus and purpose, and in this case the project worker suggested to Mrs Mansa that neither were present. The question at issue was whether or not to maintain contact using a less structured method. Mrs Mansa had previously had a year of therapy, during which she had acknowledged that while she wanted support she did not want to make any changes in her life situation. The worker did not deny that this was a legitimate wish, but explained that it would not be possible for the agency to offer that form of help.

Given that such obstacles are not present, and worker and client can agree on the structure of their endeavour in terms of problems, tasks and time limits, the model expects them to turn their attention to carrying out their plan. According to the social workers thirty clients failed to complete this stage in their work and dropped out before the final assessment. The records were therefore examined for clues as to why this occurred. The hypotheses emerging from this examination were essentially similar to those applied to the earlier drop-outs. First, there seemed to be a group of *unmotivated clients* who ceased contact because of a lack of motivation or a conflict between what they and the social worker wanted from the contact. Secondly, there was a similar group of *unassisted clients*, where the social worker seemed to lack the commitment or resources to help in achieving the client's ends. Finally, there was another smaller group of *vulnerable clients* where the social workers were deflected from their plan in order to provide long-term support. These categories are not mutually exclusive – for example, a conflict over motivation may occur because a social worker has not the power to help in the way the client wishes, or considers the client too vulnerable for this kind of work. However, in practice the categories seemed to provide a useful analytical framework, and when doubt occurred a client was allocated to the category which seemed most appropriate, or left unclassified. Table 3.2 sets out the numbers who fell into the various groups.

The unmotivated client group appeared to divide into three sub-groups. The first of these groups consisted of those clients who were either ambivalent from the beginning, or whose motivation changed in the course of the work because of a change in external circumstances. Most of these clients were involved in ambivalent marriages with a long history of comings and goings on the part of one or other spouse. Usually the wife approached the social services seeking help with separation from her husband and then later changed her mind.

Miss Chapel came into contact with the department while living in bed and breakfast accommodation. She explained that her cohabitee would not get divorced from his wife in order to marry

Table 3.2 *Reasons for Drop-Out after Problem Agreement*

Reasons	No. of cases
Unmotivated clients	
Client ambivalent/situation changes	6
Client's and social worker's views diverge	5
Social worker acting as control agent	7
Unassisted clients	3
Vulnerable clients	3
Insufficient information to classify	6
Total	30

her. He complained that Miss Chapel would not accept that his wife would not give him a divorce. It was agreed that he would remove his belongings from his wife's flat and contact a solicitor to discover his position, and that Miss Chapel would accept whatever the solicitor said. Despite – or because of – the apparent irritation of Miss Chapel and her social worker, none of these things occurred. The couple agreed that there was nothing further the social worker could do, and the case was closed.

Miss Hamble approached the department in great distress as her cohabitee had been remanded to prison. She was described as being an inadequate person much addicted to social work help, and various plans were made to see how she could cope without him. Not surprisingly, these came to nothing when he was released on bail.

A second subgroup of unmotivated clients were characterised by a divergence of views about what should be done, rather than by a conflict about what the problem was. Inevitably, the social workers sometimes assessed problems in the light of the solution which the department could provide rather than those which might be expected to appeal to the client. Thus two depressed clients were offered a day centre place to cure their depression even though one complained that she had always been shy in groups and the other that what she really wanted was to get back to work. Mrs Tapster provides a good example of such clashes of perspective:

Mrs Tapster approached the department because she was having difficulty in caring for her daughter's child. Some of her problems were financial, and the social worker suggested that Mrs Tapster could well become an official foster parent to the child and that this would improve her financial position. Mrs Tapster was dubious about this proposal, since it would mean clarifying the situation with other members of the family in a way which might disrupt the arrangements altogether. She agreed reluctantly that the social worker should go ahead, but later broke off contact.

The clash of perspectives between client and worker was even clearer in the third group of unmotivated cases, in which the social worker was either called in to assess or control the client's behaviour or felt compelled to take on this role in the course of contact. These cases included some in which the social worker was involved in deciding whether or not the client should remain in bed and breakfast accommodation, some where the social worker's view of the client's debts was that they arose from fecklessness, one where the social worker's efforts to ensure a child's school attendance were at apparent cross purposes with those of the client's family, and some which involved a risk of non-accidental injury to children. The impression from the records was that the key negotiations were often not between the client and the worker but between the worker and his or her professional colleagues.

Mrs Langley was referred to social services when she was threatening to leave her husband. The housing situation was said to be getting on top of her, and she was considerably depressed. The youngest child had apparently fallen downstairs a couple of days previously and had acquired a black eye. The social worker noted that Mr Langley was not so keen to move as his wife, and agreed to work with the family over Mrs Langley's depression and their possible rehousing. For about a month, contact continued to be focused on housing, and on the effect of the Langleys' efforts to recruit support from a councillor and others. The Langleys were told that a conference was to be called apparently to discuss their housing situation. The housing department informed them that at least 300 people were worse off than they were.

Following this initial emphasis on housing, the final interview with the Langleys revealed an important change of emphasis. The social worker reported:

'Flat newly decorated, cosy toys strewn over the floor. Grizzly children. James had bruise under right eye. The children were demanding, tearful, and Mrs Langley was rather snappy with them. I asked how James had got the bruise – he had stood on his tank and he had hurt his eye (top of cheekbone) on the skirting board.

James demonstrated how it happened, and it nearly happened a second time. (This was discussed again when Mr Langley came in, and I was satisfied by this explanation. They denied they did it when I asked.)'

This report, with its emphasis on the exact position of the bruise and the explanations which were offered for it, was in marked contrast to the earlier descriptions of Mrs Langley's situation and how she felt about it. Following the interview the Langleys avoided further contact, despite a letter and two abortive visits. The conference, it turned out, was not to consider the housing application but rather to decide whether the children should be on the 'At Risk Register'. This conflict between the social worker's wish to help the family according to their lights and her need to ensure that they did not harm their children ran through this and other records, although the social worker's hidden agenda did not always surface in such a clear way.

The unassisted clients differed from the unmotivated ones, in that the lack of motivation seemed to lie in the social worker rather than in the client. Clearly, the social workers could not give equal priority to all their clients and it was difficult to use the records to judge the degree of priority given to a particular case. In some instances, however, the social worker's enthusiasm certainly did not appear to be marked – for example, a single homeless client was told that he could not be helped with his accommodation problem, but he could come back later if he felt the social worker could be of any further help. It was not, perhaps, surprising that this client was not seen again. Other cases appeared to drift until they were closed with the clients apparently still in a dire situation and the social worker unwilling to inquire further about it.

Mrs Corrigan said that her family situation had broken down and she was described as fundamentally depressed. She was given a further appointment to work on establishing herself as an independent unit, but the social worker was ill when she came for it.

The only other entry in the file is a letter:

'Dear Mrs Corrigan, I am so sorry I was off sick at the time of your last appointment with me. I would be very happy to see you at any time you feel the need. Please do not hesitate to contact me, if you feel I can help in any way.'

Given that this client had had one fruitless journey, and was offered no definite appointment for a further contact, it was perhaps to be expected that this was the last that was heard of her.

The difficulty of carrying out task-centred casework with the group of vulnerable clients seemed to be that the worker began by formulating a plan with the client only to find that other emergencies intervened.

> Miss Archer was old, living on her own, and apparently confused. She formulated her problem as 'Being a nuisance – but I'm me. I have some worries over money. I am forgetful, and concerned about this.'

Although a task was formulated, the actual course of contact with Miss Archer did not follow a tidy plan. It turned out that a large number of people including a vicar, home help, neighbour, family, the DHSS, her general practitioner, and possibly the health visitor, were already involved with Miss Archer and considerably bothered both by her behaviour and by each other's activities. After a number of crises brought about by Miss Archer's forgetfulness and neglect of personal hygiene and the unco-ordinated activities of her support network, the original plan was dropped.

The interest of the classification which has been put forward lies not in the exact figures, which are small and based on information of uncertain reliability, but rather on the schema which they suggest for explaining the success or otherwise of task-centred casework in a particular case. Five questions seem to be relevant:

(1) Is the client basically competent to manage his or her life after a particular problem has been resolved?
(2) Is the client motivated to work on a particular problem, or is there evidence of long-standing ambivalence about it or that the problem is more in the minds of others than of the client himself or herself?
(3) Are the resources required for the solution of the problem available?
(4) Does the solution of the problem require the co-operation of others, and if so is this likely to be forthcoming?
(5) Does the social worker agree with the client's version of the problem, and is he or she committed to overcoming it?

The issue of conflict (and its opposite, agreement) runs through these questions. The conflict can be within the client, as where the client agrees to work on separating from her husband at the first interview and reverses this decision at the second interview. Other conflicts are between clients and third parties, as where the daughter wants one thing and the mother another, or where the relatives think the old lady has a problem but the old lady herself does not agree. Yet other conflicts are between the worker and the client, as where the worker's definition of a problem or its solution differs from that of the client, or the agency has not the resources to meet the client's acknowledged needs.

In some of the project cases, the social worker may have attempted to bypass these conflicts by defining the problem in terms which made it amenable to the resources available in the department and which did not necessarily involve the co-operation of others in the client's network. Table 3.3 gives the workers' own classification of the problems with which they were involved according to a scheme worked out by Professor Reid. The most interesting aspect of this table is that in only one case did a worker say that she was focusing on inter-personal conflict. As has already been made clear, many of the clients' difficulties were related to inter-personal problems, but a wife in disagreement with her husband was more likely to present herself, or at least be seen by the social worker, as having a problem of how to manage the social transition of leaving her husband, rather than as seeking marital reconciliation.

Before concluding this section, a final note of caution should be given. The outcomes described have an air of inevitability about them. The clients failed to make contact, or broke it off for no apparent reason, or only wanted a home help, or could not acknowledge a problem they plainly had. These, however, are explanations after the event and derived from the records of one of the two parties to the transactions. There remains the question as to whether or not these outcomes had to be. Would the clients who failed to make contact have responded to a quicker reply to their inquiry, or a warmer voice on the telephone, or a reminder letter? Was the lady apparently asking for a home help really lonely? Would the clients have acknowledged a problem if it had been put rather differently to them? Later chapters

Table 3.3   *Social Workers' Categorisation of Problems*

Category	No. of cases
Inter-personal conflict	1
Dissatisfaction in social relations	6
Problems with formal organisations	7
Role performance	15
Social transition	24
Reactive emotional distress	6
Inadequate resources	18
Total N	77

of Part One will return to the question of the possible effects on outcome of the skills, enthusiasm and promptness of the individual worker.

REASONS FOR DROP-OUT AFTER PROBLEM AGREEMENT

It is important to see whether the reasons for drop-out have much in common with reasons for lack of success among clients who completed all stages in the model. The present section considers the forty clients who received both a final assessment from the social worker and a follow-up interview from the independent assessor. The question is why some of these clients appear successful while others report little benefit.

The data on these clients include two different but related measures of outcome: the 'task achievement score' and the 'problem reduction score'. The task achievement measure was based on a joint evaluation by social worker and client of the work they had done together. At the final interview the social worker asked the client what they had achieved and the replies were rated on a four-point scale, from complete achievement through substantial and partial achievement and down to minimal achievement. The problem reduction measure came from the independent assessment. The clients were asked to 'Consider the one problem you most wanted help with. How is it now, compared with when you first saw the social worker?' The replies to this question were rated on a five-point scale, as 'no longer present, a lot better, a little better, about the same, worse'.

The two measures are concerned with slightly different things (one dealing with the task, and the other the problem), but as can be seen from Table 3.4, a high or low score on one almost always went with the corresponding score on the other. For simplicity, the problem reduction score will be used as the single outcome measure, being preferred to the task achievement score as being a more independent measure and one which reflects more accurately the purposes of contact between worker and client. In general, those who reported their problems as completely or substantially reduced will be called 'successes' and those who regarded their problems as the same or worse will be called 'failures'. This terminology is, of course, for convenience and does not necessarily imply that the social workers were responsible for the successes or to blame for the failures.

One variable which distinguished significantly between the successes and failures concerned the way the clients remembered their anticipations of contact with the department. The independent assessor asked them what they had expected before their first meeting with the social worker, and their replies were coded on a three-point scale: 'specific expectations, general expectations, no expectations'. Sixty per cent of those answering said they had no expectations at all and the more specific the expectations they remembered, the less likely

Table 3.4 *Problem Reduction Score by Task Achievement Score*

Problem	N	Average task achievement
No longer present	11	3·5
A lot better	11	3·3
A little better	8	3·1
About the same	7	2·8
Worse	3	1·6
Not followed up	7	2·0
Total	47	2·9

On the 5×5 table, $\tau C = \cdot 26$; $p < \cdot 05$.

they were to record a high degree of problem reduction ($\tau C = \cdot 26$; $p < \cdot 05$). In part, this finding may be explained by a wish to blame the social worker for an unsatisfactory outcome – 'If only she had done what I wanted, all would have been well' – and disappointment is clearly more likely where a specific outcome is envisaged. Nevertheless, clear expectations give the worker and client less room for manoeuvre and, as such, constitute a source of potential difficulty. Thus it is not surprising that the client who was 'just hoping and praying for a flat' and who got a number of other things instead, did not agree that her problems had been solved.

A further variable which it was thought would relate to success is the degree to which the clients reported that their worker 'understood the problem'. Some of the clients seem to have interpreted this question as referring to personal qualities – 'Is she understanding?' – and others as referring to a more intellectual grasp of the situation. Either way, only two were prepared to say that the worker did not understand, and a further two that they were not sure. The sixteen who said that the worker understood 'quite a lot' almost always explained their qualification in terms of the worker's youth and inexperience of such problems from the 'inside':

'Well, you have to live with it to really understand. How can you really see someone's problem in an hour, when you don't see the rush to the bathroom in the morning, the quarrels over the TV, us at mealtimes.'

Or again:

'She was very kind and understanding, but she was so young. I don't see how she could possibly understand the problem. The two previous social workers had experience of life.'

Twenty clients, however, had no hesitation in saying that the worker understood, although they sometimes added that they had not expected her or him to.

'I do [think she understood], and she's not married. Single people don't usually understand when you've got bills coming in.'

One of the more interesting findings of the study was that these ratings of understanding were not significantly related to outcome. In part, this may have been because of the varying ways in which the clients interpreted the question (some seemed to mean no more than that the social worker was pleasant). However, it may also be that the social worker must demonstrate a sufficient degree of understanding to involve the client in casework at all, but that given that this step is achieved understanding is irrelevant to success, or only relevant in certain kinds of case.

Once again, the variables most strongly related to outcome were those concerned with agreement. At the beginning of the independent assessment, the clients were asked how they saw their problem at the time they approached the social services. Their replies were compared with the social worker's record of the problem and rated on a three-point scale from 'agree' to 'disagree'. The clients were also asked how the social worker saw the problem, so that this, too, could be compared with the social worker's perception. Finally, the clients were asked how far they agreed with the social worker on a specific plan of action. These various measures of agreement were all significantly related to success.

Not surprisingly, the first two measures of agreement were strongly related to each other and for ease of analysis they were combined by being added together to form an agreement score. As can be seen from Table 3.5, this procedure emphasised the relationship between agreement and success even more strongly. Out of the eighteen clients who scored above the median on the agreement score, there was only one failure as against fourteen successes. The comparable figures among the twenty-two remaining clients were nine failures and eight successes.

The suggestion that a high level of agreement is almost invariably associated with success is made even more plausible by examining the one 'deviant' case: Mrs Eames, who was rated as having agreed with her social worker about the nature of the problem, but who nevertheless considered that her difficulties were worse.

Mrs Eames had had a very hard life, and had recently undergone an operation for cancer. At the time of her contact with the social worker she was involved in divorce proceedings and bothered by rent arrears and a variety of other matters. According to the social worker, Mrs Eames regarded herself as 'screwed up and in need of psychotherapy', but she was in fact referred for a discussion of job retraining which had been suggested to her at the hospital. Both the social worker and Mrs Eames described her problem in terms of a job, but the social worker's record and the independent assessment made it clear that this was probably not the issue at the top of Mrs Eames's mind. As Mrs Eames put it:

'She was a nice person, but I don't think she was switched on to my problem. There was always an urgency about her...not like you, she didn't sit back and listen...I don't know really. I expected more than I got. Maybe I am wrong. I felt rejected when she left, even though she told me it was only three months. I live on my own.'

Even if there were no doubts about the genuineness of the agreement between the social worker and Mrs Eames, the latter's difficulties were such that the case can hardly be regarded as disproving the rule relating agreement and success. This rule, however, fails to explain how some clients managed to achieve success despite initial disagreement, and how others achieved neither agreement nor problem reduction. In order to explore these questions, it was decided to look in detail at the eight cases where a high disagreement score was followed by success, and at the nine cases where it was followed by failure.

Table 3.5 *Agreement Score and Problem Reduction Score*

| | Problem reduction score | | | | | | |
| | No longer present/ a lot better | | A little better | | About the same/worse | | Total | |
Agreement score	N	%	N	%	N	%	N	%
High	14	64	3	38	1	10	18	45
Low	8	36	5	62	9	90	22	55
Total	22	100	8	100	10	100	40	100

On the 5×5 table, $\tau C = \cdot 34$; $p < \cdot 005$.

The eight cases which were successful despite disagreement seemed to fall into two groups, of which the first could be called 'the late agreers'. In two of these late agreement cases the social worker seems to have ended up doing what the client wanted in the first place, even though this did not appear to have been his or her plan at the outset. In a further two cases it was the clients who seemed to have changed their minds.

Mr Coram approached social services because, as he later said, 'I was not sexually satisfied, and was living apart from my wife'. The social worker, however, interpreted his request as 'seeking help to separate from his wife'. In the event, the comings and goings over the Corams' children seem to have given the Corams a chance to talk to each other, and they decided to stay together. Mr Coram felt that he had received 'wonderful benefits' from his interview with the social worker and, in particular, that the social worker had helped him to communicate better with his wife.

Mr Coram, however, put more emphasis on the moral support he had received from the social worker than on her problem-solving abilities:

'She didn't pinpoint the problem. She tried to get me to talk more about the welfare of the children with the wife. I never had confidence in anyone, but I was able to talk to her ... She told me she would be *my* social worker. I have no relatives over here. No one to listen to my side of the story. That made me feel relaxed. I felt someone cared.'

Another couple in this group also emphasised the role of the social worker as a support in a difficult time:

'He was unemployed at the time, and we were getting on each other's nerves. She wanted to see us together. At the time, I was determined not to, but she talked me round. She was just like a friend. We could talk over all our troubles. We've been through a bad patch – his dad seriously ill, our 4-year-old going deaf, and him with tonsilitis and unemployed.'

In the second group of late agreement cases a clear negotiation seemed to have taken place between the client and the worker, and was recognised as such by the client. All these clients felt that they had agreed on a plan with the social worker, even though they had not initially agreed about what the problem was. Mrs Fellows, for example, was referred to the social services by the school because of her son's disturbed behaviour. She had a history of broken relationships and family disasters, and an alleged addiction to barbiturates and alcohol. Despite her own problems, she had been shocked when the headmistress spoke to her about her son's difficulties. Asked how the social worker saw the problem, she said:

'She did not seem to think it was Dean at all, but me. It was; I was very low...everything seemed to be going wrong.'

Two further cases in this group involved conflicts between parents and children, and the clients again acknowledged that they were already half-willing to change at the point at which they first contacted the social worker. Cynthia, for example, was a 15-year-old girl who had been put on a short-term care order after her father had found her in possession of hard drugs and had gone to the police.

'For a few days I didn't think much about it, as I was really dosed up. When I came round I was upset ... she [the social worker] was going to help me to talk to my parents about it. I'd wanted to talk to them, but I kept it all inside me. She was trying to get me closer to my parents, and thought that was probably why I started taking drugs. [Interviewer: Did you agree?] I thought about it for five minutes, and then I thought she was right, but I wasn't conscious of it at the time.'

In this case, as in that of Mrs Fellows, the client's shift of attitude seemed to be associated not only with the social worker's understanding but with a 'shock' administered by an authoritative outsider, such as the headmistress or the court. In other cases in this group, the authority came from the social worker who took it upon herself to state the sort of care that a child needed.

'Well before, she'd found a nursery for my 2-year-old, and the nursery contacted her as I wasn't taking him on time...They started complaining as they thought it was affecting him as he was difficult to handle. And she said he might have to come into care, his home life not being settled might affect him. (I knew she wouldn't take him into care, she's not like that.) I didn't see the problem at the time, but when she talked about it, I could see that it could affect him.'

The nine cases where a high disagreement score was followed by failure seemed to break into three main groups. The first of these contained four cases all involving disagreement between spouses or between parents and children. In two of these cases the client said that the social worker had negotiated an agreed plan, but clearly it was agreed with one party only. Mr Talbot, for example, reported that it had been agreed that he should pay 50p a week off his debts. Mrs Talbot, however, reported no such agreement.

'I didn't like her when I saw her (my husband did, he thought her sympathetic). She only saw my husband's side.'

Another woman client voiced similar misgivings:

'She [the social worker] voiced several suggestions as to what the children could do. I couldn't see it as being a good idea.'

In the other two cases no agreement seemed possible with anybody, and a basically unsatisfactory situation continued unchanged.

The second group of these low-agreement failures involved only one client, Mr Johnston, a West Indian who was looking after his children after his wife had left him. For various reasons, there was disquiet about his ability to do this and the social worker's main concern was to assure herself that the children were all right. In the course of this activity she did a number of things which the client saw as helpful.

'She got me a settee and some beds and things, and told me to go to a solicitor about custody. We discussed the children. She wanted me to tell them about their mother being in Jamaica and for them to talk about her. I didn't want to at first, but after three times I did tell them ... she also suggested I petted up the eldest boy, who was throwing his food about and not eating. It was a good idea.'

Nevertheless, the client did not see himself as having a problem at the beginning of the contact and consistently maintained that the social worker had not reduced any problem. The case is of interest because it probably resembles many long-term cases in which social workers are involved for the sake of the children and because of their statutory responsibilities. Success in such cases may have different meanings for the social worker and for the adult clients.

In a final group of four cases the assessment and the social work records suggested that the social worker and client were at cross-purposes, and that the clients' central concerns had been denied or missed. Curiously, this did not mean that the clients said that the social workers did not understand them, but the overall impression was of the appearance of mutuality rather than the substance. The cases are worth examining in some detail since they illustrate the variety of ways in which true agreement can be missed. They may also represent a much larger group of cases who never reached the stage of final assessment.

In the first of these cases, the worker seems to have underestimated the force of the client's specific request. The client's husband was dying of cancer in hospital and she herself was old and crippled. She approached the social services seeking help with rehousing, in the belief that if she was rehoused she could have her husband home to live with her before he died. To judge from the social work record, however, the worker interpreted her role as helping the client to face her grief over her husband's approaching death, and saw the rehousing request as a way of getting more suitable accommodation for the client herself. There was no evidence that this clash of perspective was ever clarified:

> 'She helped me with rates and with the electricity bill, but these were trivial compared with the main problem. I was just hoping and praying for a flat ... I was just speaking to her like I'm speaking to you. She tried to comfort me.'

In the second case in this group, the social worker had got the family a gas cylinder, ensured that they should receive Family Income Supplement, negotiated a tax rebate of £180 and suggested job retraining. As a result of these efforts, the family were better off by about £12 to £13 a week. Despite these good works, the client complained that the gas holder was too heavy for her and that she had a £95 electricity bill which she could not pay. She rated her problem as 'about the same'. She also said that at the time of her contact with the social worker she had had a miscarriage and was very depressed, and that she was still thinking of asking her cohabitee to leave. None of this was mentioned in the social worker's record, nor did the client say that she had discussed any of it with him.

Depression was also a factor in the third case in this group. The client accepted that she had a problem with her rent arrears and with fuel debts. However, she said that her big problem was something that had happened two years previously and which she had not discussed with anyone except the doctor at the special investigation clinic which she attended. Obsessed with this unknown problem, she was sympathetic in a detached way towards the social worker.

'She helped me with a bed, and livened up the rent office and contacted the LEB, and she tried to motivate me into action. It was a good idea, but I'd got past that stage. I can't criticise the way she tackled it, but I don't think she helped me at all. I've always been able to think out things, but I've lost the will . . . I don't know how I would cope with me if I was someone else – not that I'm troublesome, but I've lost faith.'

The last client in this group was distinctly troublesome. She approached the social services seeking a holiday for her child, and received instead a number of suggestions to the effect that she joined Gingerbread, mobilised her church to help her, attended a day centre for mothers and children and got a solicitor. The client rejected all these offers and the interview ended on an angry note on both sides, and with the client leaving her child at the social services so that he had to be received into care overnight.

Matters were patched up, but the client was still critical at the end of the contact:

'I wanted a break for a while, and I was depressed. When I left James behind she was much better. She didn't know I'd take it like that . . . I don't think she really [understood] the first time, but she did after that. I didn't like it on the first day. I felt I was being crossexamined. When I went there, instead of going on suggesting and suggesting [she might have given more concrete help]. It was like her getting out of her responsibility.'

These last two examples highlight a potential conflict within the task-centred model, which emphasises the importance of acting in accordance with the clients' wishes and the parallel importance of enabling the clients to do things for themselves. In some instances, however, what the client wants is that the social worker should do things for them – hence, perhaps, the difficulties in the last two cases.

Thus taken as a whole this section again emphasises the crucial importance of early agreement between client and worker on the nature of the problem. In some cases, this agreement is difficult to negotiate – particularly, perhaps, when the client has clear expectations about what the social worker should do, and thus leaves the social worker little room for manœuvre. Nevertheless, it is sometimes possible to negotiate 'late agreement'. In such cases, the social worker may provide the clients with moral support over a difficult patch and carry out her negotiations when things are seen in better perspective. In other cases, the social worker may rely on her own authority or the authority of others, such as the court, to get the clients to perceive problems that had previously not been squarely faced.

In other cases, however, agreement may not be achieved. Such cases may include warring families where agreement with one party means disagreement with another, cases where the problem is really the concern of the social worker rather than the client, and the cases where the social worker seems to have missed the nature and extent of the client's desperation. Again, the question arises as to whether these outcomes are inevitable or whether they can be altered by more or less skilled work.

SUCCESS CASES: KINDS OF WORK

After concentrating on the possible reasons for which clients drop-out or fail to resolve their problems, it is time to turn to the hows and whys of success. In the independent assessment the clients were asked to reflect on the sort of help they had received. The present section is concerned with the explicit or implicit meanings which the twenty-two successful cases gave to their experience of social work, and with the different kinds of work they described.

In order to understand the clients' interpretation of their experience, it seemed better to read each interview as a whole rather than to concentrate on individual questions. This procedure gave the strong impression that the clients were perceiving their contacts with the social worker in three inter-related ways. First, they were concerned with the social worker's role which they connected with other broad roles which are more commonly understood. The words they used included 'friend', 'counsellor', 'mother', 'mate' and 'go-between'. Secondly, they described a number of valued activities or qualities which they had experienced from the social worker and which would commonly be associated with roles of this kind. For example, the social worker was a good listener or relaxed so that you could open up to her. Thirdly, they linked these roles, qualities and performances to the situation they had at the time they had approached the social services. For example, they were in a desperate state and the social worker had felt like a mother to them. Her ability to listen had helped their nerves.

In the light of this analysis the successful clients were divided into three groups, those who seemed to describe their experience in terms of 'mothering' (five clients), those who appeared to look to the social worker as an 'ally' (fourteen clients), and those who appeared to use her as an 'arbiter and catalyst' (three clients). As will be seen, there was a considerable overlap in the qualities valued in these roles, but nevertheless there seemed to be differences in the attributes which were emphasised, the problems which were tackled and the way they were approached. Each of these groups will be described in turn.

The word 'mother' was used directly by only one client. She was not, as it happened, a success case as she described her problem as only 'partially alleviated'. This woman had become very depressed and she described her feelings about the social worker as follows:

'It was just knowing she was there at any time. It was like having a mother, someone I could turn to if I needed to.'

The fundamental requirement of such a role is availability, and this was valued by the five success cases in the 'mothering' group.

'What is essential is that you have someone to go to at that precise moment.'

Or again:

'I think she was quite marvellous. By going to her, I had something to look forward to each week.'

In terms of their problems, all the cases in this group acknowledged that they approached the social worker in a considerable state of 'nerves', 'depression', or 'despair', and none of them had any clear expectation about what the social worker could do.

'I didn't expect much, really. I just thought it would be good to go and see someone.'

Or again:

'I just took it that there would be someone to help. Someone to realise how desperate I was.'

Not surprisingly, none of these clients seem to have agreed and kept a clear plan of action. One client agreed to make a break from his wife and then changed his mind. Two agreed to talk things over with the social worker to try and understand what was happening to them, and two could give no account of a plan at all. Apart from the stress laid on the importance of having someone to turn to, the clients valued the fact that the social workers were good at listening and that their actions symbolised concern. With one possible exception, they all emphasised the social worker's ability to give psychological support rather than her practical efficacy. One, for example, appeared to have flouted every piece of advice the social worker gave:

'She listened well and she gave advice. At least there was someone I could talk to. She suggested so many groups that I could join, though I didn't take up any of her offers.'

The social worker's activity in these cases seemed to be valued more for what it symbolised than for what resulted from it:

'I just found her easy to talk to, which was important to me at the time. She visited me in hospital and went to a meeting there. She saw my boy-friend while I was in there.'

Other parts of this interview suggested that what was important to this client was that the social worker cared enough to come to the hospital, rather than that she achieved anything in particular by doing so.

A further characteristic of three out of the five clients in the 'mothering' group was that they placed a strong emphasis on their relationship with a specific worker:

'If I needed to see anyone again, it would be a duty officer. In previous years there was always one social worker you knew on hand, and that was a better system. I think people like us should always have somewhere to go. We're so vulnerable ... I would like to be able to call my own social worker on the telephone. It would cut a lot of corners. When you're upset, it doesn't matter who you go to, but in the future I might have to explain it to someone new. It might stop me.'

As another client put it:

'If I ever needed her, she'd be there, but I'd like it to be her and no one else.'

The second and most numerous group of clients were classed as regarding the social worker as an ally. The main difference between this group and the last was that the alliance was formed in relation to problems with a specific practical component, and that the workers' practical skills and the way they exercised them were at least as salient as their sympathy and understanding.

'She got me rehoused. What she said, she really meant. She didn't just talk, and advise and put out a long finger.'

In this quotation, the social worker's concern is valued not just for what it symbolised (as it might have been in the 'mothering' group), but because it was associated with her ability to deliver the goods. A longer quotation may help to illustrate some of the required qualities of an ally:

'The way he tackled it, he did it very well. He took it like a real personal problem. He analysed it, how I felt. He said, let's take this problem first and sit down and talk about it. He made me realise I was in a difficult financial situation. It was a joint affair and it was good to talk to someone in my own age group with common sense. He was like a mate, he sits and listens. He'd ask a question and then he'd split it into two and four. Knowing someone was interested helped and I didn't want to let him down.'

This quotation illustrates the fact that the qualities of 'being a good listener', 'commitment' (taking it as a personal problem) and 'interest' are still valued. However, there is a new emphasis on 'common sense' and problem-solving skills, in this case taking one problem at a time and 'splitting it down into two and four'. Finally, there is an emphasis on joint action which is absent from the 'mothering cases'. Clearly, the ally role and the task-centred model should fit well together.

In practice, the qualities demanded of the ally role seemed to vary slightly with the type of problem being tackled. Three groups of problems were distinguished and seemed to relate to relatively clear-cut groups of social work activities. These groups were:

(1) Establishing a single-parent family (five cases)
(2) Making arrangements for child care (four cases)
(3) Financial and housing difficulties (five cases)

All the clients in the 'single-parent family cases' were women, and four of the five clients were clearly subject to extreme mental cruelty or were being battered. Like the 'mothering cases', they approached the social services with acknowledged feelings of desperation and depression and, with one exception, without any clear expectations of what the department could do for them. In contrast to the 'mothering group', all the clients agreed and kept a clear plan. In general, the social worker arranged for them to be placed in bed and breakfast accommodation (or, in one case, to be temporarily housed by Women's Aid), while the client undertook to see her doctor, solicitor and the DHSS, as appropriate. The social worker arranged a follow-up in order to see how the client was getting on and sometimes gave further practical help by supporting the client's refusal of an unsatisfactory rehousing offer or by obtaining furniture for the new home. The clients appreciated the fact that the social workers acted promptly and decisively ('she was *determined* to help me'), without removing their freedom of action.

> 'She saw I was in a desperate situation and I needed to get out as soon as possible, and we moved in here that same evening. I didn't expect they'd get me a roof over my head in such a short period. I thought they'd say go home and think about it and talk it over with your husband. She left it entirely up to me. She gave me no orders, but said 'I suggest you should'. Sending me here was the only help I really needed.'

Two of these clients, however, were grateful for the emotional support they received at a difficult time.

> 'Even if he hadn't done anything about accommodation, he would have helped. A problem shared is a problem halved. I didn't feel so freakish. He helped increase my self-respect. He put me on the right track.'

The other client expressed a similar thought:

> 'I knew I had someone on whom I could depend for moral support, so I've achieved an awful lot. I've had to face living on my own, looking after the boy, and keeping my job, and I haven't broken down.'

In the four 'child care cases' the clients approached social services needing baby-minders or foster parents for their children to enable their own return to work, or short-term care while they themselves were in hospital. In each case, the social workers appear to have stated their own position that children were better off with known adults, and then worked with the client to establish arrangements which could achieve this end. In each case, the arrangements involved the use of the client's own resources and those of the social services. Thus friends or boy-friends were used to care for the children overnight if necessary, and the clients were put in touch with baby-minders by the social worker who also, in one case, closely supervised the working of the arrangements. In these cases, the clients again put a high value on the fact that the arrangements were jointly worked out, and the social worker was explicit about her activities while at the same time enabling the client to play her part.

'It takes two you know. You can't leave it all to them. She gave me all the necessary things and how to go about them, and left it up to me how quickly. We worked hand in hand. I think it was marvellous. She didn't hide anything from me. She told me what she was going to do.'

Another client repeated a similar thought:

'I achieved it myself, but if I hadn't gone there I wouldn't have gone about it in the same way. I mightn't have sorted it out yet. The way she put things to me made it easier. She helped a tremendous lot, even just by sitting back listening. She was the sort of person who wanted you to feel you were doing it yourself – you're not relying on other people. I wish everyone was like her.'

Similar themes emerged in the 'ally cases' in which the social worker was involved with housing and financial problems. Here again, the clients valued in the social worker committed action, success in the acquisition of resources, and the ability to break down their complicated financial tangles into manageable pieces. They also liked clarity about what was being done and by whom, and a feeling that they themselves were in control of their fate. In so far as the problem had affected them emotionally, they valued the social worker's ability to listen.

Mrs James approached the social services with heavy debts and a number of other practical problems:

'I went to the social services in February. My eldest daughter had left school and started college and they cut my allowance by £6.70, even though my rent had gone up £5.00. The social worker did such a lot in a short time. She got shoes for the children, a maintenance grant for my eldest daughter, a bus pass. She saw the problem when I explained it. Everybody saw it, but she really helped.'

The new social worker was seen as being different from others of whom Mrs James had previous experience.

'They do everything, they ring up and somehow things get arranged. Here they involved you, told me who they were ringing, told me where I could get a birth certificate, made me feel useful. I didn't understand about holidays last year. This year the social worker found out, she sent me to speak to the headmaster, he gave me a letter and now I know what to do. I don't even mind if the children don't get a holiday this year, at least I know how to go about it next year ... When you can't do anything for yourself you feel helpless. Before I felt embarrassed.'

Two things stood out on the social worker's record on Mrs James. First, it was extremely clear and businesslike, with details of Mrs James' income and outgoings, and notes on the reasons for seeking a birth certificate. Secondly, it demonstrated considerable confidence in Mrs James, who was seen as a basically competent woman facing temporary difficulties following rehousing.

In the final group of three 'arbiter and catalyst cases' the social worker acted as a mediator with one set of spouses, and two sets of parents and children. In each of these cases, there had been a crisis: one child had taken drugs, a daughter had left home, a wife was driven by a series of family crises to go to the social services seeking temporary accommodation. The social workers enabled these couples to talk about these difficulties and interpreted each side to the other. In none of the cases did they form a clear-cut plan except in so far as this was to meet and talk things over, for example:

'She was trying to help me to talk to my parents about it.'

Or again:

She said, 'If you think I can help you, I will come round in two days' time.'

These seemed to be the only plans there were, but despite the vagueness of the task, the work was appreciated.

'She helped me quite a lot because she was a sort of go-between between me and my parents.' (daughter)

'I don't think we could even have started without her. We needed a third person and she said the right things. She was just there and easy to talk to.' (spouse)

'Mum and I have changed half and half. We're able to understand more, talk together. Before we couldn't say much together. The social worker helped a lot. She really got Mum thinking.' (daughter)

OUTCOME

A number of benefits might be expected from task-centred casework. Some of these concern process in the sense that the clients may value the emphasis on explicit joint action irrespective of its outcome; others concern outcome in that the attempt to achieve specific tasks may produce a better resolution of problems; and yet others concern the general effects of casework on the client's life in that, for example, the emphasis on joint action may enable the client to achieve greater self-respect. In keeping with these ideas, clients in the follow-up sample were asked a number of questions about process, outcome and the general effect of their encounter with the social worker on their lives. The present section examines the answers given to these questions by the twenty-two successful cases.

Not surprisingly, there were strong and statistically significant associations between the various possible measures of outcome. Thus the degree to which the clients said that their problems were reduced was associated with the degree to which they said they had achieved a great deal themselves, that the social worker had helped them, and that they liked the social worker's way of tackling the problem. The problem reduction score was also associated with the degree to which the clients said that the contact with the social worker had made a difference to their lives in general, and that as a result of seeing the social worker they had learnt something that could help them with their problems in the future.

These associations could arise in different ways. It could be that skilful task-centred work leads to a high degree of effort on the part of both client and social worker, to the completion of tasks and the resolution of problems and hence to valuable general lessons. Alternatively, clients who feel that their problems have been reduced may be more likely to speak favourably of all other aspects of the process, irrespective of whether these had produced the good effect. In order to examine the meaning of the statistical associations in more detail, it is useful to break the success cases down into the 'mothering', 'ally' and 'go-between' groups discussed in the last section and then examine the clients' replies.

The nature of the outcomes reported varied to some extent with the type of problem. In the 'mothering' group with non-specific emotional problems, the clients commented on the fact that they had learnt that help was available either from the social worker or by a process of generalisation from other people.

'I've learnt you can always go to someone for help, which before I wouldn't have done.'

'I try to hold to the conversation [with my wife]. I want to go to the complete end. I don't feel let down by the social worker. I feel as if it was someone learning to swim and now I can swim on my own.'

These clients all claimed a considerable reduction in anxiety and depression, but what they seemed to have learnt was not how to resolve problems on their own, but rather that to resolve certain problems other people are necessary.

'In a way I've learnt something, Yes. But if I was depressed again, I'd want to talk to somebody. I wasn't upset when she left, but I would have been if I'd been feeling the same way [as when I started].'

The concept that in certain circumstances one needs to talk to someone was associated with the feeling of what O'Connor (unpublished) has called 'dependency at one remove'. The social worker can be left in the confidence that he or she will be available if needed.

'I've got security. If I were sick or anything sudden should come up, I could phone him. It makes me feel less depressed.'

The theme of dependency at one remove ran through many of the interviews with clients who appeared to have some form of emotional relationship with their social workers. It was sometimes hard to determine how far the clients were hoping against hope that their social workers would be available and how far they genuinely trusted that they would be. In some cases the social worker's customary assurance that the client could always phone seems to have been used to palliate the pain of breaking a dependent relationship.

'I did feel let down [when it stopped]. Then she said, if ever I need her I could see her. I think I'll go back. She's the only person I can talk to.'

In this case, and possibly in some others, the contact was stopped, not because the client felt that it was time, but because of time limits or a judgement on the part of the social worker about the importance of avoiding dependency in the client. In other cases, dependency could be given up, either because of a belief that it could be revived if necessary, or because of a sad recognition that enough was enough, or because of the availability of alternatives.

'If ever I need her she's there. She said I could go back to see her after four weeks, but I was quite happy without arranging it like that.'

'I didn't feel let down, just disappointed like having a friend and they die.'

'I didn't feel let down as my problems seemed so trivial. Now she could go and help someone else. Now I've made a lot of friends and I'm hardly ever in.'

The alliance cases (those concerned with child care, financial/ housing and marital separation problems) were more likely than the 'mothering group' to emphasise the practical benefits of the social worker's intervention. Half the marital separation cases said that all that they needed was an establishment separate from their husband's, and that by arranging this the social worker had had a major effect on their lives, even though the transaction had been strictly business-like.

'My life is different because I live away from my husband. I didn't feel let down [without the social worker]. It would have been different if I'd got to know her over the years, but this way I get my independence.'

Even those who said they needed moral support (because their confidence was shattered or they felt 'freakish') saw the general effect of the social worker's intervention as enabling them to make an important social transition rather than as altering them of itself.

In the case of the financial/housing problems the clients could not claim that the reduction of any particular debt had a far-reaching effect on their lives. Most of them lived in circumstances whose basic nature the social worker was powerless to change and where debt was a recurring possibility. However, these clients claimed that specific financial problems had been overcome, that they had received help with the emotional stress which accompanied these problems, that they had learnt that such help was available and that they had also learnt something about how to sort out their own debts. Naturally, different clients emphasised different aspects of these benefits.

'I feel more confidence in myself. I can plan ahead and budget.'

'I've found that I can come forward instead of staying mummy. If I get into a jam, I would go back to that social worker.'

'Just because it's finished doesn't mean it's blotted out. I can contact her again. I shall miss seeing her, just talking helps. It helped my nervous situation.'

As with the marital transition cases, the resolution of temporary child care problems was seen as having a general effect on the clients' lives. In these cases, satisfactory arrangements were made for the children to be looked after while their mothers were in hospital or out at work. One client emphasised the strategic importance of such resolutions.

'I've solved that problem. I've reached a different level. I'm a lot happier and the children are a lot happier. Before I was broke. I couldn't face another office job. I was taking it out on the children. I felt they were preventing me from doing what I wanted to do. I was giving them severe thrashings for little things. I was frightened of battering them.'

Another of these clients emphasised the 'know-how' which she had got from the social worker and which, she thought, would enable her to resolve the same problem on her own in future.

'She's given me peace of mind to go to hospital. Now I've seen her I'm content to go there. In future I'd know how to go about it. I'd be able to cope on my own.'

Two more of these clients emphasised the theme of 'dependency at one remove' which characterised the 'mothering group'.

'I should say it [had made a difference]. I've got security. I didn't worry. I phoned him. It made me feel less depressed. If I should be sick or anything sudden should come up, my children would know they'd seen a social worker. They could go there straight away and tell them.'

In the final set of successes where the social worker had acted as a go-between or catalyst, the clients emphasised the fact that the social worker's intervention had produced an increase in their ability to talk to their spouse or children. These improvements were seen as having a general effect on the clients' lives.

'It's narrowed down the gap which was growing between Karen and her sisters. Karen and me can now discuss things with each other.'

'We're more relaxed. We can sit and talk to each other over problems. Before both of us thought we were hiding things from each other.'

'I've learnt to talk to my parents – how I can help myself.'

The outcomes in these various kinds of case seem both feasible and intelligible. There appears to be a natural relationship between problems, agreement between social worker and client, the nature of the role taken by the social worker and the results. The question remains whether these outcomes are determined by the problem the clients present or by other factors such as the type of client, the skills of the worker, or the organisation of the department. These are the kinds of questions which are considered in the next chapter.

Chapter 4

WHAT DETERMINES OUTCOME?

The last chapter concentrated on the accounts which worker and client gave of their transactions after their meeting, and hence on the relationship between the processes of casework and its outcome. What follows will consider the factors which may also determine outcome but which either pre-date the meeting of client and worker or which may be taken to influence their interaction without, in turn, being influenced by it. From the point of view of the study, there are two particular reasons for being interested in these 'causally prior' variables. First, measures of these variables are unlikely to be influenced by outcome. A client who has had a successful experience of casework may imagine that he or she and the social worker agreed about what should be done when in fact they did not. However, this sort of bias should not affect data on the workers' and clients' ages, or the organisation of the area office. Secondly, variables of this last kind may help in the effort to unravel cause and effect. An observer of the processes of casework can expect to improve his or her own skills, but he or she will find it difficult to know whether progress arises from the skill of the worker, the motivation of the client, the chemistry of the two, the nature of the problem, or any of a host of other variables which may be influencing the situation. A demonstration that certain workers or certain types of client are consistently associated with better outcomes may make it possible to form hypotheses about what is necessary to ensure success.

The present chapter distinguishes three groups of causally prior variables: those associated with the client, those associated with the organisational setting and those associated with the worker. Variables in each of these groups will be related to the two main outcome measures: whether or not the case became task-centred, and if so whether or not it got a 'good' problem reduction score. One advantage of employing both these outcome measures is that it makes it possible to see whether there is a 'trade off' with, for example, some workers ensuring that a high proportion of their cases become task-centred, but in consequence having a high number of reluctant or unsuitable clients with 'bad' problem reduction scores.

CLIENT VARIABLES

The quantity, quality and nature of the information which workers collect on clients varies with the purposes of their encounter; with some clients it is important to have adequate information on employment and finance, with others the focus is on family relationships, and with others on disability or mental state. Thus the standard information on all clients was sparse, covering, in essence, age, sex, marital status, living group and presenting problems. Nevertheless, the results of relating these variables to the outcome measures was of considerable interest.

Table 4.1 gives the relationship between the age of the principal client and the probability that he or she would achieve task-centred status. As can be seen, cases involving the old and the young were much less likely to become task-centred than those involving clients in the age range 20–69. Thus 42 per cent of the 106 cases with clients in the middle age range became task-centred, and this figure contrasts with 0 per cent of the eleven cases involving clients aged over 70, and 13 per cent of the fifteen cases with principal clients in their teens. These figures support the suggestion put forward in Chapter 3 that social workers were least likely to carry out task-centred work with vulnerable clients who might be expected to have the most difficulty in looking after themselves, or for whom the social workers may feel the most responsibility.

The relationship between the age of the clients and their problem reduction score was also interesting. The forty clients who had a problem reduction score consisted almost entirely of those aged 20–69

Table 4.1   *Age of Clients and their Task-Centred Status*

Age of principal client	Task-centred	Not task-centred	Total
Less than 20	2	13	15
20–29	15	19	34
30–39	16	27	43
40–49	6	9	15
50–59	5	4	9
60–69	3	2	5
70 +	0	11	11
Not known	0	1	1
Total N	47	86	133

and, as can be seen from Table 4.2, the older they were the less likely they were to think that their problems had been reduced. This correlation was highly significant. A possible explanation is that the older clients more often had chronic problems which were unlikely to change (for example, long-standing unhappy marriages or recurrent mental illness), whereas the younger clients were more often at a turning point in their lives (for example, having decided to leave their homes or husbands). There could be other explanations – the younger clients may have had a greater affinity for the young workers – but reading the case papers certainly gives the impression that many older clients had an entrenched dissatisfaction with their lot which co-existed with a long-standing reluctance to change it.

Table 4.2   *Age and Problem Reduction Score*

Age of principal client	N	Average problem reduction score
Less than 20	2	4.5
20–29	12	4·1
30–39	14	3·5
40–49	5	2·8
50–59	4	2·8
60–69	3	3·3
Total N	40	3·5

On the 6 × 5 table, $\tau C = ·29$; $p < ·05$.

In contrast to the findings on age, the sex of the principal client was unrelated to outcome. The 16 per cent of the sample who were men were only slightly less likely to become task-centred cases and just as satisfied as female clients if they did so. This fact provides encouraging evidence for the ability of female workers to deal with male clients and against too great an emphasis on the 'status similarity' of worker and client as an element in success.

The client's living group was not significantly associated with whether or not the case became task-centred or with his or her problem reduction score (thirty-four of the forty cases who were independently assessed were, in any case, in households of adults and children). As can be seen from Table 4.3, marital status was associated with task-centredness and the widowed, who were obviously on the whole the older clients, never became task-centred clients, whereas the divorced were quite likely to do so. Again, the numbers were too small to allow analysis of the relationship between marital status and problem reduction score.

Table 4.3　*Marital Status and Task-Centredness*

Marital status	Task-centredness		Total
	Task-centred	Not task-centred	
Single	11	22	33
Widowed	0	13	13
Separated	8	14	22
Divorced	8	4	12
Cohabiting	0	2	2
Married	20	31	51
Total N	47	86	133

The hypothesis that capable or motivated clients were more likely to take part in task-centred work suggested that outcome should be related to referral source. Thus it was expected that clients who made their own way to the area office should do better than clients who were sent by the courts or education welfare officer, or referred, often without consultation, by anxious relatives. In fact, however, there was no evidence that this was so. Thirty-three per cent of the self-referred clients became task-centred, as against 35 per cent of the remainder, and the average problem reduction score of the two groups was almost the same. A possible explanation for this fact is that self-referral may imply motivation on the part of the client, but this is no reason to suppose that the social worker will share the client's view of the problem, or that he or she will be able to do much about it if he or she does.

Table 4.4 sets out the relationship between outcome and problem group. As already discussed, a client's problem status is not a purely personal attribute in the same sense, for example, as their age. A client is or is not 47 years old, but if she is a battered wife she may be regarded as having a housing problem, a marital problem, a financial problem, a personality problem, or any combination of these and other problems. How she is labelled will depend, in part, on the views of those with whom she comes into contact. Nevertheless, the department did seem to be dealing with a number of relatively distinct problems which were more properly seen as attributes of the clients and the way they chose to present themselves than of the way the social workers chose to respond. 'Problem group' has therefore been treated as a causally prior variable.

Overall, the different problem groups did not differ significantly in the proportions of cases becoming task-centred. However, the reason for this failure to reach significance was almost certainly the number

Table 4.4 *Problem Group and Outcome*

Problem	N	No. task-centred	Average problem reduction score
Elderly at risk	6	0	—
Other elderly	6	2	4
Social control	17	4	3·5
Transition to one-parent family	16	9	4·3
Marital discord	15	6	2·8
Parent/child disagreement	11	1	(5)
Require care for child	13	6	4·2
Finance	20	9	3·3
Housing	9	1	—
Other emotional distress	16	7	3
Other	4	2	3
Total	133	47	3·5

$\chi^2 = 15\cdot5$; df $= 10$; p $< \cdot15$.

of categories into which the data had been divided to obtain a distinct set of categories, and the lack of numbers in the sample as a whole. Closer examination of the table suggests conclusions for some problem groups very similar to those put forward in Chapter 3.

One interesting contrast is provided by the categories concerned with family disputes. Those involving marriage (transition to a one-parent family and marital discord) were not easily distinguishable from each other on the data available at first interview. Viewed as a single category, fifteen of these thirty-one marital cases became task-centred, as against one of the eleven cases involving disputes between parents and children (a significant difference, p < ·02, Fisher's exact test). In practice, the marital cases were almost always treated on the assumption that the spouses wished to split up, and those who did so enjoyed a relatively high success rate. By contrast, only one of the fifteen marital discord cases had a high problem reduction score. Taken together, these figures suggest that task-centred work was easier and more likely when the negotiations could be carried on between the social worker and client without needing to involve others in the client's household.

A further interesting contrast (although this time the difference is not statistically significant) is provided by the relatively high proportion (nine out of twenty) of clients with financial problems who became task-centred, as against the low proportion (one out of nine) of clients with housing problems. In the case of the financial problems, the social workers sometimes had leverage over resources because the clients were not getting their entitlements. Clients, unless homeless, were not entitled to housing in the same way as to financial benefits, so that in such cases the social worker was more often powerless.

The problems which were most likely to have any positive outcome were concerned with transition to single-parent family and child care. These groups share a number of important characteristics which seem likely to be related to success in task-centred work:

(1) The problem often reflects a situational crisis, rather than the client's chronic incapacity.
(2) The problem does not necessarily involve 'control' and hence implicit conflict between client and worker.
(3) The problem usually involves young children, and hence has relatively high priority in a social services department.
(4) The problem typically involves negotiations between client and worker whose success does not depend upon co-operation with others in the client's network with whom the client is in conflict.
(5) The worker is likely to have access to the resources necessary to resolve the problem.

Thus, in such cases both worker and client are likely to want to resolve the same problem and they are not stopped by lack of resources, lack of co-operation from others involved, or the client's chronic incapacity. Such a conclusion fits the data discussed in Chapter 3 and is consistent with the statistical results on the relationship between outcome and age. Its implications are discussed in Chapter 5.

ORGANISATIONAL SETTING AND DELAY

There is little doubt that the social worker's ability to carry out task-centred casework can be influenced by the setting in which he or she is working. As explained in the introduction to this book, attempts were made to carry out similar studies in a voluntary agency and a medical social work department, and in both settings, although for different reasons, there were considerable difficulties in acquiring an adequate number of cases. Such difficulties were not found in either of the area offices in social services departments, but it is nevertheless interesting to see whether one of them could be an easier setting for task-centred casework than the other.

The main overt difference between the two offices was that in one of them the social workers took on the project cases very much more quickly than they did in the other. The data on these differences in delay are set out in Table 4.5.

It might be expected that a delay between referral and first project

Table 4.5 *Office and Delay to First Project Interview*

	Same day		1–7 days		8–14 days		15–28 days		28+ days		Not known/ no contact	
	N	%	N	%	N	%	N	%	N	%	N	%
Office 1	32	100	14	74	16	64	6	33	4	24	15	68
Office 2	0	0	5	26	9	36	12	67	13	76	7	32
Total	32	100	19	100	25	100	18	100	17	100	22	100

$\chi^2 = 39{\cdot}0$; df = 5; p < ·0001.

interview would mean that the client's initial motivation was missed and that success was less likely. However, examination of Table 4.6 suggests a more complex pattern. As can be seen, the clients who were picked up at intake and therefore had no delay had the same probability of becoming task-centred as clients in the sample as a whole. A possible reason for this surprising similarity is that the meeting of client and worker at intake was a consequence of organisational arrangements, the fact that the worker was on duty when the client came in and not an indication that client or worker were particularly motivated to work on the client's problem. Examination of the clients who were not taken into the project at the initial interview does suggest that those who were seen more quickly were more likely to become task-centred. Fifty-eight per cent of those seen within the week passed through all the stages of the model, as against 23 per cent of those who waited more than a month. This trend is very nearly statistically significant (it would occur by chance less than 10 times in 100), and it certainly seems likely that clients who were in a hurry to start with their social worker or who had a social worker who was in a hurry to start with them would be likely to succeed.

A point of some interest is that *if* there is a tendency for a long delay to be associated with a case not becoming task-centred, the association is more likely to occur because of the relationship between delay and motivation (whether of worker or client) than through the influence of

Table 4.6 *Proportion of Task-Centred Cases by Delay*

	Same day		1–7 days		8–14 days		15–28 days		28+ days		Total	
	N	%	N	%	N	%	N	%	N	%	N	%
Task-centred	13	41	11	58	10	40	7	39	4	23	45	41
Not task-centred	19	59	8	42	15	60	11	61	13	77	66	59
Total		32 100		19 100		25 100		18 100		17 100	111	100

Note: 22 cases omitted, as no contact or delay not known.

delay, as such. If the delay was in itself important in producing success because, for example, it was important to tackle problems quickly and before they became chronic, one would expect that organisational arrangements which minimised delay would be associated with outcome. However, although in Office 1 cases were taken on by their workers more quickly than they were in Office 2, Table 4.7 shows that there was very little difference between the offices in the proportion of cases that became task-centred.

Table 4.7   *Office by Task-Centredness*

	Task-centred		Not task-centred		Total	
	N	%	N	%	N	%
Office 1	33	70	54	63	87	65
Office 2	14	30	32	37	46	35
Total	47	100	86	100	133	100

$$\chi^2 = \cdot 44; df = 1; p > \cdot 5.$$

This finding should be treated with caution. No one would think that a long delay between first contact and the start of work was a good thing, and the statistical procedures used in this study are not adequate to prove that there were no differences between offices in effectiveness – for example, the differences might have become apparent with bigger numbers or if more allowance had been made for intake. However, Table 4.7 is evidence against any very marked differences in effectiveness between offices. The next question is whether there is any evidence for differences in the effectiveness of workers.

VARIATIONS IN WORKER SUCCESS

The impression given by the case examples in Chapter 3 is that task-centred casework can be successful and that it requires skill. If so, it will be expected that success will vary with the characteristics of the worker. Individual variation in success is not expected in impossible tasks – all those who attempt to jump to the moon fail – or in particularly easy ones – most people can switch on a television set. However, in tennis, cricket, acting, piano playing, politics, business management, and most other forms of complex human endeavour, it is well known that there are enormous variations in the skill of the individual performers, and that these variations are likely to be reflected in the money they earn and the results they achieve. The remuneration of social workers is almost certainly unrelated to their effectiveness, but this does not necessarily mean that they are all equally good for their clients.

Table 4.8 sets out the number of cases each worker had, the proportion of those who became task-centred, and the average problems reduction score of those which were assessed. As can be seen, the social workers differed widely in terms of the proportions of their cases who became task-centred. These differences were significant (p < ·03), but it would be unwise to place too much confidence in this test, since many of the social workers had very few project clients. However, the differences remained significant if the test was recalculated after removing social workers with less than ten cases and, although the numbers are still small, the finding should be taken seriously. The project was not designed to give some workers easier cases than others, nor was there any obvious organisational reason for differences of this kind. It is therefore important to consider how such variation might occur.

A particular reason for wishing to understand this result lies in the concentration of 'success cases' in the caseloads of very few workers. Out of the twenty-two cases with high problem reduction scores, sixteen (73 per cent) were found on the caseloads of the first four workers in Table 4.8. With these workers the chance of a case receiving a high problem reduction score was 33 per cent, with the next four workers it dropped to 11 per cent, and with the last five workers it was 3 per cent. This way of describing the figures almost certainly exaggerates the extent of the true differences between workers. With such small numbers chance will give some workers a very high success rate and others a very low one. To take an extreme example, if the last worker had taken just one more case her success rate might easily have

Table 4.8   *Outcomes by Social Worker*

Social worker	No. of cases	Percentage task-centred	Mean problem reduction score
1·6	5	60	4·0
2·5	10	60	3·8
1·1	12	58	4·2
1·2	22	50	4·0
2·2	8	50	3·0
1·5	22	36	2·8
2·4	9	33	2·7
1·3	5	20	—
1·4	17	18	3·3
2·1	8	13	—
1·8	4	0	—
2·3	10	0	—
2·6	1	0	—
Total	133	35%	3·5

been 50 per cent instead of 0 per cent. Nevertheless, the differences are apparently large and raise the question whether in the hands of some workers the task-centred method has almost no chance of success.

In this connection the last column of Table 4.8 is of interest. It suggests that workers with a relatively high proportion of task-centred cases tended to have a relatively good outcome with those that did become task-centred. This hypothesis was first tested by comparing the average problem reduction scores obtained by clients of workers who had more or less than 50 per cent of their clients task-centred (the median percentage for those workers who had any clients in the follow-up sample). This difference was significant ($p < \cdot05$). Similarly, the average for the 'good' workers was 3·92, for the others 2·93 ($t = 2\cdot6$; $df = 38$; $p < \cdot02$). However, the correlation between the client's problem reduction score and the percentage task-centred obtained by their worker just failed to reach significance ($r = \cdot29$; $df = 38$; $\cdot05 < p < \cdot1$). A decision on whether or not the 'successful' workers were really more successful should be taken on the balance of the evidence rather than this finding alone.

There are two reasons for regarding this result as important. First, it provides a firmer statistical foundation for the belief that there were genuine differences in worker success rates. If the variation between workers in their proportion of task-centred cases arose from chance, one would not expect to find an association between this proportion and their problem reduction score which is logically independent of it. Secondly, the association runs counter to a particular explanation of a variation in the proportions of cases becoming task-centred. It might be suggested that the workers with the higher proportions of task-centred cases were dragooning unwilling clients into taking part in the method. If so, one would expect that workers with high proportions of such cases would do worse with them. As has been seen, the opposite apparently occurred.

The association also provides some evidence against the idea that the variation between workers arose from the fact that some workers were taking easier cases. If this were so, one would expect the differences to be reduced by excluding the cases who failed to agree on a problem. This argument, however, is a rather indirect one and it was possible to make a more straightforward test of the possibility that differences in success rate arose from differences in the selection of the cases. In order to make this test, the workers were first divided into three groups with high, medium and low success rates. As can be seen from Table 4.9, each group involved roughly equal numbers of workers and cases. The groups were then compared to see if there were differences in the clients.

The client variables chosen for this analysis were age, marital status

Table 4.9   *Three Groups of Workers by Outcome*

	No. of cases	Task-centred N %	Complete/substantial problem reduction N %
Group 1 (4 workers)	49	27 55	16 33
Group 2 (4 workers)	44	16 36	5 11
Group 3 (5 workers)	40	4 10	1 3
Total	133	47 35	22 17

and problem group. These were the variables which were associated with outcome and they were defined in such a way as to make their association with outcome as strong as possible. For example, the groups were examined to see if they differed in the proportions of clients under 20 or over 70, or in the proportions of under twenties and over seventies taken together. Since it was the under twenties and the over seventies who had particularly bad outcomes, this procedure should have given the best chance of picking up variations between groups in terms of the difficulty of their cases.

Only one significant difference was found and this is set out in Table 4.10. The successful workers in Group 1 were very much more likely to take on problems involving transition to a one-parent family, or the provision of child care facilities. As will be remembered, these were the categories of problem which between them provided roughly half of the cases with high problem reduction scores. It therefore seemed possible that the comparative success of the Group 1 workers arose from the fact that they selected or were allocated easier cases.

In order to test this possibility, the Group 1 workers were compared with those in Groups 2 and 3 in terms of their success with the transition and child care cases, and of their success with other kinds of case. The results, set out in Table 4.11, are both surprising and interesting. The Group 1 workers maintained their superiority over other groups in each class of case, but in fact their 'lead' was more marked with the transition/child care cases. Whereas Group 1 was more likely to have successful outcomes with these cases than they were with the others, Groups 2 and 3 were not. This suggests that differences in worker success rates did not arise directly from differences in the selection of cases, but that workers whose general success rate was, in any case, high were attracted towards cases for which the task-centred method was either appropriate in itself or appropriate in their hands. More detailed analysis (involving, for example, breaking the transition/child care cases into their two distinct groups) failed to shake this conclusion.

Table 4.10   *Groups of Workers by 'Suitable' Problems*

	'Suitable' problems N %		Other problems N %		Total N %	
Group 1	16	55	33	32	49	37
Group 2	4	14	40	38	44	33
Group 3	9	31	31	30	40	30
Total	29	100	104	100	133	100

$$\chi^2 = 7\cdot49; \ df = 2; \ p < \cdot05.$$

Note: 'Suitable' problems are those involving child care or transition to one-parent family.

Table 4.11   *Groups of Workers: Task-Centredness by 'Suitable' Problems*

	'Suitable' problems				Other problems			
	Task-centred N %		Not task-centred N %		Task-centred N %		Not task-centred N %	
Group 1	12	80	4	29	15	47	18	25
Groups 2 and 3	3	20	10	71	17	53	54	75
Total	15	100	14	100	32	100	72	100

The fact that the Group 1 workers differed from the others in terms of their ability to get suitable cases suggested that they might have differed in other ways as well. The research worker who carried out the main phases of the project suggested that the Group 1 workers were, in his experience, more business-like and organised than the others. This hypothesis was tested by examining whether the Group 1 workers were more likely to achieve specificity in the problems and tasks agreed with the clients and whether they were more likely to see their clients quickly after referral. Out of three analyses, only that concerned with delay after referral showed any possible differences between Group 1 and the other workers. The results of this analysis are set out in Table 4.12

The best way to consider Table 4.12 is with considerable caution. None of the workers in Group 1 had a very high delay score, but two of those in Group 3 had comparatively low ones. This suggests that promptness in seeing clients is not sufficient to ensure success, although it may well be a necessary prerequisite. Among the workers in the first office, there was a significant tendency for low delay scores

Table 4.12 *Groups of Workers by Delay Scores*

	Average delays in days			
Group 1	1·7*,	14·1,	3*,	5·5*
Group 2	39·2,	8*,	28·8,	1·6*
Group 3	10·4*,	12·8,	—**	23·8

* Workers in Office 1.
** Delay not recorded.

Note: In each group the more 'successful' workers are listed before the less 'successful'.

to be associated with a high proportion of task-centred cases. There was no such trend in the second office. A possible explanation for these divergent results is that in the first office the delay scores were influenced by the presence or absence of enthusiasm, whereas in the second office it reflected organisational factors. If so, at least over a certain range, promptness affects outcome only in so far as it can be considered an indicator of commitment.

This conclusion is in keeping with those of the chapter as a whole. It seems likely that both workers and clients influenced outcome, but that differences between the two area offices did not.

Chapter 5

SUMMARY OF PART ONE: IMPLICATIONS AND CONCLUSION

SUMMARY

Part One has described the results of a small project jointly carried out by the National Institute for Social Work and two intake teams in an Inner London social services department. The project examined the results of task-centred casework and involved both action and research.

The social workers taking part received training in task-centred casework, but were not relieved of any of their ordinary duties. Each participating social worker undertook to carry two cases with whom he or she would try to apply the task-centred model. As soon as one of these cases was completed, he or she replaced it with the first suitable case he or she was allocated or contacted on duty. All cases were considered suitable except those thought to need simple advice or services only, and those which were the subject of social inquiry reports.

The project workers collaborated in designing forms to describe their work. These yielded data on the five major stages in the model, that is, the exploration of the clients' problems, agreement on the problem to be tackled, agreement on the tasks to be carried out, the work itself and the final review of outcome. The social workers also arranged for the clients to be interviewed by an independent assessor shortly after the last casework interview. The assessor sought the clients' views on the casework they had received and the degree to which it had resolved their problems.

These data allowed a simple 'before and after' design. The clients could be described at the point at which they approached the department, their progress through the model could be monitored and the final outcomes recorded. The report has concentrated on a description of the clients and their outcomes, and has attempted to explain why variations in outcome occurred.

Altogether 133 clients entered the project, and their characteristics are described in Chapter 2. The problems presented by the group or attributed to them were varied. They included, among other things, a number of requests to control disruptive or dangerous behaviour, despairing pleas for help from mothers at the end of their tether with their young children, complicated presentations of debts and housing difficulties, the anxieties of relatives about the elderly living alone, and the intractable disputes of warring spouses and teenagers in conflict with parents. This variety raised the issues of whether task-centred casework was appropriate to all these problems or only to some, and whether all aspects of the model were equally appropriate in all cases.

Despite the variety of cases, two things were common to the great majority of them. First, they almost always involved a person who would normally be defined as dependent, either because he or she was very young or because he or she was old and frail. Secondly, and in part as a consequence of this dependency, the social worker's concern could not usually be limited to one person. In some cases, the social worker was likely to feel responsibility for a child or old person as well as the principal client; in others (for example, the social control cases), the client's problems had been defined by someone else; in yet others, the power of a third party was likely to be such that his or her wishes had to be taken into account; and in yet others, the third party could be considered to be the social services department itself, or some other agency whose resources the client desired. These facts again raised potential problems for the task-centred model. The latter relies on the capacity of clients to resolve their problems as they define them, provided they are given an appropriate framework in which to do so. The question therefore arose of how far the model would be applicable with clients who were not necessarily seen as capable of taking control of their lives and whose problems were often defined by others with power in the situation.

Further data suggested that the degree to which these difficulties were resolved depended very much on the early contact between client and worker. Approximately two-thirds of those who did not complete the five stages prescribed by the model dropped out without reaching the second stage of problem agreement. Those who did reach this agreement did so early (in the majority of cases after one or two interviews), and with one exception also completed the next stage of task agreement. The crucial importance of the first one or two interviews was further emphasised by the brevity of the overall contact between client and worker. In the majority of task-centred cases this involved five interviews or less.

Additional evidence for the importance of getting things right at the beginning may also have been provided by the findings on 'specificity' – a concept ironically less clear than it might have been. It appeared that the less specific the problem agreed between client and worker, the more likely was the client to pass through all the stages of the model. However, among those clients who were followed up, specific agreement on problems was associated (although not quite significantly) with the reduction of problems. The most likely explanation of these two results is that a lack of specificity over problems may simply put off the evil day by disguising the fact that worker and client have failed to reach the necessary agreement about what should be done.

Overall, 47 (35 per cent) of the 133 cases completed all phases in the task-centred model, and of these 22 (17 per cent) seemed to feel that substantial inroads had been made into their problems. These figures provide some evidence for the idea that, in many cases, it is difficult to apply task-centred casework in a local authority setting. No doubt the figures are depressing if it was hoped that such casework would be a panacea; or, alternatively, encouraging if the standard of comparison was the likely success rate of a standard treatment applied to all the cases in a doctor's surgery. It was, in any case, important to try and understand the reasons for various outcomes in the light of the other data available.

Examination of the workers' records suggested that the reasons for which clients might fail to complete all stages in the model could be grouped according to a classification originally put forward by Ripple (1957). First, the clients might lack *motivation*. Some clients signified their lack of interest by failing to turn up at all, others felt that their problem had been defined by someone else and acknowledged no difficulty; others seemed interested to start with, but changed their minds when they resolved their own problems or the situation altered; others were ambivalent, so that what they wanted at one interview was not what they wanted at the next. A second group of clients lacked the *capacity* to resolve their problems according to the task-centred model. Thus a very young and insecure mother, or a confused old lady, might lurch from crisis to crisis until both worker and client had lost sight of the original problem and task. The client interviews suggested a further group of such clients – those who were simply too low and depressed to take a grip of their affairs in the way the model suggests. A third group of clients lacked the *opportunity* to resolve their problems. These included those whom the social worker judged ineligible for service, those whose problems required resources which were unobtainable, those whose problems failed to arouse commitment in the social worker, and – a much larger group – those whose problems required the co-operation of others in the family which was not forthcoming.

The interviews with the forty task-centred clients who were followed up confirmed the central importance of agreement between worker and client on what the problem was. A simple agreement scale was constructed and, with one exception, all the high scorers on this scale also reported that their problems were completely or substantially reduced.

It is of interest that some clients succeeded even without early agreement. In some of these cases the client came to see the problem the social worker's way because of a 'shock' administered by someone in authority (for example, a magistrate, headmistress, or the social worker himself or herself). In other cases it seemed to be a matter of timing: if the social worker could tide the client over a bad patch, the latter could formulate and agree a problem even though this had not been possible at first contact. In yet other cases it was the social worker who seemed to come round to the client's way of viewing the situation. The fact that client and worker can negotiate an agreed definition of the client's problem, despite initial differences in perspective, is important given that such initial differences are likely to be common. Interviews with the small number of 'failures' in the follow-up sample suggested that differences in perspective had not been negotiated in these cases, so that casework had sometimes proceeded with the appearance of agreement rather than the reality.

Further examination of the data suggested that the nature of agreement on a problem might be more complex than appeared at first sight. The model suggests that two steps are involved. First, what is the problem? Secondly, what should be done about it? It might therefore be expected that clients could agree with the worker on the problem without agreeing on what should happen next. However, as already mentioned, only one of those who reached the stage of problem agreement failed to agree on a task. The follow-up interviews suggested that in the client's mind at least, the definition of the problem to be tackled was linked with a definition of the worker's role, and therefore with a view of the qualities required for its performance.

The interviews suggested that the clients' view of their social workers' role fell into three main groups. A small number looked to their social worker as a 'mother' or general source of moral support. These clients placed less emphasis on the social workers' practical efficacy than they did on their availability and their care and concern. A larger group of clients looked to their worker as an 'ally'. Many of these clients also valued the worker's moral support, but they emphasised his or her ability to analyse problems and acquire relevant resources. They seemed a particularly appropriate group for task-centred work, and were pleased with the fact that they were treated as equal partners in a joint exercise in which the worker was clear about what he or she was doing and was ready to explain it. A final small group of clients looked to the worker as a 'go-between or catalyst' in difficult family situations. They valued the worker's tact and ability to explain each side to the other.

These broad groupings could be further divided according to the particular problem with which the worker was dealing. In the mothering group the clients were complaining of a generalised emotional distress. In the ally group they were seeking help over debts, housing, the problems of arranging alternative care for their children, or the problems of setting themselves up as an independent unit apart from their husbands. In the go-between group the difficulties centred around breakdowns in communication between spouses, or between parents and children. Each of these subgroupings seemed to involve the worker in distinct groups of activities which, in turn, were likely to depend on the possession of particular groups of skills and knowledge, and access to the appropriate resources.

The benefits the clients reported from casework varied with the type of role they saw the social worker as playing. In the mothering group the successful cases saw themselves as having been tided over a bad patch by means of the social worker's moral support. In the long term they felt that they had learnt that help of this sort was available either from the social worker or from others. In the alliance group the clients felt that their immediate problems had been resolved and in some cases that, in future, they would know how to resolve such problems for themselves. Spouses who had succeeded in separating and mothers who had placed their children in day care so that they could go out to work saw the resolution of their immediate problems as strategic, in the sense that it would make a major alteration in their future lives. The group who saw the social worker as a go-between or catalyst felt that they had learnt to talk things over with others in their family, and that this also was a strategic change which would have long-term effects.

The hypotheses suggested by the workers' and clients' accounts of their experiences were on the whole supported by the statistical analyses reported in Chapter 4. One finding was that the over-seventies and the under-twenties were difficult to engage in task-centred work. Another was that the younger task-centred clients were more likely to report a successful outcome than were the older. It was suggested that the very young and the very old were more likely to be vulnerable clients who had difficulty in managing their affairs, whereas in the middle age range the younger clients were more likely to be facing an acute crisis for which a good outcome was possible, and less likely to be involved in long-standing and intractable situations.

A further result reported in Chapter 4 was that 'success cases' were more likely to come from the problem categories of 'transition to one-parent family' and 'need for alternative child care arrangements'. This finding did not quite reach statistical significance, but was in agreement with earlier discussion of the conditions likely to promote or discourage task-centred work. In these problem categories the clients were unlikely:

(1) to be at cross-purposes with the social worker about the nature of the problem or the desirable solution;
(2) to be basically incapable of managing their affairs;
(3) to require resources which the department or other agencies were unwilling or unlikely to provide;
(4) to require the co-operation of others for resolving the problem to a degree which was unlikely to be forthcoming.

Perhaps the major finding reported in Chapter 4 concerns the influence of individual workers on outcome. Some workers got a relatively high percentage of their clients into task-centred work, and these clients were likely to report considerable problem reduction. Other workers had a relatively high proportion of drop-outs, and those clients who did not drop out were less likely to be satisfied with the results. As a result of these two processes, the 'successes' were almost completely concentrated in the caseloads of four out of the thirteen workers. By contrast, the 'worst' five workers had only one success case out of forty. For statistical reasons these figures almost certainly exaggerated the extent of the difference between the 'good' and 'bad' workers, but they do underline the potential importance of worker differences in the outcomes of task-centred work and the need to examine this in further research.

The research social worker felt that the successful workers were 'better organised' and 'more businesslike' than the others. Statistically, these workers were more likely to select or be allocated cases with problems relating to needs for alternative child care arrangements or to transition from a two- to a one-parent family. In comparison with the other workers, they were particularly successful with these cases. In one office, but not the other, the successful workers were more likely to see their clients quickly. These findings may provide leads on which further research can build.

IMPLICATIONS

The evidence which exists, much of it contained in the next two parts of this book, suggests that task-centred casework does not reduce behavioural symptoms such as delinquency or parasuicide in the face of which traditional casework has lost so much of its reputation. However, task-centred work can enable clients to resolve their problems more successfully than they would without casework (Gibbons *et al.*, 1978), or with other supportive attention (Reid, 1978). The present study has been exploratory and descriptive rather than evaluative, and much of its evidence comes from case studies of very small groups. Nevertheless, the project may further help to clarify what objectives are feasible in task-centred work and what needs to be done to make these objectives more easily achieved.

The project suggested a set of quite stringent conditions for task-centred work to be efficacious. The client must have a problem which he or she wishes to resolve, the social worker must share this view of the problem and be skilled in that particular type of work, the problem must not require resources or the co-operation of others when these are unlikely to be available. If long-term change is desired, the problem selected must be relevant to this change, its resolution should be strategic in terms of its effect on the client's life, and the client should not be vulnerable in the sense of being subject to recurrent emergencies which he or she is unable to handle. On the other hand, casework will be redundant if the client can resolve his or her problems unaided.

It may well be that the coincidence of these conditions is rare, and particularly so in the sort of statutory work in which casework has traditionally been tested. In such work the problem (for example, delinquency) is usually selected by others, the clients are often very vulnerable and by the time anyone thinks of involving a social worker the situation may well be chronic. These considerations may explain the recurrent failure of experiments in social casework to detect much improvement in their subjects and the rather low proportion of clients in the present experiment who reported a substantial or complete reduction in their problems.

Nevertheless, some clients in this study did say that they had been helped and, although it could be argued that they would have resolved their problem in any case, most of them said that this outcome arose partly from the social workers' efforts. There was evidence that some workers were having an effect, whether this was for good or ill, and it is perhaps more productive to concentrate on the implications of this evidence of effectiveness rather than on a post-mortem on social work's past aspirations for the impossible.

In considering these implications, it is important to remember that social work is not simply about helping people or solving problems. It may also, for example, involve ensuring a fairer distribution of scarce resources, monitoring situations which may deteriorate, attempting to control deviant behaviour, facilitating the work of the courts, or satisfying a variety of anxious and sometimes angry people that as much as possible is being done about an apparently hopeless situation. These and other social work activities may be regarded by clients as the reverse of helpful, but they are nevertheless not the whole story. As has been illustrated in this report, social work can help.

Theoretically, this help could do three things: resolve the clients' problems so that they could carry on their lives in their former equilibrium; maintain clients in a precarious equilibrium by recurrent bouts of help in particular emergencies; produce a strategic change in the clients' life so that they could achieve a new equilibrium. A reading of the first account of task-centred casework (Reid and Epstein, 1972) suggests that task-centred casework was designed to return clients to a former state of equilibrium. If so, it would, perhaps, be inappropriate for those whose usual state of being gives rise to long-term concern.

The present project, however, suggests a somewhat wider application for task-centred work. Certainly, a number of basically competent clients who had suffered temporary misfortunes were able to use the help offered to resolve their immediate problems and return to their former condition. However, a number of clients were also helped to make quite radical changes in their circumstances which could be expected to lead to long-term benefits.

There is particular interest in the possibility that task-centred casework could contribute to the long-term maintenance of clients which seems characteristic of much long-term local authority social work. These clients, like those seen at intake, may suffer from attacks of depression, difficulties in arranging care for their children, financial set-backs and breakdowns in communication with others in their families. It seems likely that many of these problems could yield to a task-centred approach, even if this had to take place against a background of long-term support. This could enable these clients to contain their recurrent emergencies and perhaps build up skill in handling them over a period of time. Mattinson and Sinclair (1979) suggest that work of a similar kind can be effective with long-term clients, although they argue that it needs to be supplemented by other techniques.

In developing task-centred work it is necessary to take account of possible differences between individual workers. There is considerable evidence that psychotherapists differ in their effectiveness (Bergin, 1971; Truax and Mitchell, 1971), and also that the individual characteristics of those who run small residential institutions have a massive impact on the well-being and behaviour of the residents (Sinclair, 1971 and 1975; Tizard, 1975). Curiously, investigation of individual differences in the effectiveness of social workers appears to have been neglected despite the crucial relevance of this subject to social work training. The present study suggests that there probably are such differences and that they are important.

The study has less to say on what exactly are the qualities and skills required of the task-centred worker. Reid (1978, p. 300) provides a list of skills which he considers central to task-centred work and he has apparently used this list successfully in training his students. The list is the product of considerable experience and research and it would be wrong to modify it without better evidence than this study could provide. Nevertheless, it may be useful to summarise the areas of skill to which the study is relevant and to which further inquiry could be applied.

First, the study has underlined the paramount importance of getting clear what the client wants and of avoiding the temptation to define these wants in terms of what the agency can provide. It has also suggested that conflict between client and worker, or client and significant others, over the nature of the problem and its solution is very common. For this reason, workers also need to be skilled in understanding the client's view of the problem and in negotiating an agreed version of it. Workers also require skill in timing these negotiations, in that some clients may initially be unwilling to adopt a task-centred approach but come round to this after one or two inter-views. Skills related to timing and to negotiation might perhaps be given greater prominence in Professor Reid's list, although these skills certainly appear in his examples.

A second way in which later work may modify the list concerns the emphasis on specificity and time limits. It may be that the English social workers were less certain than their American counterparts in their use of these concepts. However, there was no evidence that cases where a time limit was agreed were more successful than others which had reached the stage of problem agreement, or that workers who succeeded in agreeing specific problems or tasks were particularly successful. Examination of the follow-up interviews suggested that the clients cast the workers in different roles which, in turn, were associated with a variety of problems. If this differentiation is confirmed by later research, it may be found that particular aspects of task-centred work are only appropriate with certain problems, so that one of the social worker's skills may need to be the selection of the type of role he or she may play in particular situations.

Finally, examination of the workers' records suggested that they had particular batteries of techniques and knowledge which they applied in relation to particular problems. For example, the problems of dealing with transition to a one-parent family, of providing alternative care for children and of tackling financial difficulties, all called forth different kinds of expertise. Workers using task-centred methods will need expertise in a wide range of different problems in order to have confidence in applying the method and to avoid the temptation to define problems so as to fit the worker's competence rather than the client's difficulties.

FURTHER WORK

In the light of all the evidence there seems little doubt that task-centred casework can play an important part in alleviating the problems of some clients. Certainly no one could read the records in this study and fail to think that some of the clients had been helped in important ways. The tasks which remain for research are to specify even more precisely the range of problems for which this technique is appropriate, the situations in which it needs to be modified and the characteristics of the workers who are successful with it.

It may be that this endeavour would proceed more fruitfully, if more slowly, by concentrating on specific groups of problems (for example, the need for short-term child care) and attempting to identify the social work skills and the external resources which are required for their resolution. Such a programme would build on and clarify the expertise which social workers undoubtedly possess in relation to particular problems but which, in its detail, rarely gets written down. Obviously, a programme of this kind would be of little use unless it was translated into training. The National Institute for Social Work has begun to develop training in task-centred work and to encourage support groups for workers interested in it. The costs of development and of the skill training itself are high, and progress is therefore slow. However, if individual differences in skill are important, progress in this field is essential.

REFERENCES: PART I

Bergin, A. E. (1971), 'The evaluation of therapeutic outcomes', in A. E. Bergin and S. L. Garfield (eds), *Handbook of Psychotherapy and Behaviour Change: An Empirical Analysis* (New York: Wiley), pp. 217–70.

Fischer, J. (1976), *The Effectiveness of Social Casework* (Springfield, Ill.: Charles C. Thomas).

Gibbons, J. S., Butler, J., Urwin, P., and Gibbons, J. C. (1978), 'Evaluation of a social work service for self-poisoning patients', *British Journal of Psychiatry*, vol. 133 (August), pp. 111–18.

Glampson, A., and Goldberg, E. M. (1976), 'Post-Seebohm social services: 2 the consumer's viewpoint', *Social Work Today*, vol. 8, no. 16, pp. 7–12.

Goldberg, E. M., Mortimer, A., and Williams, B. T. (1970), *Helping the Aged: A Field Experiment in Social Work* (London: Allen & Unwin).

Goldberg, E. M., Walker, D., and Robinson, J. (1977) 'Exploring the task-centred casework method', *Social Work Today*, vol. 9, no. 2, pp. 9–14.

Goldberg, E. M., and Warburton, R. W. (1979), *Ends and Means in Social Work* (London: Allen & Unwin).

Jones, M. A., Neumann, R., and Shyne, A. W. (1976), *A Second Chance for Families: Evaluation of a Program to Reduce Foster Care* (New York: Child Welfare League of America).

McKay, A., Goldberg, E. M., and Fruin, D. J. (1973), 'Consumers and a social services department', *Social Work Today*, vol. 4, no. 16, pp. 486–91.

Mattinson, J., and Sinclair, I. A. C. (1979), *Mate and Stalemate: Working with Marital Problems in a Social Services Department* (Oxford: Blackwell).

Mayer, J. E., and Timms, N. (1970), *The Client Speaks* (London: Routledge & Kegan Paul).

O'Connor, P., 'The Brown *et al.* vulnerability model: observations and reflections' (unpublished).

Parsloe, P. (1978), 'Some educational implications', in O. Stevenson and P. Parsloe (eds), *Social Service Teams: The Practitioner's View* (London: HMSO) pp. 329–59.

Reid, W. J. (1978), *The Task-Centered System* (New York: Columbia University Press).

Reid, W. J. and Epstein, L. (1972), *Task-Centered Casework* (New York: Columbia University Press).

Reid, W. J., and Shyne, A. W. (1969), *Brief and Extended Casework* (New York: Columbia University Press).

Ripple, L. (1957), 'Motivation capacity and opportunity as related to the use of casework services: theoretical base and plan of study', *Social Work*, vol. 2, no. 1, pp. 87–94.

Sainsbury, E. (1980) 'Client need, social work method and agency function: a research perspective', *Social Work Service*, no. 23, pp. 9–15.

Shaw, M. J. (1974), *Social Work in Prison*, Home Office Research Study No. 22 (London: HMSO).

Sinclair, I. A. C. (1971), *Hostels for Probationers*, Home Office Research Study No. 6 (London: HMSO).

Sinclair, I. A. C. (1975), 'Influence of wardens and matrons on probation hostels', in J. Tizard, R. V. G. Clarke, and I. A. C. Sinclair, (eds), *Varieties of Residential Experience* (London: Routledge & Kegan Paul) pp. 122–40.

Sinclair, I. A. C., Shaw, M. J., and Troop, J. (1974), 'The relationship between introversion and response to casework in a prison setting', *British Journal of Social and Clinical Psychology*, vol. 13, no. 1, pp. 57–60.

Stein, J., and Gambrill, E. (1977), 'Facilitating decision making in foster care', *Social Services Review*, vol. 51, no. 3, pp. 502–11.

Tizard, J. (1975), 'Quality of residential care for retarded children', in J. Tizard, R. V. G. Clarke, and I. A. C. Sinclair (eds), *Varieties of Residential Experience* (London: Routledge & Kegan Paul) pp. 102–21.

Truax, C. B., and Mitchell, K. M. (1971), 'Research on certain therapist interpersonal skills in relation to process and outcome', in A. E. Bergin and S. L. Garfield (eds), *Handbook of Psychotherapy and Behaviour Change: An Empirical Analysis* (New York: Wiley) pp. 299–344.

Wood, K. M. (1978), 'Casework effectiveness: a new look at the research evidence', *Social Work*, vol. 23, no. 6, pp. 437–59.

Wootton, B. (1960), *Social Science and Social Pathology* (London: Allen & Unwin).

PART II

TASK-CENTRED CASEWORK
IN A PROBATION SETTING

*by E. Matilda Goldberg and Stephen J. Stanley with
the assistance of Jenny Kenrick*

ACKNOWLEDGEMENTS: PART II

This study was jointly undertaken by the National Institute for Social Work and the then Inner London Probation and After-Care Service. It was mainly financed by the DHSS and partly by ILPAS. This project could not have flourished without the active and persistent collaboration of the staff of the experimental probation unit in which it took place and the encouragement and good will of the ILPAS management. Unfortunately, the departure of the workers to various new posts deprived us of opportunities for continued collaboration and consultation during the writing-up stage which would have undoubtedly enlivened and enriched the following pages.

Chapter 6

EVALUATING THE EFFECTIVENESS OF PROBATION

Most of the problems discussed in the Introduction in relation to the effectiveness of social work also apply to the field of probation. Martinson (1974) in his review of 231 studies reported from 1945 to 1967 concludes that 'with few and isolated exceptions, the rehabilitative efforts that have been reported so far had no appreciable effect on recidivism' (p. 17). Similar conclusions are reached from a survey of published research carried out in the Home Office Research Unit by Brody (1976). In a more hopeful vein Lipton and his colleagues (1975) also suggest that casework and individual counselling may be associated with reduction of recidivism if directed towards the solution of immediate problems such as housing, finance, jobs, or illness which have high priority for offenders. For our purposes in this chapter we shall only select a few salient points for discussion which help to highlight issues which have also become apparent in the task-centred casework project.

The first point relates to the aims, and hence to the outcome criteria, of probation. It has been pointed out repeatedly that although the reconviction rate is the only reliable objective outcome measure available, it is doubtful whether it measures reformatory effect. However, an important question is whether the probation officer's intervention is primarily aimed at the prevention of delinquent acts. In our case discussions at the Differential Treatment Unit (DTU) where the task-centred probation project took place, we could at times only find a tenuous relationship between the problem areas the client wanted to work on, the tasks to be undertaken and the delinquent behaviour. In their report on the IMPACT experiment, Folkard and his colleagues (1976) point out that although the participating probation officers most frequently mentioned reconviction record as a criterion of success, many of them attached little importance to reconviction. Other objectives often mentioned were changes in inter-personal relationships, reduction of presenting problem, improvements in the client's social situation, and so on. But it is not established, as yet, how such improvements in inter-personal relationships and in the client's immediate social situation are related to delinquent behaviour. For instance, although the ratings of the supervising officers in the IMPACT experiment indicated that the situations of the experimental group in relation to family, leisure and work had improved significantly compared with the control group, yet significantly more of the experimentals spent some time in custody during the supervision period than did the controls. Similarly, in the community treatment project in California the experimental group, though rated more successful in some respects, was committing more offences than the control group, but they were not always being counted as failures because apparently a more lenient policy was adopted towards them. Current reappraisal of the treatment or rehabilitative model with its dubious results has led to a renewed emphasis on retribution or punishment within a justice model which it is suggested should be separated from any 'treatment' an offender might seek voluntarily for any problems in living (Bean, 1976; Folkard, 1980).

The second point we wish to consider is the nature of the input and its appropriateness for the aims pursued. As in other forms of social work and inter-personal forms of help it is extremely difficult to describe, let alone classify or measure, what actually goes on in the interaction between social worker and client. Yet, as Brody aptly says, 'various types of treatment have been discussed and evaluated as if their characteristics were precisely known, in the same way as the properties of pharmaceutical drugs are understood and exploited' (1976, p. 55). In Reid and Shyne's brief and extended casework experiment it was at least certain that the input in the experimental group was much less than in the continued service group (422 interviews compared with 1,562 interviews). Reid and Shyne (1969) were also able to show differences in intervention methods used in the two groups. Similar considerations apply to a field experiment in social work with the aged (Goldberg *et al.*, 1970).

However, in the IMPACT experiment, although the probation officers engaged in more 'situational' treatment, that is to say meeting their clients outside their office and becoming more involved with their families and associates, the extra time available appears to have been channelled mainly into the traditional areas of marital and family help, leaving areas such as work and accommodation relatively untouched. For example, in the London IMPACT sample 51 per cent of the clients were unemployed at the time of their current offence, yet in the subsequent probation order only 8 per cent received extra help related to work. Two consequences flow from these facts. First, that it was not possible to show that the experimental and comparison groups had definably different types of treatment, yet testing the effects of two demonstrably *different* methods of intervention is the essence of an experimental design. Secondly, as in the social work experiments discussed in Chapter 1, one could question the appropriateness of the treatment offered, as well as the immediate objectives.

Lastly, we want to touch on the problem of specificity: which methods work best, carried out by whom, in what kinds of problem situations, with what kinds of people, in what types of settings? Certain pointers are emerging on some aspects of this topic. For instance, evidence is accruing from studies in social work and criminology which indicate that an intermediate group of offenders (or social work clients) who are neither first offenders nor confirmed recidivists (neither people experiencing minimal transient problems nor chronically disturbed people) are the best targets for successful intervention. As will be seen later, there is even a hint in our own modest findings that a middle group, those with one previous offence, were likely to do best.

The other findings in relation to specificity which are possibly of some significance are those related to personality types of clients. There is some evidence (Shaw, 1974; Sinclair *et al*., 1974) that offenders with a high degree of introversion respond better to counselling towards the end of a long-term prison sentence than extroverts, as reflected in significantly lower reconviction rates. It is of interest that these findings were not confirmed with short-term prisoners (Fowles, 1978). In the IMPACT experiment a suggestion emerged that offenders with low criminal tendencies and many personal problems had a more successful outcome than probationers with moderate or high criminal tendencies and average or few personal problems. Conversely, offenders with moderate or high criminal tendencies and average or few personal problems did significantly worse under intensive situational treatment than under normal probation supervision. These findings are echoed in our small task-centred study, which indicates that an acknowledgement of problems and a readiness to work on them, in conjunction with low criminal tendencies, seemed to be associated with favourable outcome.

There is also the personality and style of the key workers, be they hostel warden, social worker, or probation officer. A variety of studies suggest that success and failure is more dependent on such personality factors than had been previously supposed and that these may be relatively independent of skill training. Although the samples in the task-centred studies are small and findings have to be interpreted cautiously, there are indications that worker variables are associated with outcome and that these are possibly more important than the methods used.

Chapter 7

SETTING AND AIMS OF
THE PROJECT

THE SETTING

The probation project took place at the Differential Treatment Unit (DTU), an Inner London probation office which was especially set up as one of the experimental units for an earlier probation experiment. The DTU continued as a special unit with a brief to innovate and develop new practices, and was already experimenting with short-term probation orders of six months' duration at the time when one of us (EMG) was looking for a group of probation officers able and willing to explore the application of task-centred casework to probation. The unit, situated in Islington, consisted of six trained and experienced probation officers of whom one was a senior. They operated with reduced caseloads compared with ordinary probation officers, carrying no more than about twelve active cases; they held frequent case discussions and they had developed a method of 'shadowing', that is to say each case taken on by an officer had a shadow appointed with whom the officer could discuss, and if necessary share, the case.

The group was keen to explore the task-centred method. After all the members of the DTU had read the basic text by Reid and Epstein (1972), discussions took place about the method and the feasibility of setting up a joint project between the Inner London Probation and After-Care Service and the National Institute for Social Work. A pilot study was begun in February 1976 in which the probation officers tried to apply the method to new referrals; during this phase the recording instruments to be used were adapted to the probation setting. Fortnightly meetings of the whole unit with the two authors were instituted and, at first, were used to explore and discuss the main elements of the method, both in relation to theory and practice, since it departed in important respects from the methods of casework this group had used in the recent past. By April 1976 all the administrative details had been sorted out, including discussions with the magistrates concerned, and the main study began.

The aims of the study were:

(1) To explore whether the task-centred model, which was designed for 'voluntary' clients who wished to do something about acknowledged problems, can be used in the context of 'involuntary' clients who have come to the attention of social workers because society is concerned about their behaviour and where the casework is part of a judicial order.

(2) To find out how helpful the method is in alleviating specified target problems as judged:
    (a) by the clients themselves at the end of the probation period;
    (b) by the probation officers;
    (c) by reconviction rates.

THE DESIGN OF THE STUDY

As already explained in Chapter 1 it seemed important first of all to try out and possibly refine and adapt the task-centred method to the requirements of the probation setting before embarking on a tightly controlled study comparing task-centred casework methods with other ways of carrying out probation supervision. Hence the design of the study reported here was a simple before-and-after one which compared the state of the problem(s) specified at the beginning of the probation period with the problem situation, as assessed by the client in an interview with an independent assessor, at the end of the period. This measure of problem reduction was related to another outcome measure which is the degree to which, in the opinion of the probation officer and the client, the tasks undertaken to alleviate a specific problem or problems had been achieved.

We also attempted to relate these outcome measures to a number of independent background factors and to the amount and type of input in terms of number of interview, intervention methods used by different workers and, finally, to the independent criterion of reconviction rates.

In the following chapter we shall describe, first, the administrative organisation of the project, how all the referrals coming in for enquiry reports from the courts were assessed, and how the sample of 100 short-term probation orders was arrived at.

We then discuss the input, showing how the short-term probation orders fared, how the task-centred model was used within the constraints of a probation setting, and what turned out to be the outstanding features of task-centred intervention. In Chapter 14 outcome is discussed and in Chapter 16 some conclusions are drawn about possible future policies and research.

Chapter 8

SAMPLE AND FLOW OF
REFERRALS

REFERRAL PROCEDURE

While experimenting with short-term probation orders, the staff of the Differential Treatment Unit (DTU) had already come to a special arrangement about referral procedures with the local magistrates' courts and the probation teams serving them:[1] the first two or three offenders appearing on specified days of the week at these courts who were remanded for a social enquiry report (SER) and were not currently known to another probation officer were referred to the DTU.[2]

In order to allow the DTU staff to develop short-term probation methods a further agreement had been reached with local magistrates that the court would make a probation order for one year (the minimum period then allowed by law) on the understanding that it would normally be terminated by conversion to a conditional discharge after six months. It was understood, however, that under certain circumstances an order would be allowed to run its full course.[3]

When an offender was referred to the DTU for an SER, the probation officer concerned used the remand period to carry out a careful problem exploration to establish whether a target problem and a task, or tasks, designed to tackle the problem could be agreed with the offender. If an agreement was reached, the probation officer would suggest in the SER a 'short-term probation order', usually setting out in the recommendation the problem and tasks to be worked on, as shown in the following example;

In discussion . . . we have agreed to concentrate in the first instance on obtaining employment and then to find more satisfactory social situations in which she can make new relationships. Mrs A has agreed to be supervised intensively in order to meet the above objectives, and in the event of the court agreeing to make a probation order, I would respectfully ask that it should be for a short period.

If the court accepted the officer's recommendation, a one-year probation order was made with the client's agreement, on the understanding that it would normally be terminated after about six months.

THE SAMPLE

The aim was to study 100 short-term probation orders. From information available about referral rates and the proportion of cases in which probation was recommended, it seemed likely that a year's intake, together with some cases taken on just before the starting date, would provide the sample required. Assuming that each probation order lasted six months, the fieldwork was expected to end after eighteen months by October 1977.

It soon became apparent that the original estimate of the time required to obtain 100 short-term probation orders was over-optimistic. While in the period preceding the project approximately half the SERs prepared by the DTU had resulted in probation orders, during the project period the proportion was more like one in four or five. Hence, it was agreed to extend the fieldwork phase by six months. As the numbers still fell short of the required 100 by that date, all probation orders made during a further three months were added, so that fieldwork continued for over two years.

DATA COLLECTION

Information was collected about SERs and cases in the project, from case papers, interview schedules, task formulation sheets, final interview summaries, follow-up interviews and team discussions. Finally, in 1982 data about reconvictions were added. (See Chapter 10 for further description of the method.)

DATA ANALYSIS

Quantifiable information was recorded for analysis on edge-punched (Copechat) cards.

In addition, the follow-up interviews were analysed separately, scaling quantifiable responses not yet in scaled form on the interview schedule. Before analysing these results, the two researchers and the independent assessor rated the responses independently; any disagreements arising in a small number of cases were then thrashed out in discussion until agreement was reached.

Finally, qualitative data from the discussion notes and case records were used, as described more fully in Chapter 11.

To summarise, the progress of a probation case through the project would be as follows:

(1) Referred for SER
(2) Problem exploration during remand
(3) Recommendation of short-term probation order if a problem and task had been formulated or were likely to be formulated and probation was otherwise appropriate
(4) One-year probation order made if magistrate accepts recommendation
(5) Task formulation completed
(6) Work on task(s)
(7) Final interview; client asked about follow-up
(8) Order converted to conditional discharge after about six months
(9) Independent assessor informed if client agrees to follow-up
(10) Independent assessor attempts to contact client
(11) If contact established, independent assessor interviews client
(12) Analysis of data
(13) Relating outcome data to reconviction rates.

REFERRALS TO THE MAIN SAMPLE

During the period 1 April 1976–30 September 1977, a total of 435 offenders were referred for SERs to the DTU, and 406 (93 per cent) reports were prepared (see Figure 8.1). Fourteen offenders failed to appear (3 per cent); seven were transferred to other probation teams (2 per cent); in eight cases no information was available as to why the report was not prepared (2 per cent). These 406 reports produced eighty-six 'short-term' probation orders, as well as ten other probation orders, eight extending over one year, and two with special conditions of treatment attached. Thus a probation order was made in 24 per cent of cases on which SERs were prepared. In six of these eighty-six short-term orders no task formulation was undertaken, and they were rejected from the sample as not being task-centred. A further fourteen short-term task-centred probation orders were made on clients referred shortly before 1 April 1976 and six on clients referred after 30 September 1977, and these brought the total of such orders to 100. As Figure 8.1 shows in 93 (23 per cent) of the 406 SERs, the probation officers recommended a short-term probation order; but only seventy-four (80 per cent) of these recommendations were accepted by the magistrates. The probation officers recommended other types of disposal (including eight long-term probation orders) in 313 cases, and

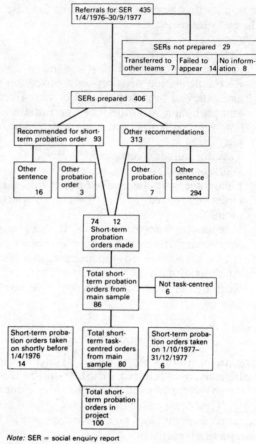

Note: SER = social enquiry report

Figure 8.1   *Progress of main sample cases*

in twelve of these the magistrates decided on a short-term probation order.

The first question we asked was whether offenders for whom probation was recommended differed in their social and demographic characteristics from those for whom other recommendations were made. The results of this analysis are shown in Table 8.1.

It can be seen from this table that the two groups were remarkably similar. The major difference is that those for whom short-term probation was recommended were less likely to be in employment.

Table 8.1   *Characteristics of Offenders and Probation Officers'
Recommendations*

	Short-term probation N=93 %	Other disposals N=313 %	All referrals: N=406 %
Client lives:			
Alone	8 9	23 7	31 8
In family with children under 17	38 41	130 42	168 41
In family without children under 17	15 16	43 14	58 14
In other private household	12 13	54 17	66 16
In residential accommodation	9 10	9 3	18 4
In other accommodation (e.g., squatting, no fixed abode)	11 12	50 16	61 15
Not stated	— —	4 1	4 1
Client is:			
Male	65 70	233 74	298 73
Female	28 30	80 26	108 27
Aged 17–20	39 42	103 33	142 35
21–24	14 15	56 18	70 17
25 or over	40 43	150 48	190 47
Not stated	— —	4 1	4 1
Divorced/separated/widowed	17 18	40 13	57 14
Single	49 53	175 56	224 55
Married	15 16	64 20	79 19
Cohabiting	12 13	32 10	44 11
Marital status not stated	— —	2 1	2 —
Employed	30 32	151 48	181 45
Unemployed	50 54	127 41	177 44
Housewife	4 4	10 3	14 3
Unsupported mother	7 8	16 5	23 6
Student/OAP	2 2	6 2	8 2
Not stated	— —	3 1	3 1
Client has:			
No previous convictions	21 23	96 31	117 29
One previous conviction known	23 25	50 16	73 18
More than one conviction known	47 51	153 49	200 49
No information on convictions	2 2	14 4	16. 4

There is also an indication that they were more likely to be second
offenders and less likely to be first offenders.

Those actually placed on a short-term probation order differed in
more respects, however, from those who were not (Table 8.2). They
were more likely to be female, aged 17–20, second offenders and

Table 8.2 *Characteristics of Offenders: Magistrates' Disposals*

	Short-term probation N = 86 %		Long-term probation N = 10	Other disposals N = 310 %		All referrals N = 406 %	
Client lives:							
Alone	5	6	1	25	8	31	8
In family with children under 17	36	42	3	129	42	168	41
In family without children under 17	16	29	—	42	14	58	14
In other private household	9	10	2	55	18	66	16
In residential accommodation	6	7	4	8	3	18	4
In other accommodation (e.g., squatting, no fixed abode)	14	16	—	47	15	61	15
Not stated	—	—	—	4	1	4	1
Client is:							
Male	55	64	8	235	76	298	73
Female	31	36	2	75	24	108	27
Aged 17–20	39	45	5	98	32	142	35
21–24	15	17	2	53	17	70	17
25 or over	32	37	3	155	50	190	47
Not stated	—	—	—	4	1	4	1
Divorced/separated/ wjdowed	16	19	1	40	13	57	14
Single	46	53	9	169	55	224	55
Married	11	15	—	66	21	79	19
Cohabiting	13	13	—	33	11	44	11
Marital status not stated	—	—	—	2	1	2	—
Employed	25	29	4	152	49	181	45
Unemployed	46	53	6	125	40	177	44
Housewife	5	6	—	9	3	14	3
Unsupported mother	7	8	—	16	5	23	6
Student/OAP	3	3	—	5	2	8	2
Not stated	—	—	—	3	1	3	1
Client has:							
No previous convictions	25	29	2	90	29	117	29
One previous conviction known	23	27	2	48	15	73	18
More than one conviction known	38	44	6	156	50	200	49
No information on convictions	—	—	—	16	5	16	4

unemployed. In particular, the magistrates' choices show a shift towards probation for women, towards first and second offenders, and away from older offenders and those with multiple convictions.

Unfortunately, no comparable information is available about the characteristics of offenders remanded for SERs by magistrates' courts in Inner London in 1976 to show how far our main sample is typical of such a population. In 1980, however, the Inner London Probation Service carried out a survey of SERs prepared by probation officers, and we have studied the figures from this survey in respect of cases in the north-east division of Inner London (covering the Boroughs of Hackney, Islington and Tower Hamlets), in terms of the following variables: age of offender, employment status, previous convictions, sex, and accommodation.

These figures show that offenders referred to the DTU were more likely to be living in fixed accommodation (80 per cent against 72 per cent), more likely to be female (27 per cent against 20 per cent), more likely to be aged over 20 (65 per cent against 58 per cent) and more likely to be first offenders (29 per cent against 18 per cent); and also less likely to be unemployed (44 per cent against 52 per cent). None of these differences are statistically significant and some may be attributed to the fact that the DTU only took on cases that were not already known to a probation officer.

Twenty-eight per cent of the SERs in the 1980 Inner London sample, contained recommendations for probation compared with 25 per cent in our main sample. Twenty-three per cent were specifically recommended for short-term probation and these reports were also compared with the recommendations for probation in the Inner London study. We found that the DTU reports contained fewer clients in non-fixed accommodation (20 per cent against 29 per cent) more clients aged 21 or over (61 per cent against 53 per cent), but about the same proportion of unemployed (50 per cent against 51 per cent) and only slightly more first offenders (23 per cent against 21 per cent). The percentages of women in the two groups were similar.

The figures suggest that while the sample of cases referred to the DTU may not be entirely typical of all SERs prepared for magistrates' courts, the profiles of those cases in which probation was recommended are very similar in terms of age, sex and previous convictions. Thus there is no evidence from this analysis that the clients for whom DTU officers recommended probation were consistently better or worse risks than those for whom probation was recommended in the 1980 sample. The cases taken on by the DTU therefore appear to be within the 'main stream' of probation cases.

REASONS AGAINST RECOMMENDING PROBATION

As already shown, probation was recommended in about a quarter of the cases in the main sample. Officers had undertaken to recommend a short-term probation order when they had reached agreement with the client on a problem area – and preferably also a task – to work on, and when probation was not for other reasons impractical or inappropriate (for example, because of the nature of the offence committed or because the client lived too far away). The DTU team and the researchers carried out a systematic examination of the reasons for not recommending probation in three out of four cases. We first tried to

Table 8.3   *Main Reasons against Recommending Probation*

Reason	N	%
Client denies offence	8	3
Trivial offence	3	1
Client *has* no or only slight problems*	27	9
Client *perceives* no problems	51	16
No agreement on problem area	27	9
Problems are identified but client does not want to do anything about them	16	5
Client can cope by himself	41	13
Problems solved in enquiry stage	5	2
Problems regarded by probation officer as too severe/ pervasive	13	4
No task identified (although problems were)	3	1
Other social work agency more appropriate	26	8
Other judicial disposal more appropriate	18	6
Insufficient contact with client	5	2
Situational obstacles to realistic problem exploration	7	2
Client hostile to probation officer/order	24	8
Probation physically impractical	6	2
Other reasons	15	5
No main reason	4	1
No reason identifiable	6	2
No information	8	3
Total number where probation not recommended	313	100

* as far as could be ascertained by probation officer and client.

identify all the possible reasons for not recommending probation and then distilled them into usable categories. These were tested for reliability and modified in the light of this test. The coding was based primarily on the content of the SER and wherever possible carried out by the probation officer responsible for preparing the SER. Officers were asked to code *every* reason affecting the decision as well as the main reason. Out of a total of 313 cases 305 were examined, as there was insufficient information on which to base a judgement in 8 of them. The results of this analysis (Table 8.3) show that while in 14 per cent of the cases other disposals or agencies were seen as more appropriate, the *primary* reason (in 59 per cent of SERs) for rejecting probation as a mode of treatment was an inability to locate or agree on a problem to tackle. This could arise from a variety of circumstances: because there were no major problems to resolve (other than the one of being before the court); because the client seemed able to resolve his or her problems without any help from the probation service; because although others saw a problem, the client did not acknowledge it; because no agreement could be reached between probation officer and client; because the problems were solved during the remand period; or because they were so pervasive and chronic that short-term work had little or no chance of effecting any changes.

NOTES: CHAPTER 8

1 The three courts of Clerkenwell, Highbury Corner and Old Street Magistrates' Courts cover the London Borough of Islington and parts of the Boroughs of Camden and Hackney.
2 Social enquiry reports (SERs) are prepared either before trial or after conviction, but before sentence on defendants in criminal cases, to aid the court in sentencing by presenting information about the defendant's social background in relation to the offence. All SERs on defendants aged 17 or over appearing before the courts are prepared by the probation service. Probation officers have been encouraged by the Home Office to make recommendations as to the appropriateness or otherwise of a probation order in each case, and if the court requires, to comment on the defendant's suitability for a community service order or for a particular custodial sentence. This has been generally (but not universally) interpreted to give probation officers the power to recommend other sentences or disposals to the courts.
   In the Inner London Probation Area SERs for magistrates' courts are (unless the defendant is already well known to the probation officer and herself or himself requests a pre-trial report) prepared after guilt has been established – but before sentence is passed. To enable the report to be prepared, defendants are remanded for two or three weeks on bail or in custody. When an offender is remanded for an SER, the court's request for a report is passed to a probation team covering the area in which the offender lives, or to an officer already supervising the offender. In this study the process by which an offender is remanded for an SER and the request for the SER is passed to a team (in this case the DTU) or officer is called a *referral*.

3   At the time of the project the minimum length allowed for a probation order was
    one year. The probation order could be discharged by the court or substituted by a
    conditional discharge before the end of the period set for the order, and might also
    be replaced by another (harsher) sentence if the client reoffended or otherwise
    breached the conditions of the order.

    The 1977 Criminal Law Act gave the Home Secretary the power to reduce a
    minimum length of probation order to six months and this change came into force
    on the 1 May 1978. (It seems likely that the introduction of the six-month probation
    order was aided by the experience of the DTU in working in this way.)

Chapter 9

THROUGHPUT AND ANALYSIS OF 100 SHORT-TERM PROBATION ORDERS

The intention was to work on task-centred lines with all the 100 cases in which a short-term probation order had been made and to discharge the order at the end of six months. These plans did not always work out, as Table 9.1 shows.

Table 9.1 *Disposal of 100 Short-Term Probation Orders*

	N
Order converted at end of 6 months	64
Order continued on initiative of magistrate, probation officer, or client	17
Order ended in breach, another sentence, or client disappeared	17
Order transferred	2
Total N	100

Almost two-thirds of the orders were converted to conditional discharges at the end of six months as planned. The remaining thirty-six fell into roughly two groups: in the first either the probation officer or the magistrate decided to carry on the order for the full year, mainly because the probationer's delinquent behaviour or other social circumstances gave cause for concern; the second group consisted of those who either committed further offences and received custodial sentences or who disappeared.

The first question then is: Did those for whom short-term task-centred probation did not work out differ from those who successfully completed the short-term order? They did differ in important socio-demographic respects, as Table 9.2 indicates.

More of them were single people (72 per cent compared with 44 per cent), between the ages of 17 and 20 (56 per cent compared with 34 per cent), far fewer lived in families (33 per cent compared with 73 per cent), more belonged to ethnic minorities (39 per cent compared with 22 per cent), and more were unemployed (64 per cent against 47 per cent).

Table 9.2 *Socio-Demographic Characteristics of 100 Probationers in Two Disposal Groups*

	Order converted at 6 months		Order not converted at 6 months	
	N = 64	%	N = 36	%
Age:				
17–20	22	34	20	56
21–34	30	47	13	36
35–64	11	17	3	8
65 +	1	2	—	—
Sex:				
Male	39	61	23	64
Female	25	39	13	36
Marital Status:				
Single	28	44	26	72
Married	10	16	1	3
Cohabiting	9	14	5	14
Divorced/Separated	15	23	4	11
Widowed	2	3	—	—
Living in family setting	47	73	12	33
Not in family setting	17	27	24	67
From ethnic minority group	14	22	14	39
Not from ethnic minority group	50	78	22	61
Employed at start of order	19	30	11	31
Unemployed at start of order	30	47	23	64
Unsupported mother	9	14	1	3
Housewife	4	6	—	—
Student	1	2	1	3
Retired	1	2	—	—

As Table 9.3 shows, more of those whose order was not converted at six months were remanded in custody for the preparation of a social enquiry report (SER) (31 per cent and 20 per cent), and more had over four previous convictions (36 per cent compared with 14 per cent). It is also of interest that of eight prostitutes taken on for probation, six belonged to the group which did not successfully complete the six months' short-term order.

Thus it would seem that the thirty-six whose order was not converted at the end of six months were more socially disadvantaged and their problems were probably less amenable to short-term casework.

If we look at the problem areas (according to the Reid typology described in the Introduction, pp. 5–9), we also detect some

Table 9.3   *'Criminal' Characteristics of 100 Probationers in Two Disposal Groups*

| | Order converted at 6 months | | Order not converted at 6 months | |
	N = 64	%	N = 36	%
Offence:				
Against property	51	80	25	69
Against persons	4	6	1	3
Other offences	9	14	10	28
Remanded in custody	13	20	11	31
Remanded on bail	51	80	25	69
Recorded previous convictions:				
None	20	31	9	25
One	19	30	10	28
2 or 3	16	25	4	11
4 or more	9	14	13	36

differences between the two groups (Table 9.3). More of the probationers whose cases remained open singled out difficulties in role performance, mainly related to work, as their most pressing problem. On the other hand, none of them identified inter-personal conflict as the main focus of difficulty, while this problem area was the focus of task-centred work in seven of the short-term cases. (Since these problems usually centred on marital conflict, this difference is probably associated with the fact that far more of the short-term probationers lived in a permanent marital or cohabiting relationship.)

Table 9.4   *Problem Area of 100 Probationers in Two Disposal Groups*

| Problem area | Order converted at 6 months | | Order not converted at 6 months | | Total |
	N	%	N	%	N
Dissatisfaction in social relations	20	31	11	31	31
Difficulties in role performance	14	22	13	36	27
Inadequate resources	9	15	5	14	14
Inter-personal conflict	7	11	—	—	7
Reactive emotional distress	6	9	3	8	9
Problems of social transition	6	9	1	3	7
Problems with formal organisations	—	—	1	3	1
Behavioural problems	1	2	2	6	3
Unclassifiable	1	2	—	—	1
Total	64	100	36	100	100

The casework with sixty-four probationers could be regarded as task-centred since the following criteria were fulfilled: a contract in the form of an agreement on problem and task had been made, there was evidence that work on the task had been carried out, and the probation order was converted into a conditional discharge at the end of about six months.*

As Table 9.2 showed, the majority were under the age of 35; three-fifths were men; although fewer than half (44 per cent) were single, only 16 per cent were married in the conventional sense of the word. The rest either cohabited or were divorced and separated. Nevertheless, nearly three-quarters of these sixty-four lived in some kind of family setting. Practically half were unemployed at the start of the order. Over two-thirds had at least one previous conviction, and half had two or more previous convictions. Most – about three-quarters of them – had committed some form of theft, or other offences against property. Well over half of these delinquents came from very disrupted backgrounds, for example, they had been separated from one or both of their parents for long periods during their childhood.

As far as we have been able to ascertain, the social and demographic characteristics of this sample of offenders are similar to other groups of probationers and delinquents studied. In terms of the proportion unemployed this is similar to probationers in the IMPACT experiment (Folkard *et al.*, 1976), while the prevalence of parental separation echoes the strong association between this factor and delinquency observed by West and Farrington (1973) and many others. It seems, then, that our sample was not a highly selected group of first-time offenders living in supportive environments. Many of them were socially or emotionally adrift, without a job or settled way of life and on bad terms with their families.

How then did the task-centred method work out among a group of clients with such widespread social and emotional difficulties, none of whom had asked for help in the first place?

The typologies of problem situations and intervention techniques developed by Reid and Epstein (1972), described in the Introduction and in Appendix A respectively, were used in the analysis. Ideally, in order to check on the reliability and validity of the intervention

---

*Although the intention was to convert the order at the end of six months, administrative delays occasionally postponed the date for a month or two.

techniques coded by the workers, a sample of interviews should be tape-recorded so that independent assessors can listen to the responses and assign them to the various intervention categories (Reid and Shyne, 1969). It soon emerged that regular, or even occasional, tape-recordings of interviews with clients did not prove feasible, especially as the researchers were not prepared to apply undue pressure which could have jeopardised the whole enterprise. A compromise was worked out, according to which probation officers estimated after each interview what percentage of the session had been devoted to the various intervention techniques. This method can only convey the probation officer's *subjective* perception of what actually went on, but it may tell us something about the worker's preferred style which, in turn, may be related to outcome. We also asked the probation officers to indicate which of the various modes of intervention used seemed the most important in each interview. As will be shown later, the importance of a particular type of intervention is not necessarily associated with the amount of time taken up by it – particularly in those interviews which took place after the exploratory remand period.

In addition to completing interview schedules, the probation officers continued to write narrative accounts of their interviews with clients and usually two-monthly summaries. Wherever possible a final interview was conducted along structured lines which traced once more the original target problem, explored what the probationers had got out of the probation experience, how much they felt they had contributed themselves, and how they saw their future. Finally, the probationer and probation officer usually discussed and scored the degree of task achievement; the probation officer also scored how much the problem(s) originally identified had been reduced in his or her view.

Fortnightly group discussions were held with Tilda Goldberg and Stephen Stanley in which most of the 100 cases came up for review and these were written up by Stephen Stanley after each session. In the beginning stages of the project the focus was on problem exploration and on the evolution and formulation of tasks. Later on, when cases tended to be discussed near the closing stage, the emphasis shifted towards an assessment of the whole course of intervention and its outcome and how the task-centred method had contributed to this outcome.

In summary: we have a few quantitative measures of *input*, such as numbers of interviews, and proportion spent on task(s); the distribution and importance of different intervention techniques, and the write-ups of the case discussions. Finally, there exists a vast amount of unstructured narrative material. Several attempts were made by the authors to devise a systematic framework for analysing this descriptive material, but none of the approaches proved satisfactory within the limits of the time and resources available.

The main *outcome* measures used were the task achievement scores arrived at in the final interview with the probation officer and, in the cases which were followed up by the independent assessor, the clients' judgements on the status of their original problems. In addition, we were able to score ten of the clients' answers to the assessor's key questions about the process and outcome of their probation experience. Finally, we obtained reconviction rates up to three years after the start of the orders.

In the following analysis of input and outcome we have tried to arrive at a compromise between qualitative and quantitative data. We look at the process of adopting and adapting the task-centred model to the probation setting, we describe typical problem situations and tasks and highlight some of the characteristics of the task-centred method as seen by clients, probation officers and the independent assessor. Finally, we use quantitative data associated with input and outcome on task-centred criteria and relate these to the independent and external measure of reconviction.

Chapter 10

TASK-CENTRED CASEWORK IN A PROBATION SETTING

As was already suggested in the Introduction, probation officers usually deal with clients who have been declared problematic or 'deviant' by other members of society and who are referred to the probation officer for enquiries and a report within the framework of a court of law. These features are at first sight far removed from the aims and methods of task-centred casework intended for clients who perceive problems in themselves or in their environments they wish to resolve. However, long before task-centred casework was thought of probation officers were selective about the offenders they recommended for probation. Although the criteria were never clearly stated, this selection appeared to be associated with the client's ability to 'co-operate' with the probation officer; but the aim of this collaboration remained vague. The criteria for selection were usually derived from clinical hunches related to the offender's previous history and behaviour patterns, and were rarely brought out into the open and discussed with him or her. In any case, the offender was often not aware of the 'underlying' problems that were thought to cause his or her difficulties, and still less was the client considered able to articulate what he or she might contribute to alleviate these problems (Bottoms and McWilliams, 1979).

The important change resulting from task-centred casework and other developments towards a more openly shared contractual type of casework is that the probation officers in this project only recommended those cases for probation where, after careful exploration, a specific problem could be identified which the client recognised and acknowledged as something he or she wanted to tackle and where some kind of probation objective could be defined.

For example, in the case of a married woman in her late forties who was caught shoplifting, although she and her husband were quite well off, the offence seemed to be related to a marital crisis. The probation officer's report concludes:

Both husband and wife have expressed considerable enthusiasm to attempt to see if there was some way they could improve their current matrimonial situation and would welcome assistance from the Probation Service to try and achieve this. The court might feel reluctant to order a period of probation supervision considering this is Mrs A's first offence. Nevertheless, I feel that the legal structure of such an order would greatly help her to try and contain some of her anxiety which sometimes seems to her as if it spills everywhere and is uncontainable.

Or, in the case of an 18-year-old youngster involved with others in the theft of a motor car the proposed 'contract' reads as follows:

During the remand period Mr B. had co-operated in having his reading and writing skills assessed by a colleague. He expresses a keenness to undertake further instruction which can be provided by the Probation Service. He has also expressed a willingness to co-operate in looking for work with the assistance and direction of myself. These undertakings would necessitate his attending this office three times per week until he found employment and twice thereafter until his reading skills are improved. Mr B. has agreed to be supervised intensively in order to meet the above objectives.

Finally, here is an example of a task contracted by a very depressed and disturbed young man who committed criminal damage to premises of people by whom he felt rejected – a task which he later found impossible to tackle in his state of mind. (See p. 127).

I feel that Mr C. is essentially an intelligent and sensitive man who has been deeply affected by a disturbed family history. I have some confidence that once he is able to begin to unravel his confused feelings and can start to build up some degree of self-confidence, he will be able to live a more creative and satisfying life for himself. His psychotherapy has just begun and he needs time to settle into this and to begin to build on it. *At the moment he perceives his greatest problem to be one of an inability to relate to other people in any satisfying or fulfilling way*. He feels very isolated and unable to make contact with people. He has expressed a wish to try and become involved in some form of voluntary social work as a way of reaching out to others. He sees this as a way of not only helping others, but also of helping himself. I see this aim as an expression of a positive urge to try and do something about his current predicament and a second period of probation could be a way of testing out this aim, to see (a) if he can achieve this, and (b) whether or not he can sustain it. As he is already receiving treatment and support from St Bartholomew's Hospital, I do not consider probation should be imposed for rather ill-defined 'support' reasons. If he can be encouraged to achieve one specific aim in his life at the moment, I would consider it likely that such an achievement might have very positive results on his life in other areas.

Such provisional agreements presented to the magistrate approximate to the task-centred model in which clients are motivated to engage in problem-solving activities with their social workers. As we shall see later when discussing outcome, some offenders had chosen a 'problem' to be worked on as a means of escaping other less pleasant ways of being dealt with, but once on probation gave unmistakable signals that they had no intention of changing anything. Others were too disturbed and entangled in their multiple personality problems to be able to make use of this focused method of tackling problems.

Most offenders did not approach the probation officer because they had a problem they wished to resolve; some had learnt to look on probation as a soft option ('better than prison', 'way out from prison') involving them in a fairly cosy relationship in which they would go on talking about their difficulties ('soothing your mind – stopping you worrying'). Others expected a punitive type of police supervision – a 'telling off'. Yet others expected 'nothing much' to happen as their previous experience of probation had been 'going in, reporting how I was getting on, and out again'. Hence a good deal of preliminary work was required before a contract could be formulated. It often took a number of interviews to: (1) disentangle the offender's present situation and attitudes and the antecedents of his or her offence; (2) discuss the possible recommendations the probation officer might make to the magistrate and convey to the offender that probation was going to be an active and demanding problem-solving endeavour; (3) evolve a target problem which the offender really wanted to tackle, usually among a welter of other difficulties; and (4) to establish a realistic and achievable objective or task. In a number of cases the first attempt at a problem formulation led along blind alleys, partly because offenders tried to conceal vital aspects of their lives or previous offences, sometimes because social enquiries led to un-realistic formulations and tasks (several, but not all, of these were cases remanded in custody), and partly because the lives of some of these young men and women were so chaotic that as soon as one problem was selected other crises seemed to take precedence.

As Table 10.1 shows, in over half the task-centred cases it took four

Table 10.1 *Interview at which Task Was Formulated*

| Interview no. | Order Converted at 6 months | | Order not converted at 6 months | | Total |
	N	%	N	%	N
1	—	—	2	6	2
2	19	30	9	25	28
3	10	16	12	33	22
4	12	19	5	14	17
5	11	17	4	11	15
6+	10	16	3	8	13
Not known	2	3	1	3	3
Total N	64	100	36	100	100

or more interviews to arrive at a task formulation and in ten out of the sixty-four, six or more interviews. It is worth noting that this time span can be sufficient to complete a piece of task-centred intervention in situations which do not require the presentation of a social enquiry report (SER) to a court before the 'real' work can begin. Indeed it seemed to the outside observer (Tilda Goldberg) that sometimes the impetus of problem search, agreement on problem and task, followed by work on the task was lost because officer and client had to go through the ritual of preparing an SER and were inclined to stall while awaiting the court's decision. One officer suggested that the (orthodox) SER containing a detailed social history demanded the gathering of so much information that it became difficult to focus on one problem area and virtually ignore many others revealed by this lengthy exploration.

Another element inherent in the court-bounded probation setting affects the way in which the task-centred model is applied. One of its main dynamics is the fixing of time limits for the achievement of the task(s) being undertaken. It is this positive expectation of being able to alleviate problems within a given time span that spurs both worker and client to considerable efforts. However, since the agreement with the magistrates was that the probation order would normally be discharged after six months (and not until then), the time limit was dictated by the administrative exigencies of the probation order rather than by the nature of the task. In a number of cases tasks were accomplished within two or three months, after which the client and the probation officer had to agree to 'tread water', as it were, until the order could be converted into a conditional discharge.

The consequence of the long exploratory period and the six-month time limit is that the mean number of interviews in the sixty-four cases (seventeen) was very much greater than in the other task-centred projects discussed in this book where the average number of interviews was under ten, and the duration of contact usually under three months.

In his later book, *The Task-Centered System*, Reid (1978) defines the intervention strategies even more clearly and concretely than in the original text. He lays great stress on the identification of 'specific problems arising from unrealised wants', which are then defined in terms of specific conditions to be changed. Change, he suggests, is effected by problem-solving actions or tasks the client and practitioner undertake mainly *outside* the interview. The practitioner is there to assist the client in task implementation, and the aim is always to develop and augment the client's own action. He emphasises that this process is facilitated by a relationship in which the client feels 'understood, accepted, respected and liked'. The challenge of task-centred casework is that this atmosphere of 'non-possessive warmth' must be activated within a treatment relationship that is problem focused, task-centred and highly structured. The practitioner expects clients to work on agreed problems and tasks, and conveys these expectations implicitly and explicitly and tries to hold the client (and himself or herself) to the contract. Reid suggests that if the client's goals are related entirely to existential issues (who am I, why am I the way I am?), the important shift from 'what is wrong to what is needed' cannot be made, and thus the method may not be appropriate. He also suggests that deep emotional disturbances which lead to great distortion of reality, as well as profound needs for dependence and nurture, are probably not amenable to the method. All these points were amply confirmed during the project, as the outcome data will show.

Most of the probation officers participating in the project were psychodynamically oriented, used to exploring their clients' problems and past experiences in considerable depth; they subscribed to the theory that insight into the nature of their past difficulties and their possible link with the present was an important step towards resolving current problems in living within the therapeutic client/worker relationship. Thus the task-centred goal setting, 'the shift from what is wrong to what is needed' and the step-wise work to achieve what is needed, were not necessarily part of their strategies. On the other hand, at the start of the project the workers were already acutely aware of the vagueness of the goals they were pursuing and they were also questioning the somewhat paternalistic and protective relationship in which they often found themselves involved. After the first flush of enthusiasm, when the probation officers undertook some concrete and successful pieces of work associated with clearly articulated aims, with the clients working hard on the tasks and the officers experiencing a new feeling of sharing and partnership, a reaction set in. This reaction was partly occasioned by complex and difficult situations which did not yield to the new methods of working. The officers also noticed that they tended to be preoccupied with the mechanics of the method to the detriment of a warm responsive relationship. One probation officer said that at first when working with clients she kept getting caught up in the question 'Is this task-centred?'; but then she went to the other extreme of following her usual style of work and asking 'Does this fit into the task-centred model?' at the end of it! The officers also complained of feeling restricted and 'de-skilled' by the method, which seemed to paralyse their imagination. They tended to be more rigid, they thought, and less sensitive to their clients' needs. Since exploration of the past and the clients' feelings and attitudes had been such a central concern in their previous methods of intervention, they felt impoverished by the new emphasis which was on goals and how to achieve them rather than on a continuing exploration of behaviour and attitudes.

All kinds of false starts were made: in several instances, there was an enthusiastic rush into tasks before problems had been adequately specified and acknowledged by the probationers. It also became apparent that in a number of cases the tasks embarked upon were too ambitious and not achievable, so that the review sessions on task achievement became mainly reviews of failure. The group gradually realised that one of the important features of task-centred casework was to help clients to set themselves achievable goals and thus narrow the gap between expectations and reality.

After the project had been going for about four months, during which time the group had struggled with their disappointments and doubts, one member brought forward a case in which he thought the method had yielded results: it made him realise how much he used to act as a parent who knows best rather than treating his clients as potential self-directing adults, and how he had been unable to 'let go' when a client had in fact achieved the agreed task. This was a young man who had been charged with taking and driving away a motor car. Having realised, with the help of the probation officer, how much he accepted delinquent behaviour as normal, he now wished to distance himself from the delinquent gang with whom he was associating. (The problem area was therefore classified as dissatisfaction with social relationships.) The task was to accept the job which was on offer and to develop at least two constructive leisure activities. The probationer threw himself into these tasks with great energy, and soon worked all hours as an assistant in a small shop and became interested once more in his old hobby of weight-lifting. At this point the client declared the original agreement 'redundant' – he had achieved the tasks set. At first the probation officer felt somewhat nonplussed and rejected. Later on, when reviewing the case in retrospect, he realised that this was the point at which ideally the probation order should have been brought to an end. However, since there were still three more months to go, a further problem search led to a new task around the problem of managing his money; he used to spend his wages within a few days and then relied on his relatives to tide him over. The awareness of this problem seemed to be related to a desire to become more independent of his family; some work was done on budgeting and on confronting his dependence/independence dilemma. These discussions only took up a few sessions; the remaining time of the order was spent encouraging and rewarding the client for his achievements, and the probation officer felt no need to 'fish' for further problems.

Gradually, partly as a result of constant critical discussion and analysis of case material, the probation officers became more ready to let the clients arrive at a formulation of their problems rather than to 'put words into their mouths', and to confront clients more openly when the focus of the work vanished, when tasks were pushed aside or when confusion reigned supreme in a welter of problems and happenings so that both worker and client lost the thread. With increasing confidence in the method and its possibilities, they became freer and more imaginative in its use. The growing tendency towards active collaboration in tackling tasks and solving problems was marked by the increasing use of the word 'we' when referring to contracts and work on tasks.

Another noticeable development was the explicit work on the ending of the order, reviewing any achievements or learning that had taken place, the meaning of the probation experience, and looking at the positive gains of becoming self-directing and independent. (The process of closing cases is a notoriously neglected field in casework practice. Social workers often 'fade out' and clients are not sure whether their cases are still 'open or closed' — McKay et al., 1973).

Although these developments affected all the members of the probation team in some measure, it became clear that some officers felt much more at home with this sharply focused and very open method of working than others who still preferred more implicit, tentative and less specific ways of relating to clients and their problems. It is true to say, however, that all of them became more focused and goal-oriented, striving for greater clarity about what they were trying to do, and being less satisfied with the development of a vague and aimless relationship as the main ingredient of a probation order. Above all, they were less inclined to do things *for* their clients. Increasingly, the officers commented with satisfaction on their ability to resist the attempts of some clients to get them to rush around and arrange things for them. Instead they encouraged, supported and, if necessary, taught clients how to negotiate with the housing authorities, the DHSS, the social services or with estranged relatives, and so on. Confirmation of the impact this way of handling practical problems of everyday living had on their increase in self-confidence was often expressed in the clients' interviews with the independent assessor (see Table 14.5 and the subsequent discussion, p. 145).

Chapter 11

PROBLEMS AND TASKS

Adopting Reid and Epstein's problem typology, we found (see Table 9.4, p. 107) that dissatisfaction with social relations and difficulties in role performance were identified as target problems in over half the cases. Next came inadequate resources and interpersonal conflict, and the rest of the problem categories were relevant in less than 10 per cent of either the short-term group or those whose orders were not converted at six months. Dissatisfaction in social relations often manifested itself as a feeling of unease with the kind of life into which the offenders had drifted, a lack of self-confidence, or a failure to assert oneself and to become independent and self-directing. The probation officer would note: 'he feels like a child, not allowed to speak for himself – nobody listens to him'; 'Shyness – frightened to apply for jobs'; 'Feels rejected and unwanted by family.' Or the client would say: 'I want to be able to do something and know it's *me* that's done it.' Others expressed feelings of isolation: 'I need something – a holiday? – to get out more and meet more people.' Or from the probation officer's observation: 'Feels isolated, aimless, extremely lonely.' Feelings of loneliness and lack of confidence were associated with drinking problems in a number of cases: 'Drinks too much, gets lonely'; 'Drinks too much, it gives him confidence and helps him to get on with people'; or, as described by the probationer: 'I drink too much, makes me feel big.'

Tasks were aimed at exploring and confronting the social situation which distressed the client, and helping him to do something about it. For example, in the case of a backward youngster (aged 17 whose offence was indecent exposure) who felt he was not allowed to speak for himself, the plan was to meet as a family, to establish better communication, with the aim of helping the probationer to speak up for himself and encouraging the family to let him do so. The client who felt she needed to get out more and meet more people was a single mother aged 23 (her offence was criminal damage and assault on a police constable). She first worked out a task with her probation officer of 'getting into some form of voluntary service in the community'. Having found (with the help of the probation officer) voluntary work in a toy library for handicapped children as well as a very supportive maternal friend in the woman who ran the service, it turned out that another problem in the area of social transition was nagging at her persistently. This girl, who had been in the care of a local authority for many years could not come to terms with the fact that she did not have a social worker any longer. (Once more the social worker had faded out rather than establishing clearly what the basis of any future relationship was to be.) So the second task to be tackled was to have it out with the social services exactly where she stood in relation to support from them. Another young chap who felt that he drank too much, partly because he got so lonely (offence: taking and driving away, and theft) decided with his probation officer that he would systematically reduce drinking by exploring other activities and finding other ways of spending money.

Difficulties in role performance were mostly connected with work, but in several instances also with an inability to lead a reasonably orderly, settled way of life, to manage money and, more rarely, with roles as a parent or spouse. The tasks were often defined in very concrete, practical steps: 'Find work and devise a strategy to get up in time', or for someone whose difficulty was that he could not work for his A-levels as he was feeling hopeless and depressed: 'Keep a list of hours worked on A-level studies and give reasons why not on particular occasions.' For those whose role performance was severely impeded by their inability to read and write, literacy classes and exercises constituted the task. Various ways of budgeting and of dealing with formal organisations about methods of payment constituted aims in debt management. An important lesson that was learnt in relation to youngsters who had not worked for years and had not established any settled ways of living, let alone work habits was to break the task down into small achievable steps. Thus it soon became clear that a task formulated as 'Find a job and keep it' was much too big and ambitious. Many of the tasks had to be how to begin to look for a job, how to determine one's suitability for a specific job, how to behave in an interview, and even how to use the telephone in an effective way.

The problems of inadequate resources were more often related to unsatisfactory living conditions than to lack of money or of other resources. Most of the tasks were again of a very practical kind – to take all manner of steps to procure and keep accommodation, or to find work as a means of paying debts. Sometimes the task was formulated in terms of intermediate steps towards obtaining more adequate resources, for example, to find a day nursery for a child to enable a single mother to go out to work.

Problems of social transition were experienced by people who had committed a delinquent act in a phase of severe disequilibrium while facing traumatic changes in their lives, or while attempting to come to some vital decisions about possible changes in their lives. For example, one young woman who had embezzled money from her employer described her problem as wanting to leave her common-law husband but being unable to take practical decisions, and the task was to devise a plan to get away from her husband with her child. In another case, a young man with many previous convictions and a stormy marriage entailing many separations said that he had 'no job, no accommodation' and that he needed to come to terms with living alone. The contract was to find a job and accommodation and become independent of his wife by the end of the probation order. While the task of finding accommodation and a job proved to be along the right lines, the aim of separating from his wife did not turn out to be what he wanted, and he worked through to a decision to return to her. Similarly, the young woman just quoted was not able to make up her mind to sever her links with her husband; it emerged that her inability to make any decisions was due to a severe state of depression for which she needed psychiatric help.

It seems, then, that however thorough the problem exploration and however genuine the agreement about intended changes in attitudes and behaviour, targets can easily shift as feelings, attitudes and plans are explored and tested in real life.

Problems and tasks can be more reliably defined when a specific traumatic event necessitates a considerable readjustment. For example, a man who perpetrated a driving offence under the influence of drink following separation from his wife formulated his targets as needing to move into a smaller place, return to work and build a new life. The task was 'To help the client to feel that he is again master of his own destiny and that things are not being done to and for him'. This sounds very much like the language of the probation officer, but it is indeed quite similar to the task described by the man in the follow-up interview: 'Try to stand on my own two feet and to get back my self-respect.'

Very few – barely 10 per cent – of the probationers were categorised as experiencing problems of reactive emotional distress. The difficulties revolved around fear, embarrassment, or depression about certain actions or events. For example, a young boy with several previous convictions felt convinced that he had venereal disease but was ashamed to visit a clinic. Another client saw his problems as depression since the breakdown of his marriage and an inability to pull himself together. In the case of a young widow, a bizarre driving offence proved to be clearly related to unacknowledged distress over her husband's death. Interestingly, there is only one case in which the emotional distress was directly related to the offence: the probationer had stolen and destroyed some precious ornaments belonging to his father and felt deeply distressed about what he had done to him.

Five of the seven problem areas identified as inter-personal conflict related to marital difficulties and two to parent/child conflicts. In practically every case, the task was directed towards achieving better communication and enhancing the probationer's awareness of the effects his or her attitudes and behaviour were having on the other family members, with the aim of changing behaviour patterns. Although tasks were usually defined in somewhat general terms (see case example, p. 124), the work was more focused than in other problem areas and often led to the formulation of subtasks: couples were to note certain behaviours; talk to each other for a certain length of time each day; engage in specific joint activities; work out plans for allocation of routine jobs, and so on. For example, in the case of the family who could not let a backward member speak for himself or assert himself, one of the subtasks was to allow him to accomplish jobs on his own, such as washing up.

The almost universal tendency to define problems in terms of lack of work, unsatisfactory human relations, or lack of resources – problem areas which may or may not bear a direct relationship to the offence – gives food for thought. We shall return to the nature of the relationship between offence, problem, task and outcome in Chapter 16.

Chapter 12

OUTSTANDING FEATURES OF TASK-CENTRED INTERVENTION

(1) CLARITY OF PURPOSE AND TASK

Scrutiny of the case material and the follow-up interviews suggested that the more clearly the problem and the work on the task was specified, the more able the client was to describe such work at the follow-up interview and to recognise his or her own part in it as well as the probation officer's role. For example, a single mother with three children who had dishonestly used a Barclaycard and who was entangled in many material and emotional problems, decided that she wanted to tackle her indebtedness. The probation officer described the initial task: 'She needs a specific area where success can be experienced, and budgeting successfully will enable her to feel she has control over her situation.' The client saw it from a more down-to-earth perspective: she commented at the follow-up interview that, for her, budgeting, which was just one of the many areas in which she felt a failure, was the obvious problem to concentrate on as it was the one that led to her offence. It is noteworthy that there were many tempting psychological and emotional problems related to this woman's childhood and broken marriage which the probation officer wanted to explore later on, but he refrained on a signal from the client in response to his probing that she felt a great increase in self-confidence and was now able to manage on her own. At the follow-up she referred to her achievements with much satisfaction.

In another case, an important but comparatively small area of difficulty was clearly specified and worked on within a plethora of other problems, which according to the social enquiry report 'have already received very long-term open-ended investigation without the client feeling any relief or that she could feel that anything could ever change'. This was a woman of 45, charged with shoplifting of goods which she later gave away to old-age pensioners. She produced innumerable problems, including depression and a horrific childhood background. The client said at the follow-up interview: 'I did not see no way out of my problem.' The probation officer, in recommending probation, said in his report: 'The legal structure of such an order would greatly help her to try and contain some of her anxiety, which sometimes seems to her as if it spills everywhere and is uncontainable' (see p. 112). Structured work with specific tasks and subtasks succeeded in holding the focus which remained concentrated in the here-and-now rather than in the client's unhappy past – the sterile and resistant area on which another agency had previously concentrated. Attention – after discussions with both husband and wife – was directed towards their distant relationship rather than to the problem the woman had first wanted to work on – why she had become pregnant as a teenager, and so on. Although the main task was rather vaguely formulated as 'to see what can be done to improve the couple's relationship', various specific subtasks were evolved, for example, for the clients to set aside ten minutes each day listening to each other and to have some sort of physical contact once a day. (This was a conjoint marital case in which a male and female probation officer worked with both husband and wife.) At the follow-up the couple were amazed how far they had progressed in such a short time, contrasting this experience with that of two years' casework at a voluntary agency. 'They [the probation officers] were very much to the point and very kind with it.' Although the couple were not totally together yet – for example, they were still facing considerable sexual difficulties – they were quite clear about the ways in which they wanted to continue working on the remaining problems on their own, and they were equally aware that this would entail a great deal of effort.

In the case discussions the two probation officers involved pointed out that they could have become bogged down in exploring how the clients' past had contributed to their present behaviour and attitudes towards each other, but instead they had concentrated on bringing about some small changes in their present relationship, which took a great leap forward.

(2) COLLABORATION ON THE TASK WITH THE PROBATION OFFICER

In practically all the cases in which tasks were clearly established and worked on, the clients, though aware of their own efforts, stressed the collaborative aspect in their follow-up interview: 'We did it together.' The single mother above who tackled budget problems said, 'We seem to have worked together...he did not tell you what to do...he wanted me to suggest things. Then you know that you want to do something and you do it.' Or again, 'The ideas came from him but I had to do the applying', or 'We really worked on the problem [difficulties at work] and solved it'. Much of this collaboration was rooted in a great deal of reinforcement and encouragement by the probation officer to continue with the efforts. After a discussion with a client who had difficulties at work, the probation officer wrote: 'I stressed that what he had done he had done primarily on his own, and that I had merely been there to point out certain aspects of his behaviour and to encourage him to behave in a different way.' The client at the follow-up, referring to his relationship with the probation officer, said, 'It instils confidence to solve problems'. Another important aspect of this collaboration is that both client and worker have tasks to perform as this snippet from a write-up illustrates: 'She had not made a list of things as agreed, neither had I done my side of the work. I used this to illustrate how we both had to have a clear agreement on what we are going to do and a commitment to do it if we are actually to achieve a change.'

Clients also often referred to the feeling that they had been treated as equal adults. Thus one client said: 'He gave advice about what I could do. He was giving me my own free will; he makes you feel more grown up and wiser ... it is as if I have grown up ten years in the last year.' 'He put the ideas up and we discussed them. He took trouble to set up the classes with the tutor, even though it was my final decision what I do. He thought about me in the daytime – he did some work for me. He didn't fold up the file and put it away when I had gone. He didn't look down on me, he said, "let's see what *we* can do" – not "what are *you* going to do" ... I learnt a lot from him – I suppose I always had it there. I think I'll be able to handle most of the problems that come up.'

(3) SETTING LIMITS TO VENTILATION OF FEELINGS AND EXPLORATION OF THE PAST

Although the task-centred method tries to solve problems, mainly by reference to the present situation rather than to the past, not infrequently unresolved emotional difficulties, originating in the recent or more remote past, can hinder progress on a specific task. In these circumstances the probation officers evolved a method of explicitly setting aside a number of interviews to explore such problems and relationships in the hope that work on the task could then be resumed. This proved an excellent device, since it delineated the space available and avoided the pitfalls of getting lost in a maze of past traumatic events and associated feelings about which little could be done – at any rate, in a probation setting. On the other hand, such ventilation – in one instance, the circumstances surrounding a husband's death and, in another, past difficulties in the father/son relationship – cleared the way ahead. As the latter client said: 'I have got it out of my system.' It was noticeable that none of the clients wished to exceed the number of sessions reserved for such explorations and ventilation of feelings, and quite naturally returned to the problem of the present.

(4) BREAKING DOWN PROBLEMS

This was a novel idea to several clients: 'I'd never done anything like it before.' The very process of listing and ranking problems in order of urgency and adopting a step-by-step approach towards their solution seemed to encourage hope and initiative. It helped to protect both client and worker from being overwhelmed by the multiplicity and complexity of the problems in living which many clients experienced.

(5) THE USE OF DIRECTION

Several, especially of the less articulate and possibly less intelligent clients, liked to be kept to the task and to have to report on their progress; but a few, particularly those who did not make a success of things, resented the task orientation: 'Telling me to stick to my job and that rubbish.' Another client complained that his officer was 'nagging' him. A few wanted a listening ear, but they did not wish to make any effort to solve any problems. One or two of the probationers were looking for a deep emotional involvement and resented the task-centred limitations of the relationship and felt greatly rejected when the order came to an end.

(6) THE CONCEPT OF ACHIEVEMENT

A considerable number of clients (thirty-eight of the forty-four clients followed up at the end of six months) commented with satisfaction on the feelings of achieving an objective, however small: 'I achieved all of it ... I know what the problem was and I know that I had to do something about it ... she put the options in front of me – it was up to me whether to take them or not.' 'With a little push behind I did quite a lot.' Or, 'We did it together. I did the work and reported back to her. Each week we talked over what I was achieving – it used to feel really good.' 'Going up there and doing it was an achievement.' Clearly these feelings did not prevail among those who had either no wish to engage in any effort to achieve anything: 'Only thing that would have helped – to lock me up'; or those who expected to be 'fed', to be given things: 'I wanted immediate help if my giro did not come and I had no money for food ... I needed the understanding and did not get it'; or those who thought society should change: 'They thought taking drugs was more serious than I do...these should not be problems, society needs to change'; or those who wanted to engage on a long journey of self-exploration: 'I had to teach her my problems'; or those who were in a state of deep depression and despair: 'In my state of mind at the time I took the line of least resistance.' This client went along with the probation officer's suggestion (to do some voluntary social work), 'but I did not think I was in a state of mind to deal with anyone else's problems when I couldn't deal with my own.'

(7) FAMILY INTERVENTION

In nine cases two probation officers worked with either a couple or a whole family, using task-centred principles. One such case has already been described on p. 124. In another situation of marital conflict in which the problem was described as 'No mutual sharing, exchanges resulting in conflict, living in the past', the couple described in the follow-up interview how they made a list of each other's faults, tried to discuss them and do something about them. After joint interviews they found they could talk more easily together. The wife said: 'Normally you just think about it without telling or have a row ... we have learnt to be able to talk without rowing.' However, in cases where one partner had made up his or her mind (covertly) that the marriage had really ended, joint work could lead to greater hostility between the marriage partners. In one such case, individual work (after an abortive attempt at joint sessions) to help the wife with both the practical and emotional tasks flowing from her separation was seen as much more helpful by the client in the follow-up interview. The comments of the independent assessor are illuminating on the family case in which the aim was to make the young offender more independent and able to speak up for himself and be able to get a job (see p. 97): 'A most successful family group – usefully task-centred. Objectives had been clear to all the family, including T...I was impressed by the whole family's commitment to work for T. Father's attitude seemed least changed probably – he still seemed to find T "different". I think maybe sister had gained most – she was intelligent and perceptive and particularly clear about the methods used by the POs. But the old habit of speaking for T persisted. I had to work hard to get his feelings.' Perhaps the last sentence is a useful reminder that even comparatively task-centred intervention spread over a few months, though it can sow a few seeds, cannot overcome a family's habits formed over a life-time.

(8) PRACTICAL HELP

As already mentioned, many concrete tasks were undertaken by both probationers and officers. These were largely related to finding accommodation, dealing with officers of the local DHSS, job search, and so on. The main objective of the officer was always to try and get the clients to undertake as many of the tasks as were within their capability, but to recognise when they became disheartened by failure and to be prepared to share difficult tasks.

For example, a lone mother who was overwhelmed by financial and other material difficulties after her husband had gone off with her 'best friend' said, 'I can now deal with Social Security or the gas people on my own.' In the past she could only approach them through her social worker. (It should be added that, as well as gaining the capacity to deal with her material problems, the relationship with the probation officer had enabled her to trust people again which she rated at least as high in importance.) Or take the comment of one of the many probationers who had almost given up trying for jobs and whose habits of sleeping late, and so on were not exactly conducive to keeping a job. Not only was the simple device of an alarm clock suggested, but 'he helped me to put out a bit more personality when applying for jobs', that is, he encouraged him to smile! The client thought there had been a slight improvement: 'I am better at looking for jobs'!

(9)   USE OF COMMUNITY RESOURCES

As already indicated in the discussion on problem and task formulation, the probation officers used tuition in literacy skills as an important means of improving role performance. For some clients learning to read and write was the main task and their most important achievement; they spent more time during the order with the voluntary associate who did the tutoring than with the probation officer. Additional resources, mainly within the probation service, were also used to tackle employment problems. An ancillary worker and a voluntary associate conducted regular job-search sessions at the probation office. Clients would be encouraged to scrutinise newspapers for job advertisements, to use the phone or write letters of application, and to undertake further job explorations between sessions. A number of clients were placed with Bulldog Manpower Services, a voluntary scheme organised by the Inner London Probation Service with Home Office funding to provide employment opportunities for clients with poor work records and to equip them to move eventually into the open labour market.

Lastly, when clients expressed a wish to do voluntary work the probation officers linked them up with such work in various settings. These endeavours to create openings for constructive and rewarding activities are in contrast to the almost exclusive emphasis on self-exploration and 'talking' treatment prevalent in more orthodox probation casework.

DISCUSSION

At this juncture many readers will suggest that the characteristics of task-centred casework do not differ greatly from other methods of casework or counselling, to which Laura Epstein has given the wonderfully descriptive label of 'mush'. Such methods can include family thereapy, practical assistance, use of community resources, and also contracts with clients about aims and content of the work to be done. On the other hand, the behaviourists have argued that task-centred casework is largely watered-down behaviour therapy in which behavioural techniques such as extinction, reinforcement, modelling, rehearsal, and so on play an important role. The answer is a qualified 'yes' to both propositions. It has never been claimed that task-centred casework is a new method of intervention, but rather a framework capable of accommodating a variety of techniques to achieve explicit and modest aims. As discussed already, the framework which supports the task-centred approach has four planks: a thorough problem exploration leading to an agreed problem(s) to be tackled, an agreed formulation of an objective or task to be achieved within a set time limit, and the encouragement of the greatest possible degree of client effort. No rules have been laid down as to how these four aims should be approached, except that explicitness and honesty rather than implicit assumptions and a 'double agenda' should inform the proceedings.

Chapter 13

TASK ACHIEVEMENT AND PROBLEM OUTCOME

The main outcome measures were based on two ratings: one by the practitioners in consultation with the clients on how far the task(s) worked on had been achieved, and the other by the client in the follow-up interview in which the answer to the key question, 'How is the problem(s) now compared with how it was when you first saw the probation officer?', was rated. Finally, these, in the main, self-rating assessments were related to an independent and external outcome measure – the occurrence of reconviction within a three-year period.

TASK ACHIEVEMENT

It will be remembered that a follow-up visit was only achieved in forty-four of the sixty-four cases whose order was converted at six months. Hence, in the twenty cases not followed up we were limited, in the main, to the ratings on task achievement jointly made by probationers and the probation officer in the final interview. As Table 13.1 shows, complete and substantial task achievement scores were lower in this group (40 per cent) than among those followed up (61 per cent). It will also be noticed that two-fifths of the cases not followed up clustered in the middle, as 'partial achievement', in contrast to only 16 per cent in the group which was followed up. The socio-demographic characteristics of this group of twenty did not differ from the forty-four who were seen by the independent assessor. However, these twenty missed more appointments with their probation officer than the other group, an average of over six compared with four, and, not surprisingly, in the majority of cases the reason for the unsuccessful follow-up was failure to keep appointments, to answer letters, or just being out when the assessor called. Only one refused outright to be seen by the assessor. A scrutiny of the case material also suggests that tasks were less clearly defined among these twenty cases than in the group which was successfully followed up. In a number of cases (fifteen) it proved difficult to keep any focus and

Table 13.1 *Task Achievement of Sixty-Four Orders Converted at Six Months and Seventeen Orders Continuing for One Year**

Task achievement	Order converted at 6 months				Order not converted at 6 months	
	Followed up		Not followed up			
	N	%	N	%	N	%
Complete	9	20	4	20	1	6
Substantial	18	41	4	20	3	18
Partial	7	16	8	40	4	24
Minimal	5	11	—	—	3	18
None	5	11	2	10	1	6
Not known	—	—	2	10	5	29
Total N	44	100	20	100	17	100

* Task achievement was not assessed in the 17 cases which ended in breach of probation, another sentence, or disappearance.

problems were not really grappled with either by reflective discussion aimed at change in behaviour or by practical tasks designed to alter the social situation. Thus it may have proved difficult to arrive at a clear-cut picture of the degree of task achievement.

It is also of interest to glance at the outcome on task achievement for the seventeen probationers whose order ran for a whole year.* Their task achievement was still lower than among the twenty cases just discussed: barely a quarter (24 per cent) achieved their tasks either completely or substantially (Table 13.1). The average number of missed appointments was substantially higher – 8.5. The hope that in difficult cases introduction of the probation order could achieve more positive results than a six-month probation period has not been realised in this small sample. These findings are similar to those reported by Gibbons in this volume (see p. 209).

CONGRUENCE BETWEEN TASK ACHIEVEMENT AND PROBLEM REDUCTION

The rest of the discussion on outcome will be concerned with the core group of forty-four short-term probationers who had an independent follow-up interview. We first of all explored the relationship between task achievement, as assessed by probation officer and client in their final review, and problem reduction as assessed by the client at

*No outcome measures on task achievement or problem reduction are available for the seventeen clients who did not complete their order either because they disappeared or because they were arrested for further delinquency (see Table 9.1).

the follow-up interview. Table 13.2 shows considerable congruence between these two measures. In sixteen of the fourty-four cases there is complete agreement, and in another twenty there is only one point of difference in the ratings between task achievement and problem reduction, indicating that these measures are highly correlated. It is likely that there was a considerable carry-over from the probation officer/client evaluation in the final session to the independent assessment interview, which usually took place only a few weeks after the end of the order. However, it would be extraordinary if in the 'successful' cases, at any rate, there was no correlation between task achievement and problem reduction, since the objectives pursued were designed to ameliorate specific identified problems.

The following three examples illustrate the fit between task achievement as discussed with the probation officer, and the problem reduction as estimated by the clients in their interviews with the independent assessor.

First, a young man of 19 who was involved in a succession of offences connected with taking and driving away motor cars while experiencing a very unsettled period at work, said to the probation officer in his final interview: 'I have achieved what I set out to do. I have now got a job with good money.' (The task was rated as completely achieved.) To the assessor he said that the plan was to get a job, which he did immediately, and he rated his problem as 'no longer present'.

The next example is somewhat more complex, particularly as the interview with the probation officer did not strictly follow the outlines of the interview schedule. A 19-year-old assistant technician in a computer firm whose abiding hobby was to build a portable discothèque

Table 13.2   *Task Achievement and Problem Reduction of Forty-Four Short-Term Probation Orders Converted at Six Months and Followed Up*

Task achievement (assessed by probation officer and client)	Problem reduction (client's assessment at follow-up interview)					
Task	No longer present	A lot better	A little better	About the same	Worse	Total
Completely achieved	2	5	1	1	—	9
Substantially achieved	6	9	2	1	—	18
Partially achieved	—	3	4	—	—	7
Minimally achieved	—	1	3	—	1	5
Not achieved	—	3	1	—	1	5
Total N	8	21	11	2	2	44

for commercial use in clubs, had acquired various expensive pieces of equipment dishonestly. In his last interview with the probation officer he identified his initial problem as 'my head wasn't ticking over properly and I couldn't get things together'. To the independent assessor he described his problems in a more prosaic manner: 'I was seeing things I wanted and could not afford and taking them.'! Secondly, he suggested that he had to get himself sorted out and 'find out in what direction I was heading'.

In the long final interview with the probation officer the tasks were rated as completely achieved: he had conquered his delinquent tendencies and felt secure 'having got his equipment legal'; he and his group had instituted a saving scheme for buying equipment and he had made progress in his job. In his interview with the assessor he rated his stealing problem as 'no longer present' and also gave top rating to his job promotion (he had got on a special course which was leading to promotion). The problem about saving he rated 'a lot better'. In addition, he described in both interviews how he had learnt to sort out his muddles. To the assessor he put it this way: 'She showed me what I could do by letting me talk about what I had in mind for the future. I had had ideas but had previously no one to sort things out with.'

The last example illustrates congruence in a somewhat unsuccessful case. A very unsettled and rootless young Irishman of 21 had spent many years in the care of the local authority and had then led an itinerant life, moving from hostel to hostel and sometimes sleeping rough. He had a very poor work record and had got into trouble for burglary, criminal damage and other offences on several occasions. The probation officer had put much effort into helping him to settle in a hostel, to organise his money better and to be more persistent in looking for work and keeping it. In his very monosyllabic final interview with the probation officer he identified his problem as 'moving about and that', and he felt that he had partly achieved the task of 'staying in one place a while'. He had actually managed to stay in one hostel for three months. He also mentioned that he had kept out of trouble but seemed somewhat uncertain about the future. (He was in trouble again within two months and sent to Borstal.) In his interview with the assessor he described his problem in a similar vein: 'I had nowhere to settle; I was getting in a bit of trouble.' He detailed the tasks which had been agreed with the probation officer during the course of the probation period with considerable accuracy: to live in a hostel, to save up money to get a place of his own, to try to organise his money better, and to settle and stay in one place for a while. He was very realistic about his achievements, how he had been thrown out of the first hostel because he did not pay the rent, how he had not been able to save at all and that he was hardly better able to manage his money. But he did stress that he had stayed in his present hostel for four and a half months (by the time he saw the assessor) and that it was the longest time he had stayed anywhere during the last eighteen months. So he rated his accommodation problem as a lot better, his money problem as a little better, and he added his present problem of not keeping a job for good measure!

Both interviews convey a kind of bleak hopelessness, and towards the end of his talk with the assessor he said that he had not changed: 'I have got worse – I'll be truthful.'

We shall take up the more general problem this case also illustrates, namely, whether task-centred casework has any contribution to make to a footloose drifter, isolated from his fellow beings and with severe personality difficulties.

It is instructive to explore further the eight cases where there was a discrepancy of more than one point between task achievement and problem reduction. Table 13.2 shows that five were rated as task minimally or not achieved in the final interview with the probation officer, while the problems were estimated a lot better (4) or a little better (1) by the clients in their interview with the independent assessor. On the other hand, in three instances problem reduction was rated lower than task achievement. A careful study of all the case material available throws a good deal of light on these discrepancies. It seems that with one exception the lower assessments on task achievement in the final interview with the probation officers reflect the reality of the situation. In four cases a change in circumstances unrelated to the tasks to be achieved had brought about a temporary alleviation of the problems, but basically nothing had really changed. For example, a client with many previous convictions, some of them related to his heavy drinking, was facing a situation of chronic marital conflict. The problem area was eventually defined as inter-personal conflict, and some conjoint work was carried out with husband and wife. At the end of the probation period his wife and children had left him and he was again drinking heavily, getting into further trouble, and both he and the probation officer felt that nothing had been achieved. When he saw the independent assessor a few weeks later his wife had returned once more, they were in a kind of honeymoon period and maintained that things were better between them, that they were able to talk more easily to each other without having a row; the wife realised that her nagging aggravated his drinking, and so on. The independent assessor in her comments sensed that they still seemed very insecure in their relationship and that they were almost too keen to prove to her that things were better between them. Subsequently, there was a further separation, the client lapsed into serious alcoholism, and when he saw his probation officer after a further offence he assured him that he had given him a very good write-up in his interview with the assessor!

Another young man who grew up in a very delinquent environment and had eleven previous convictions to his credit had not achieved his task of cutting down his drinking and finding other interests by the end of the probation period. However, he told the independent assessor that his problems had lessened, but mainly because a cousin of his had thrown him a lifeline and 'I grabbed at it'. This cousin had offered him work and advice, and it was this person rather than the probation officer who was seen as the helping agent and so he rated his problem as a little better.

Another similar example is that of a lone mother who had agreed to an unrealistic task of starting nurse training, which was soon abandoned when she met up with 'Jack'. She rated her problems as a lot better since she had found a new companion, but her task achievement was nil, although she felt that the relationship with the probation officer had been a helpful one.

Another unsupported mother who felt that she was living in chaos with huge debts and drug problems, and that she was being harrassed by her neighbours (her baby had died under what neighbours might interpret as suspicious circumstances), agreed with her probation officer that the task was to try and get some order out of chaos and to find ways of doing this little by little. In her interview with the assessor she mentioned three problem areas: her baby's death, the neighbours' attitudes which made her want to move to another flat, and difficulties with the social security. But she stressed that basically her financial problems were the cause of all her troubles and she felt that she had not received any help in this respect from the probation officer: 'The probation officer was no help, she did not understand.' Although the baby's death was one of her causes of distress when she first met the probation officer, she did not involve her in her feelings about this: 'I did not think she ought to bring up about the baby unless I did.' Whenever the probation officer did mention the baby she became emotional but seemed unable to discuss it. Yet when it came to her assessing her problems in the follow-up interview, she rated her distress about the baby's death as 'a lot better' because time had elapsed; her troubles with the social security as 'a little better' because there were not as many problems as at the time immediately following the baby's death; and the housing and neighbour troubles she said were 'a lot better' – she had decided to stay where she was: 'They are talking about someone else now!' The probation officer in the final case discussion at the DTU was completely aware of the total lack of contact and meeting point between her and the client, and felt that 'the whole case was disastrous'. Thus, in fact, the probation officer, assessor and client all agreed that nothing had been achieved as a result of probation. Here are the assessor's comments made after the interview: 'Help offered by the probation officer and method of working did not seem relevant to client who felt that her problems could only be resolved by immediate action – cash.'

These case examples illustrate how the task-centred method, with its explicitness about aims and honesty between client and helper about tasks, can elucidate which changes can reasonably be ascribed to their joint work and which problem resolutions are associated with fortuitous external influences.

In the fifth case, although the discrepancy seems considerable – the client rating his problem as 'a lot better' in his interview with the assessor, and the probation officer rating task achievement as 'minimal' – yet there is a good deal of congruence in what the client said in his final interview with the probation officer and to the assessor. In both interviews this client (who after the break up of his marriage had started drinking heavily, had become very depressed, and committed a small shop burglary on the day he was discharged from hospital still under the influence of drugs after a suicidal attempt) described how he had only begun to work on his problems in earnest during the last five weeks of the order, how he had cut down drinking, joined various organisations and started a class in the Welsh language with some others and 'took a more realistic view of life'. However, possibly the probation officer's rating was the more accurate assessment of this client's achievements, for he was soon in trouble again which was related to heavy drinking and depression. One wonders whether an extension of the probation period would have helped to consolidate the late spurt.

The three instances in which the probation officer and client together rated task achievement as complete or substantial, while the client felt in his interview with the independent assessor that his problem was little or no better, were mainly due to different areas being rated in the two interviews. Thus one client saw his problem area as being related to his drinking and the task to work for alternative interests and sources of satisfaction. The high achievement rating was based on the fact that he had obtained a job, while the modest rating on problem reduction (a little better) was related to his drinking, which had hardly changed.

Someone surrounded by debts who was not prepared to take any action herself to sort things out met what her probation officer described as 'passive resistance' on her part with this client, so that eventually this girl had to take various steps herself, to see the DHSS, the housing department, and so on. In her final interview with the

probation officer she felt that although she was still in financial difficulties they were not so pressing, and that she could now 'face up to
responsibility' and do things for herself. However, when it came to
seeing the independent assessor she said, 'I am still in the same mess'
and rated her problem 'about the same'. She added, 'they tried but
they can't really help with financial problems'. But she did let fall
during the interview that she went to see the housing authorities
herself, adding 'that is the best way – you don't have to keep running
to other people'. The interviewer's comments were that the client's
problems were so huge that no limited achievements seemed to count.

The third client whose self-rating on problem reduction was much
lower than his rating on task achievement with the probation officer is
of very great interest, since he is practically the only one who related
his achievement directly to conquering his delinquent tendencies. He
was a young clerk aged 17 who was fascinated by motor cars, had
already several convictions for taking and driving away, and this time
had been apprehended for going equipped for theft (car keys). He
described his problem graphically as 'not getting into more trouble
with cars and remembering the experience of being in custody'. This
fascination for cars was in marked contrast to his responsible and
hard-working behaviour at work which mirrored his family's ethos.

The tasks were first of all addressed to three questions – Why do I
like cars? What can I do instead of driving cars? Why shouldn't I drive
cars? – and on deciding on the homework to be done between sessions
as a result of answering these questions. (Sheets were filled out with
these questions and the kind of homework he was undertaking.) His
final interview with his probation officer is worth quoting in full. In
answer to the first question to look back on what had been achieved in
general, he said: 'It taught me to speak my mind and made me realise
that other people care for their goods as well as I care for mine.' (One
of the tasks he undertook was to build himself a pedal bike as a
substitute for the motor bikes he used to pinch, and this bike was stolen
from him!) In answer to the second question in the final interview, to
consider once more what the problem was when he started probation,
he said: 'I could not keep away from cars – it was as if they were the
only things in my life.' To the question as to whether he felt that this
was the problem he most wanted to have help with, he replied: 'Yes.'
Next came the question on how much he thought had been achieved:
'A lot; I have gained will-power and am not so tempted by cars.
Because they have not been on my mind, I have got time to do other
things – training, buying clothes, going out, decorating my room,
building a bike, being best man at a wedding.'

To the question as to what part he himself had played in tackling his
difficulties, he answered: 'I have done all the resisting – put all the

will-power into it, and said no. All these things I have done have helped me to say no.' In reply to the question whether the work done had made any difference to his life, he said: 'It needed someone to really talk to me about driving for me to take it seriously. It helped me to work out what to do with all my spare time and energy.' The questionnaire then asks, 'What about the future?'. He replied: 'I feel sure I won't get into trouble with cars – I think twice now before doing anything which might get me into bother. Also, after six months' probation, it would be like working for a week and getting no wages.'

To the question, 'How do you think you will be able to cope?', he answered: 'I have enough to occupy myself with, and there are people I can talk to (including you) if I need to.' And invited to appraise the method of work, he replied, 'You have treated me as an adult. When other people treated me like a kid I tended to react by behaving as a kid. I changed with being treated as a grown up.'

In his interview with the assessor, which unfortunately took place nearly five months later as this boy had missed several appointments, he rated his problems as 'the same' since he was still paying off fines and repaying damage done to a motor bike. But, at the same time, he was full of positive feelings about his probation experience which had 'made me feel more grown up and wiser'. He also talked enthusiastically about the tasks he had undertaken with much support from his probation officer. The explanation for his cautious rating was probably that by the time this interview took place he was in further trouble and confessed to being easily led.

This case raises the much wider problem of how much task achievement, even if it is quite closely related to overcoming delinquent behaviour, can really touch the springs of such behaviour. We shall pursue these questions further in Chapter 16.

The general conclusion we draw from this exploration of discrepancies in the ratings of the task achievement with the probation officer and problem reduction with the assessor is that basically the evaluation of both the content and the outcome of the task-centred work was remarkably similar in both interviews, despite the differences in ratings which often dealt with different facets of change at a different point in time.

Chapter 14

FACTORS ASSOCIATED WITH SUCCESSFUL OUTCOME

Table 13.2 (p. 132) showed that half (twenty-two) of those clients whose order was converted after six months and who were followed up had high ratings on both task achievement and problem reduction. Although numbers are very small and any findings can only be regarded as suggestive hunches, we compared these twenty-two 'successes' with the other twenty-two probationers in relation to the following factors:

(1) Social background including previous offences.
(2) Agreement on problem and task as recorded in the task formulation sheet and as described to the independent assessor in the follow-up interview.
(3) Problem areas selected for task-centred work.
(4) Missed appointments and offences committed during probation period.
(5) Employment situation.
(6) Number of interviews and percentage spent on the task.
(7) Methods of intervention.
(8) Type of worker.
(9) Views of probationers.
(10) Reconvictions.

(1) SOCIAL BACKGROUND

Table 14.1 shows hardly any differences between the 'successes' and the rest. There is a slight suggestion that the former tended to live in family settings. The successful cases were more likely to be second offenders and fewer of them had committed more than two previous offences. (It should be remembered, however, from Table 9.2 (p. 106) that there were marked differences in social background between the sixty-four offenders whose order was converted after six months and the thirty-six probationers whose order was not so converted.)

Table 14.1 *Social Background and Previous Offences of Forty-Four Probationers whose Orders Were Converted and Followed Up in Two Outcome Groups*

	'Successes'* N = 22	*The rest†* N = 22
Age:		
17–20	9	6
21 +	13	16
Sex:		
Male	14	14
Female	8	8
Living in family setting	18	14
Not in family setting	4	8
Employed at start of order	5	7
Unemployed at start of order	12	9
Unsupported mother	3	4
Housewife	2	1
Student	—	1
Recorded previous convictions:		
None	6	6
One	10	4
Two or more	6	12

* Task achievement 'complete' or 'substantial'; problem 'no longer present' or 'a lot better'.
† Lower ratings on task achievement or problem reduction.

(2) AGREEMENT ON PROBLEM AND TASK

It is often suggested that genuine agreement between social worker and client on the target problem and task is a precondition of successful task-centred casework. We could put this suggestion to the test, since the agreed problem area and task formulation were recorded on the task formulation sheet at the beginning of the order; in the independent follow-up interview the client was asked about the problem that worried him or her most when starting probation, and what the probation officer had seen as the main problem; similar questions were posed about the 'plan'. The clients' retrospective reports to the independent assessor on whether they agreed on problem or task with the probation officer did not differentiate between the twenty-two clients with high ratings on problem reduction and task achievement, and the rest. Indeed, the proportion of cases in which there was – in the client's view – complete agreement between

Table 14.2   *Congruence of Problem and Task Description in Probation Record and Follow-Up Schedule*

Congruence	'Successes' N = 22	The rest N = 22
Problem completely congruent	17	13
Problem not congruent	5	9
Task completely congruent	16	12
Task not congruent	6	10
Problem *and* task completely congruent	14	8
Problem *and* task not congruent	8	14

himself or herself and the probation officer on the main problem was almost identical in the two groups – thirteen and fourteen. Similar results emerged when asked about agreement on the plan or task – fifteen and thirteen. However, when we compared what was actually recorded as main problems and agreed tasks on the task formulation sheet (near the beginning of the order) and in the independent assessment schedule (as told to the interviewer), the results were somewhat different: while agreement on either problem or task taken separately again did not differentiate between the successes and the rest, agreement on both problem and task taken together did differentiate, as Table 14.2 shows. There was complete congruence in relation to both problem and task in fourteen of the twenty-two successes, but this only applied to eight of the rest of the cases, possibly supporting the hypothesis stated above.

(3)   TYPE OF PROBLEM AREA

Table 14.3 shows hardly any difference between successful outcomes and the rest in relation to problem areas, with the possible exception of problems of social transition where four of the five cases so categorised had a successful outcome. Once more we emphasise that numbers are much too small to draw any conclusions. It is interesting, however, to speculate about the very different picture emerging in a previous pilot study of twenty-three task-centred cases in an area office of a social services department (Goldberg *et al.*, 1977). Here the problem area of inadequate resources was associated with the most successful results, while problems of social transition proved very resistant to the task-centred method. Most of these social service clients facing problems of transition had to make painful adjustments to irreplaceable losses and possibly to a rather barren future. They

Table 14.3   *Problem Areas for Forty-Four Short-Term Probation*
Orders in Two Outcome Groups

Problem area	'Successes'	The rest
Dissatisfaction in social relations	6	8
Difficulties in role performance	3	6
Inadequate resources	3	2
Inter-personal conflict	3	3
Reactive emotional distress	2	1
Problems of social transition	4	1
Behavioural problems	1	—
Unclassifiable	—	1
Total N	22	22

Table 14.4   *Change in Employment Status among*
Thirty Unemployed Offenders

	Followed-up: successes	Followed-up: the rest	Not followed up
Unemployed at *start* of order	12	9	9
Client got a job *during* the order	6	4	6
Client still in work at *end of order*	5	4	4
Client in work at *follow-up*	7	2	?

were very vulnerable individuals who felt unable to cope with their
change of circumstances and who wanted to cling to the social workers
as listeners and sources of support in a prolonged and dependent
relationship. In the much younger probation group, problems of
social transition were mainly related to marital breakdown: the
opportunity to grapple with the necessary emotional and material
readjustments or with the process of decision-making was used to
good purpose, and none of these clients wished to prolong the
relationship. The one unsuccessful case of problems in social
transition was that of the young lone mother, already mentioned, who
was to start a 'new' life by becoming a nurse; but, as she revealed in
the follow-up interview, she never seriously entertained the idea, and
as soon as a suitable man came along the task (never started on her
part) was abandoned.

(4)   MISSED APPOINTMENTS AND OFFENCES COMMITTED DURING PROBATION PERIOD

Once more numbers are too small to draw any conclusions from the

slight differences emerging: the twenty-two probationers with successful outcomes missed fewer appointments on average (three) than did
the rest (five). Only one probationer in the former group reoffended
during the order compared with five among the rest.

(5) EMPLOYMENT SITUATION

Over two-fifths (21 = 43 per cent) of the forty-four clients whose
orders were converted at six months and who were followed up were
unemployed at the start of their orders (these excluded housewives and
lone parents as well as students and pensioners). In twelve of these,
employment was mentioned in the initial or a subsequent problem
formulation as a problem area, although not always worked on as a
task; in a further four cases, finding a job became a task during the
order, although unemployment had not been identified explicitly as a
problem area.

Ten of these twenty-one unemployed clients found work during
their probation period and by the end of the order nine were still
working, one having been made redundant.

Table 14.4 shows that during their orders the frequency with which
unemployed clients found and kept work during the order was similar
for both the twenty-two successes and the rest. At the follow-up
interview, a higher proportion of the initially unemployed offenders
were still at work in the successful group (seven out of twelve)
compared with the rest (two out of nine). The difference is not, however, statistically significant.

(6) NUMBER OF INTERVIEWS AND PERCENTAGE SPENT ON THE TASK

The average number of interviews was similar for the successes and
for the rest – approximately eighteen. There is some evidence that the
work in the successful group was more task-centred: the average
number of interviews where work on the task was recorded was twelve
for the successes and eight for the rest. There is, however, considerable variation within each of the two groups, and these results, while
in the right direction, are again not statistically significant.

(7) METHODS OF INTERVENTION

An analysis of the methods of intervention used by probation officers
in the forty-four cases was carried out using the ratings in the interview schedule as to which of the five activities – exploration,
encouragement, structuring, direction and enhancing awareness –
were the most important in the officers' interviews with clients.

The only significant difference emerging was that officers rated 'direction' as the most important activity more often with low scorers on task achievement and problem reduction (20 per cent of cases) than among high scorers (10 per cent). It is tempting to associate this result with the low scorers' non-achievement of their tasks; but, even among this group, 'direction' was overall a less important activity than 'encouragement' (which might be regarded as reinforcing task achievement) and 'enhancing awareness'.

Thus, apart from this one observation, there appears to be no direct overall association between task-centred success and the methods of intervention used; it is possible that the one significant difference emerging is associated with differences in workers' styles.

(8) TYPE OF WORKER

The ten officers in the project (counting all students who participated as one officer) achieved differing rates of success, ranging from officer A with four successes and no cases in the less successful group, to officers H, J and K with no successes at all. These officers varied also in the emphasis they gave to each of the five activities, but we could not discover any consistent association between the importance officers gave to different activities and the outcome of their cases. In particular, one of the most successful officers (officer B with sixteen cases overall) rated 'direction' as the most important activity in 27 per cent of interviews with clients; only one other worker (J with nine cases) reached this level, yet he was one of the least successful officers in terms of outcomes.

We must conclude, therefore, that if there is a relationship between type of input, worker style and outcome it is not a simple or direct one, at least as a predictor of task achievement and problem reduction. This issue is discussed in more detail in Appendix B.

(9) VIEWS OF PROBATIONERS ON SUPERVISION AND OUTCOME

A substantial amount of material from the follow-up interviews has already been used in previous sections. Here we shall concentrate mainly on the quantifiable data which could be scored and compared. Seven of these items (in addition to question 11 on problem reduction) discriminated significantly between those with high scores on task achievement and problem reduction, and the rest (Table 14.5). Twenty of the twenty-two among the high scorers felt that probation worked out well or quite well compared with ten among the rest. Looking at questions 12 and 13 ('How much do you feel you achieved for yourself?' and 'How much did the probation officer help?'), possibly the most interesting finding is that the feeling of having achieved a great deal oneself goes hand in hand with the awareness that the probation

Table 14.5 *Probationers' Views on Supervision and Outcome*

			'Successes' N = 22	The rest N = 22
Q2	What do you think the probation officer saw as your main problem?	Congruent	13	14
		Fairly congruent	6	2
		Minimally congruent	2	2
		Not congruent	1	3
		Not stated	—	1
Q4	Did you agree with the probation officer about what could be done?	Agreed	15	13
		Some agreement	3	2
		Minimal agreement	1	3
		No agreement	1	2
		Not stated	2	2
Q6	How did it work out?	Well	11	3*
		Quite well	9	7
		Partially	1	4
		Not well	1	8
		Not stated	—	—
Q9	Was the six-month probation period too long?	Too long	2	5
		About right	14	11
		Too short	6	5
		Not stated	—	1
Q12	How much do you feel you achieved for yourself?	A lot	14	3*
		Quite a lot	7	7
		Something	1	8
		Nothing	—	3
		Not stated	—	1
Q13	How much did the probation officer help?	A lot	15	5*
		Quite a lot	6	7
		A little	1	9
		Not at all	—	1
		Not stated	—	—
Q14	Did you like this way of tackling your problems?	A lot	13	4*
		Quite a lot	6	6
		Partly	3	7
		Not at all	—	4
		Not stated	—	1
Q15	How much did you feel the probation officer *really* understood your problem?	Completely	17	8*
		Quite a lot	4	2
		A little	1	7
		Not at all	—	5
		Not stated	—	—
Q16	Has contact with the probation officer made any difference to you or your life in general?	A lot	11	6*
		Quite a lot	7	3
		Some	3	7
		None	1	6
		Not stated	—	—
Q17	As a result of seeing the probation officer have you learnt anything that might help with problems in the future?	A lot	10	2*
		Quite a lot	7	5
		Something	5	5
		Nothing	—	9
		Not stated	—	1

* Denotes that differences in responses between successes and the rest were statistically significant at at least the 5 per cent level of confidence on a two-tailed χ^2 test.

officer too contributed a lot to the success. The successful group had very much higher scores on both these questions than the rest. This association between self-help and support again points to the importance of partnership in working on tasks and achieving aims. It seems that both the sense of having achieved something by one's own efforts as well as the enhancement, help and understanding from an outsider are important ingredients in successful outcome. We have already quoted many comments to this effect in the section on collaboration (pp. 124–5). Again, while twenty-one of the twenty-two high scorers on problem reduction and task achievement felt that the probation officer had understood their problems 'completely' or 'quite a lot' (question 15), this only applied to ten among the rest. Similarly nineteen in the successful group said that they liked the way the probation officer tackled their problems, compared with ten among the others. Similar differences obtain in the answers to the questions about the immediate felt effect of the probation experience (question 16) and in regard to future problem-solving (question 17). These answers contrast even more sharply with the replies given by the six probationers who scored lowest on task achievement and problem reduction. None of these six clients felt that they had achieved much, that the probation officer had helped them or had understood their problems, and none liked the task-centred approach. Most of the twenty-two successful clients spoke with obvious pleasure and animation about their probation experience, which had enhanced their confidence and coping ability, and specifically mentioned regaining confidence compared with two among the rest. The six clients with the lowest scores on the outcome measures spoke with detachment, depression, or bitterness about their supervision. Two were severely depressed people, isolated and unhappy; another wished to explore his needs, ideas and his malaise in a continuing therapeutic relationship; one was a drug-taker who saw no need to change but felt that society had to change; another had severe drinking problems; and the sixth was a young man without purpose or direction who responded negatively to what he called the 'nagging' of the probation officer who reminded him of his mum. It seems that at least five of these six were profoundly disturbed people, possibly needing other forms of intensive and prolonged help. It is of interest – in view of parallel findings in a number of other studies – that this unimproved group had more interviews, a mean number of twenty-four compared with eighteen for the whole group. The probation officers seemed to work harder and more desperately at trying to establish a specific problem with which help was most wanted among the welter of pressures and difficulties and to keep these clients to some kind of focus or task. Only one-third of the interviews contained evidence of work on the tasks that had apparently been agreed upon.

Somewhat unexpectedly the probationers' views on the length of the probation period did not discriminate between the two groups. The comments made were however illuminating, since probation was not merely a period of help but a court sentence. Several used the word 'relief' at the end of the order but, at the same time, expressed a sense of personal loss and sadness at parting with the probation officer, 'like saying goodbye to a friend'. A few who considered six months' probation just right said that it might have become boring if it had gone on longer, indicating that towards the end they were going over familiar ground. Others mentioned that if they had gone on longer you might 'lean on them or take advantage of them', or 'I would have relied on it too much if it had gone on longer', and another suggested that he would have become too involved, adding 'I said all I had to say'. Those who considered the period too short indicated that they still had problems and needed further help; but all acknowledged that the probation officers had left the door open and that they could consult them if they had any problem with which they could not cope themselves. Those who considered the period too long – mostly in the less successful group – sometimes felt that probation had not achieved much and that, on the whole, it had been a waste of time.

Lastly, the clients' vivid descriptions of the nature of their achievements defy quantification.

The main themes were first of all, and most frequently mentioned, that they learnt how to *sort out problems*: 'I have learnt to work things out on my own. Before, I had to run away from problems'; or, 'I know how to sort things out – sit down and think'. When this client thought he might be laid off work he went to the union to talk it over – this was his own idea. Another young man who had tuition in reading and writing and worked hard at it described vividly how surprised he was to see something coming off the end of the pencil when it never did before. And then he went on to say: 'You can express your feelings rather than arguing or punching a guy or nicking a car as you walk down the road. I can talk about things and sort them out.'

Next, a majority of clients commented on how they had learnt to use their own initiative in *dealing with formal organisations* such as the DHSS, the housing authorities, and so on. Some contrasted this way of mobilising resources by their own efforts with their experiences in the local authority social services: 'Things did not change with her'; 'My social worker does not work the same way.' (This man had explained how the probation officer pushed him a little to do things and also gave a lot of support: 'He gave ideas and asked how it turned out.')

The third main area of learning mentioned was *how to handle relationships* and to 'see yourself as others see you'. In several marital cases the partners felt that they could talk more easily to each other, recognising each other's faults and virtues and, as a result, had tried to change their behaviour.

(10) RECONVICTIONS

The toughest and most objective outcome measure of probation – though hotly contested as a legitimate measure of effectiveness by some – is the prevention of further delinquency. This is usually indicated by the percentage of ex-probationers who are reconvicted within specified periods of time. (The difficulties inherent in this concept as a true measure of delinquency were discussed in Chapter 6.) With the help of the Home Office Statistical Department, information about subsequent convictions for 'standard list' offences (that is indictable offences and some serious non-indictable offences) of ninety-six task-centred cases in the sample was collected for a period of up to three years after the key offence which brought these clients into task-centred probation. (Two cases which were transferred to other offices early on and two who died during the order were excluded.)

The results of this exercise are encouraging and suggest that short-term task-centred probation in this small sample was associated with no worse – and possibly rather better – reconviction rates than long-term probation not conducted along task-centred lines. The findings also point to a possible association between outcome measures on task-centred criteria (degree of task achievement and problem reduction) and reconviction rates.

. The evidence for these statements is as follows: Table 14.6 shows that the overall reconviction rate recorded for all the ninety-six cases in which task-centred probation was attempted was 42 per cent, that is to say, two-fifths of the probationers had offended again at least once by the end of three years. These ninety-six included five outcome groups: Group A (twenty-two) who had high scores on task achievement and problem reduction at the end of six months and who were followed up by the independent assessor; Group A2 (twenty-two) who did less well on these criteria and who were also followed up; Group B (twenty) whose task achievement was about average, but whose problem status could not be ascertained as no follow-up contact was made; Group X (seventeen) whose probation order ran for a full year mainly because of their lack of progress at six months and Group Y (fifteen) who were in custody or had been lost sight of. Ideally, one should compare the reconviction rate of this sample of offenders with that of a similar control group which received long-term probation, not conducted on task-centred lines. As explained in the Introduction, such an experimental design did not prove feasible. We therefore did

Table 14.6 *Comparison of Reconviction Rates Over Time of Probationers as Observed in Three Studies*

	Task-Centred Casework Project[1]	Home Office Reconviction Study[1]	IMPACT (London Sample)[2]
	N = 96	N = 258*	N = 313†
Cumulate percentage reconvicted after:			
one year	26%	33%	40%
two years	40%	47%	—
three years	42%	53%	—
six years	—	63%	—

* Number of *male* probationers convicted of standard list offences in a total sample of 5,000 (4,425 males and 575 females); females were excluded from the detailed analysis shown in Phillpotts and Lancucki (1979).

** Combines both control and experimental cases for the London subsample of the IMPACT experiment. The observed reconviction rates for control and experimental groups were 36 per cent and 43 per cent respectively.

(1) Reconviction data based on Home Office Offenders' Index.
(2) Reconviction data based on Criminal Records Office, supplemented by information from probation officers.

the next best thing and compared reconviction rates of the task-centred sample with those of the subjects in the IMPACT experiment and with those obtained in a larger-scale, six-year follow-up study of the effects of different sentences including probation (Phillpotts and Lancucki, 1979). (It should be noted that the IMPACT sample consisted entirely of high-risk offenders with previous convictions.) At the very least, these comparisons (Table 14.6) indicate that the subjects of this project were no more likely to reoffend than were probationers in the other two samples. Indeed, the figures suggest that they may be less likely to do so.

The next question is: Did those whose task achievement and problem reduction were rated as complete or substantial have a lower reconviction rate than the rest? Table 14.7 shows that the most successful project group (A1) had by far the lowest reconviction rate – 18 per cent, less than half the average rate of 42 per cent for the whole of the task-centred sample. Surprisingly, the rest of the forty-four who had a follow-up visit (A2) came out nearly as badly as those whose behaviour had led to a long probation period (X) and those who were apprehended or disappeared (Y). Group B (no follow up) came out quite well, with a 25 per cent reconviction rate. The reasons for this are partly explained below.

The large Home Office study referred to above had shown that reconviction rates are related to age and previous criminal record.

Table 14.7 *Reconvictions Over Three Years of Ninety-Six Probationers in Five Outcome Groups Analysed by Age within Previous Convictions*

	0 or 1 previous convictions						2 or more previous convictions						All cases		
	Age 21+			Age 17–20			Age 21+			Age 17–20					
	Total	Reconvicted		Total	Reconvicted		Total	Reconvicted		Total	Reconvicted		Total	Reconvicted	
Outcome Group	N	N	%	N	N	%	N	N	%	N	N	%	N	N	%
A1	10	—	—	6	1	17	4	1	25	2	2	100	22	4	18
A2	6	1	17	4	3	75	9	6	67	3	2	67	22	12	55
B	9	—	—	4	2	50	4	1	25	3	2	67	20	5	25
X	4	1	25	7	4	57	1	1	100	5	4	80	17	10	59
Y	1	—	—	6	2	33	7	6	86	1	1	100	15	9	60
Total	30	2	7	27	12	44	25	15	60	14	11	79	96	40	42

Hence, in Table 14.7 outcome is related to age and number of previous convictions. Interesting and suggestive results emerge, although numbers are very small and caution in interpretation is indicated. We note first of all that one group, namely those over 21 for whom the key conviction was the first or second, has a spectacularly low reconviction rate – 7 per cent – and that this good record holds for all outcome groups. It is apparently well known that people who have reached the age of 21 before they commit their first or even a second offence are unlikely to offend again. The table shows that nearly half of the A1 Group (ten out of twenty-two) and of the B Group (nine out of twenty) were in this good risk category while they only formed a quarter or less of the poorer outcome groups. It seems likely, therefore, that this high proportion of low-risk cases is partly responsible for the lower reconviction rates of those who scored well on task-centred outcome criteria. However, when these good risks are excluded from the analysis, the difference between the reconviction rates of the task-centred 'successes' and all the other groups is still considerable – one-third (four out of twelve) against nearly two-thirds (thirty-four out of fifty-seven) – but the result is no longer statistically significant and thus could have arisen by chance.

Favourable outcome on task-centred criteria seems to be associated, in particular, with low reconviction rates of people aged 17–20 who have none or one previous conviction. This group could be termed a 'middle-risk' one; but the table and other statistical evidence (West, 1982) suggests that persistent offenders in this age range present the worst risks and their reconviction rate seems to be unaffected by the outcome of task-centred probation (Table 14.7).

Next we asked; Did those probation officers who were most successful with their clients obtain better results in relation to reconvictions? Table 14.8 shows that the clients who were supervised by the four most 'successful' probation officers (A to D) had an appreciably lower reconviction rate (30 per cent) than the rest (51 per cent). This difference was almost wholly due to the good results achieved with young offenders, under 20, who had no or one previous offence – the middle-risk group: as the table shows, none of the seven in this category, who had been looked after by the most successful officers, were reconvicted, compared with twelve out of twenty among the other officers' clients in this middle-risk group. It is just as instructive to note that the successful workers did hardly any better in relation to reconvictions of persistent offenders than their colleagues.

The final step, ideally, would be to relate all three variables we have considered – outcome of task-centred casework, relative success of different probation officers and reconviction rates. Numbers are too small to do this, but it is likely that there is an association between the

Table 14.8 Reconvictions Over Three Years of Ninety-Six Probationers of More or Less Successful Workers Analysed by Age within Previous Convictions

Workers	0 or 1 previous convictions						2 or more previous convictions						All cases		
	Age 21+			Age 17–20			Age 21+			Age 17–20					
	Total N	Reconvicted N	%	Total N	Reconvicted N	%	Total N	Reconvicted N	%	Total N	Reconvicted N	%	Total N	Reconvicted N	%
A–D	17	1	6	7	—	—	10	6	60	9	6	67	43	13	30
E–K	13	1	8	20	12	60	15	9	60	5	5	100	53	27	51
Total	30	2	7	27	12	44	25	15	60	14	11	79	96	40	42

three variables: for example, whilst four of the seven youngsters of the medium-risk group who were supervised by the four most successful workers had high ratings for task-centred outcome and did not reoffend again, this only applied to two of the twenty comparable middle-risk cases supervised by less successful probation officers. Thus one hypothesis well worth exploring further suggests that there is a middle-risk group who respond well to task-centred probation, especially when carried out by skilled officers. Such a proposition is well in line with findings on social psychological intervention with other client groups. Such intervention appears to make most impact on medium-risk groups rather than on those with transient problems, or on those who experience long-standing multiple troubles or intolerable living conditions.

In summary: it has proved difficult to establish any clear relationship between background factors, input variables and outcome as measured by scores on task achievement and problem reduction. There are some indications that amount of input, methods used and type of worker are related to outcome, but numbers were too small to clarify these issues in any definitive way.

There is a suggestion that those who obtained high scores on task achievement and problem reduction were somewhat better risks from the point of view of living circumstances and delinquent behaviour before and during the probation period. Conversely, very disturbed and rootless people or persistent delinquents did badly. Full agreement between offender and probation officer on both problem area and task(s) seems to be associated with successful outcome, while there appeared to be no connection between type of problem and outcome.

Those who achieved their tasks and felt that their problems were much reduced displayed significantly more positive attitudes towards the task-centred probation experience than those who had done less well. The former group singled out the ability to sort out problems, to deal with formal organisations and to 'see yourself as others see you' as the most valuable learning experiences.

A study of reconviction rates suggested that they were no higher (and possibly lower) having regard to this sample's age range and criminal records than reconviction rates after long-term probation. There are indications that good outcomes on task-centred criteria were associated with lower reconviction rates than poor outcomes.

Chapter 15

SUMMARY OF PART TWO

This exploratory study sought to describe and evaluate task-centred casework in a probation setting. In particular the project aimed (1) to explore whether the task-centred model, originating from work with 'voluntary' clients who want to do something about acknowledged problems, can be used in the context of a judicial order; (2) to find out how effective the method is as judged by the clients themselves, by the probation officers and by reconviction rates.

The design of the study was a simple before-and-after one which compared the state of the problem(s) and aims of probation at the beginning of the probation order with the situation at the end of the order and with reconviction rates three years later.

The project was carried out under the joint auspices of the National Institute for Social Work (supported by a DHSS grant) and the Inner London Probation and After-Care Service in an experimental probation office – the Differential Treatment Unit (DTU) located in the Borough of Islington. The officers in this unit carried reduced caseloads and devoted most of their time to the exploration and application of task-centred methods to their probation work.

After a pilot phase in which task-centred methods were studied and tried out and recording instruments adapted to the probation setting, all the offenders referred for a social enquiry report (SER) from the courts served by the DTU were approached within the framework of the task-centred model.

The probation officers used the remand period for a thorough problem exploration; if a problem area and a task could be agreed with the offender and the case was considered suitable for probation, the officer would recommend a short-term probation order in his or her report to the court, which would normally terminate after six months. Contrary to expectations it took over two years to assemble a sample of 100 completed short-term probation orders, since only 23 per cent of the court referrals resulted in short-term probation orders – a percentage which is in accordance with the general norm in Inner London.

The 100 offenders who were placed on probation with a view to discharge after six months were broadly similar in their social and demographic characteristics to those who received other sentences. The main reason why three out of four clients were not recommended for probation was an inability to locate or agree on a target problem or to formulate feasible tasks. In some situations no problems, or only trivial ones, could be detected; in others, problems appeared to exist but were not acknowledged by the offenders, or problems were so pervasive and chronic that short-term probation could not hope to alleviate them.

Almost two-thirds (64) of the 100 short-term orders were terminated at the end of six months and were considered to be task-centred as they fulfilled the following criteria: a target problem or problems and tasks were agreed between worker and probationer, there was evidence that work on the task(s) had been carried out, and the order was converted to a conditional discharge after six months. In most of the remaining orders further delinquency or adverse circumstances either led to the probation period running for a full year or to the clients' disappearance or to custodial sentences. These thirty-six offenders for whom the task-centred method did not work out differed in some socio-demographic respects from those who successfully completed a short-term task-centred probation order. There were more persistent delinquents among them, they were younger, far fewer lived in families, more belonged to ethnic minorities and more were unemployed.

The majority of the sixty-four task-centred clients were under the age of 35; three-fifths were men. Practically half were unemployed at the beginning of the order; over two-thirds had at least one previous conviction, and half had two or more previous convictions. Most had committed some form of theft.

Dissatisfaction in social relations and difficulties in role performance, mostly related to work, were identified as target problems in over half the cases. Tasks were aimed at gaining some insight into the clients' behaviour and working out a strategy with them for bringing about some small and specific changes in their activities and relationships. Tasks in connection with the work role were mainly of a practical kind, such as work search sessions, literacy classes for those who could neither read nor write, and social skills training of various kinds.

The social work was carried out by nine experienced probation officers, only three of whom (including the senior) remained at the DTU throughout the project period. Some students also participated in the project. The officers, who had been used to an exploratory stance with the aim of achieving insight as the central concern, found the task-centred goal-setting and the 'shift from what is wrong to what is needed' difficult to incorporate into their skills. They discovered that they had to help clients to scale down ambitious and global targets to small, achievable aims; they experienced some initial discomfort in 'letting go' rather than to fish for further problems when their clients had in fact achieved the agreed tasks. Although they differed in their use of task-centred methods, all officers acknowledged that this model had helped them to become clearer about what they were trying to do, to share their thinking and feelings more openly with their clients, and to encourage more self-help and problem-solving in the clients themselves.

Certain features of the task-centred method stood out clearly:

(1) The more sharply the problem(s) and the task(s) were specified, the more clearly the clients were able to describe their task-centred efforts at the follow-up interview.

(2) Although clients stressed their own effort and initiative in achieving their tasks, they also emphasised the probation officers' participation and their encouragement. The reciprocity and equality experienced in the relationship were often commented on.

(3) The probation officers evolved a successful device for dealing with emotional obstacles to task achievement by setting aside a finite number of sessions for exploration and ventilation of these difficulties.

(4) The process of listing and ranking problems in order of urgency seemed to protect both workers and clients from being overwhelmed and to encourage hope and initiative.

(5) The idea of being kept to the tasks seemed to appeal particularly to the less articulate and intelligent clients, though a minority resented the focused task orientation.

(6) The well-prepared ending of the order and the final review of progress (or lack of it) in relation to initial problems and objectives of probation were generally experienced as helpful by both client and worker.

(7) The great majority of the forty-four clients who were followed up commented with satisfaction on their feelings of achieving an objective, however small, and on their increase in self-confidence.

The main outcome measures were based on two ratings – one by the practitioners in their final interviews with the clients on how far the task(s) had been achieved, and the other by the independent assessor in the follow-up interview with the client in which the answer to the key question 'How is the problem(s) now compared with how it was when you first saw the probation officer?' was rated. These two measures were only available for forty-four of the sixty-four task-centred cases as twenty failed to keep their appointments with the independent assessor. An additional independent outcome criterion was the proportion of offenders in the whole sample who were reconvicted up to three years after the offence for which the probation order was made.

There was a high degree of congruence between task achievement scores and problem reduction scores in the forty-four cases which were followed up. Any discrepancies (eight cases) were largely explained either by circumstances unrelated to the tasks undertaken, bringing about a temporary alleviation of the problem, or by different problem areas being rated in the two interviews in which outcomes were assessed.

Half (twenty-two) of those clients whose order was converted after six months and who were followed up had high ratings on both task achievement and problem reduction. The other twenty-two had lower scores, but only six clients had the lowest possible scores on both task achievement and problem reduction. The results were mirrored in the reconviction rates which were considerably lower for the twenty-two who had come out well on both task achievement and problem reduction than for the rest, although this is partly explained by the larger number of low-risk clients among the former group.

It was difficult to establish any clear relationships between backgrounds, type and amount of input and successful or unsuccessful outcome. There was a hint that those who obtained high scores on task achievement and problem reduction were somewhat better risks from the point of view of living circumstances and delinquent behaviour before and during the probation period. Full agreement between offender and probation officer on both problem area and tasks to be undertaken seemed to be associated with successful outcome, while there appeared to be no connection between type of problem tackled and outcome.

There were few indications that amount of input, methods used, concentration on the task and worker style were directly associated with outcome. However, some officers achieved better results in relation to both project outcome and subsequent reconvictions than other officers. Numbers were unfortunately too small to clarify these issues further; carefully designed experimental studies may throw some light on them.

Not unexpectedly, those who achieved their tasks and felt that their problems were much reduced displayed more positive attitudes towards task-centred, short-term probation than those who had done less well. Thus almost all of the twenty-two high scorers felt that probation had worked out well, compared with only half among the rest. The satisfaction of having achieved a great deal oneself went hand in hand with the recognition that the probation officer, too, had contributed much to the success, which highlights the part reciprocity and partnership played in working out problems and achieving aims. The importance of congruence between client and worker perspectives was underlined by the fact that practically all the high scorers felt that their probation officer had understood their problems, compared with less than half among the rest. In stark contrast none of the six lowest scorers felt that they had achieved much, or that their probation officer had helped them or had understood their problems, and none liked the task-centred approach.

A study of reconvictions in this sample over a three-year period suggests that this time-limited method is at least as effective in preventing further convictions as are long-term probation orders. There are strong indications that favourable outcomes of task-centred probation are associated with an avoidance of reconvictions and that this effect is mainly evident in a middle-risk group of younger probationers who are first or second offenders. Clearly, these hypotheses need extensive experimental testing.

Chapter 16

CONCLUSIONS OF PART TWO

CAN TASK-CENTRED CASEWORK BE USED IN THE CONTEXT OF A COURT ORDER?

The first question we wished to answer in this exploratory study was: Can task-centred casework be used in the context of a court order? The answer is a qualified 'yes', supported also by recent helpful clarifications of the current ideologies and practices in the probation service by Hardiker (1977), Bottoms and McWilliams (1979), Parsloe (1979), Harris (1980) and Folkard (1980). Arguments continue within the probation service whether the four primary functions of probation officers, namely, 'the provision of appropriate help for offenders, the statutory supervision of offenders, diverting appropriate offenders from custodial sentences and the reduction of crime', can be combined – especially the care and control functions (Bottoms and McWilliams, 1979). There is also doubt whether the fourth, the prevention of crime, is a relevant or achievable aim. However, a sufficient consensus seems to be emerging in support of the following propositions. (1) accepting that the probation service (and *mutatis mutandis* some aspects of the personal social services) has important control functions and that probation officers 'are and always have been law enforcement agents' (Bottoms and McWilliams, 1979), then, at the very least, any personal help offered must not conflict with this agency function. (Some practitioners and theoreticians take a more positive view and maintain that helping functions which respect the individual's right to self-determination can be fruitfully combined with control functions.) (2) In face of the growth in the prison population and the ineffectiveness of custodial sentences for many groups of delinquents, the role of probation officers as pioneers in non-custodial alternatives such as community service, day or hostel care and community development directed towards crime prevention, is an expanding one. It follows that a probation order need not necessarily (if it ever was) be regarded as a quasi-compulsory individual treatment order. Thus, if we regard the probation service as we do the personal social services as providing a range of options and functions, then casework help becomes only *one* of the options available. It would only be considered in circumstances where the client wishes to tackle certain problems in living with the help of a social worker or probation officer. Indeed, most of the authors mentioned above argue succinctly, very much as the originators of task-centred casework have done, that unless personal help is based mainly on the client's determination of problems which he regards as relevant to his well-being, the helping relationship will either lead to a coercive one with the control element lurking underneath the surface or to a dishonest one in which the helper pursues a hidden agenda of 'underlying problems' and the client obliges with an endless exploration within a maze of subterranean problems. In any case, most evaluative studies show clearly that social service clients as well as clients within a judicial setting mostly define help in terms of achieving a solution to immediate practical problems.

As we have seen, in about a quarter of the court referrals for SERs offenders did identify problems or situations which they seemed anxious to change with the help of the probation officer. Since half of these 100 offenders had at least two previous convictions it is not surprising that about a third (36) of them fell by the wayside. However, the majority of the sixty-four clients whose order was terminated at six months registered some task achievement and amelioration of their problems. The way in which these probation clients responded and evaluated the effects of the task-centred method did not seem essentially different from the reactions expressed by clients in other settings (Goldberg *et al.*, 1977; see also Parts One and Three in this volume). Hence we conclude that task-centred casework is possible within the framework of a judicial order and is regarded as a helpful experience by a small proportion of those – mainly young – people who are referred to probation officers for SERs. The openness and honesty of the relationship between client and worker makes it more likely that the boundaries set by the agency functions and the probation order are made explicit rather than swept under the carpet. Such considerations are also relevant in cases of statutory supervision in the personal social services. It is possible that problem-solving along task-centred lines may also be feasible and helpful in some cases where initially other non-custodial community-based methods are considered more appropriate. For example, offenders in day facilities, in hostels, or doing community service may, at some stage, become aware of problems or situations which cannot be tackled in these settings and which they wish to resolve either individually or in groups with some outside support. We therefore agree with those writers who suggest that such a personal helping service should be available for those who wish to use it as part of a broad and diversified court social service.

The second question we set out to answer was: How helpful was the method as judged by the probation officers and clients? From the worker's vantage point the task-centred approach stimulates clarity of thinking, more explicitness about aims and ways of achieving them, and more forward planning of individual cases; it invites greater participation by the clients, who are encouraged to accomplish as much as possible by their own efforts. The method discourages an aimless pursuit of a 'relationship' for its own sake and the continuing exploration of problems of which the clients may not even be aware.

The probation officers felt that the method helped to clarify the contributions of both clients and workers and led to greater equality between client and helper. Since the objectives were relatively modest they felt less oppressed by the multiplicity of problems and areas they had not been able to affect in their work with clients. Many problems were deliberately left unexplored, however tempting the unravelling of the psychopathology of the underlying problems may have been. Finally, the probation officers felt that the positive work on the ending of the order, looking back over what had been achieved and forward to the clients' ability to solve problems on their own in future, was an important addition to their helping repertoire.

The method by which personal help could only be attempted on problems which the clients considered as relevant to their life situations led to a clearer recognition of problems where either control and surveillance or other community services seemed more appropriate and it resulted in less collusion with clients to treat probation as a soft option.

From the client's point of view, the clarification of the purpose of the undertaking, the sorting-out process, the working partnership with the probation officer and the resulting sense of achievement seemed to enhance a feeling of confidence and autonomy. However, it seemed that such methods were more likely to work with clients whose personalities were not grossly disordered and whose life circumstances were not too disrupted. Among clients who were not able to make use of the help offered were those who longed for a continuous nurturing relationship, who were in the grip of addictions, who experienced profound despair and depression or whose material circumstances seemed impervious to any small-scale attack.

SOME POLICY ISSUES ARISING FROM THE STUDY

Although caution is indicated as numbers were small and the study mainly an exploratory one, there were few, if any, indications that the results of a prolonged period of probation were substantially different from those that had been achieved at the end of six months. In addition, almost all studies of prolonged counselling or casework show that most of the 'work' is done during the first months; also Reid and Shyne's most disturbing finding in their study of brief and extended casework (1969), was that deterioration was significantly greater in the long-term, open-ended treatment group. Other recent studies of long-term social work have similarly raised many question marks about aims and outcomes (Glendinning, 1981; Fisher *et al.*, 1983).

Since this study was completed six months probation orders have been introduced, but so far less than 5 per cent of orders take advantage of this option. Yet, from the cost aspect alone, in view of the evidence available so far should the six months' order not become the first option – provided always that active, goal-oriented social work rather than passive, vague surveillance, forms the content of such orders?

But we would go further than this and suggest that the time limits of probation orders should remain flexible, even within the six months' period and be capable of discharge even before the six months are up if probationers and probation officers can show clear evidence that the targets specified in the original contract have been achieved. Such a possibility would mean that successful problem-solving rather than rigid administrative considerations would dictate the discharge of an order. These ideas contrast with those propounded by recent discussions in the literature – for example, Folkard (1980), which maintain that length of 'sentences' should be in accordance with sharply defined legal criteria and not with possibly subjective treatment criteria and that personal social work help should constitute a voluntary 'extra'.

Flexibility also seems desirable at the beginning of an order. As we have seen, not infrequently the gap between SERs and the formulation of a potential contract specifying target problems and tasks, and the making of an order, can be several weeks during which the momentum of the task-centred enterprise can be lost. Would it be feasible to explore the possibility – always with the offender's agreement – of beginning task-centred work immediately after agreement is reached on problems and aims? If an order is made later on then such an order should date from the beginning of the problem-solving work.

Finally, a more general policy point became very evident: since it seems fairly firmly established that those who have never been convicted or only once up to the age of 21 are rarely reconvicted, should these findings not be heeded by magistrates instead of using up a good deal of expensive manpower on this very low-risk group?

UNRESOLVED ISSUES AND FURTHER RESEARCH

The design and scope of this study did not enable us to clarify further how much it is the *person*, how much the *method* and how much a combination of the two, which is the crucial input factor associated with outcome.

In the absence of more adequate recording methods (and, in particular, tape-recordings) doubts remain as to how rigorously the task-centred model was applied and indeed can be applied. It needs to be acknowledged that many interviews read like general discussions and that work on the task – either directly or by discussion – occupied less than half of the time spent with clients. However, it seems fairly certain that in most cases a purpose and focus were established and conscious attempts made to adhere to them, or, in the light of altered circumstances, to enter explicitly into a new agreement. Hence the recording of modes of intervention, left entirely to the subjective judgement of the worker leaves a lot to be desired; more work needs to be done both on the appropriateness of the categories of intervention used and ways of recording and rating them. In order to clarify what actually goes on in the interchange between client and worker, more tape-recordings of at least a random sample of interviews seems essential. It would be very instructive to involve clients as well as workers and their colleagues in the process of rating responses from listening to tape-recordings. Such endeavours would once more generate more partnerships between workers and clients and make the rationale of tape-recordings more comprehensible to clients.

In general, it seems to us that the foundation has now been laid for controlled experimental as well as cross-sectional studies to investigate further the association between good outcome in task-centred probation and reconviction in different risk groups. The hypotheses to be tested would be that while task-centred probation does not differ significantly from other methods of probation supervision in its impact on reconviction rates in the lowest-risk groups (people 21 or over who have never been convicted or only once), and with the highest-risk groups (young people who are persistent offenders), it can influence the reconviction rates of medium-risk groups. In this group the hypothesis would be that short-term, task-centred probation is at least as effective as long-term probation and is thus more cost effective.

Another area which needs further exploration is the relationship between the problems dealt with in the probation context and the offending behaviour for which the order was made. There was usually only the most general relationship detectable between the problem chosen to be tackled, the tasks attempted and the offending behaviour. It may prove feasible to mount an experiment in which task-centred casework is focused on problems which are clearly related to the offence or offending behaviour. Outcomes measured in various ways – behaviour, clients' opinions and probation officers' judgements, as well as reconviction rates – would be compared with those obtained in the comparison group, where the problems tackled would be chosen with no specific regard to their relationship with the offence, on the assumption that the resolution of problems that place stress most heavily on clients are likely to reduce offending behaviour.

REFERENCES: PART II

Bean, P. (1976), *Rehabilitation and Deviance* (London: Routledge & Kegan Paul).

Bottoms, W. E., and McWilliams, W. (1979), 'A non-treatment paradigm for probation practice', *British Journal of Social Work*, vol. 9, no. 2, pp. 150–203.

Brody, S. R. (1976), *The Effectiveness of Sentencing*, Home Office Research Study No. 35 (London: HMSO).

Fisher, M., Newton, C., and Sainsbury, E. (1983), *Mental Health Social Work Observed* (London: Allen & Unwin).

Folkard, M. S. (1980), 'Second thoughts on IMPACT', in E. M. Goldberg and N. Connelly (eds), *Evaluative Research in Social Care* (London: Heinemann Educational Books).

Folkard, M. S., Fowles, A. J., McWilliams, B. C., Smith, D. D., Smith, D. E., and Walmsley, G. R. (1974), *IMPACT. Intensive Matched Probation and After-Care Treatment. Volume I: The Design of the Probation Experiment and an Interim Evaluation*, Home Office Research Study No. 24 (London: HMSO).

Folkard, M. S., Smith, D. E., and Smith, D. D. (1976), *IMPACT. Intensive Matched Probation and After-Care Treatment. Volume II: The Results of the Experiment*, Home Office Research Study No. 36 (London: HMSO).

Fowles, A. J. (1978), *Prison Welfare: An Account of an Experiment at Liverpool*, Home Office Research Study No. 45 (London: HMSO).

Glendinning, C. (1981), *Resource Worker Project, Final Report* (Social Policy Research Unit, University of York, Dept of Social Administration and Social Work).

Goldberg, E. M., Mortimer, A., and Williams, B. T. (1970), *Helping the Aged: A Field Experiment in Social Work* (London: Allen & Unwin).

Goldberg, E. M., Walker, D., and Robinson, J. (1977), 'Exploring the task-centred method', *Social Work Today*, vol. 9, no. 2, pp. 9–14.

Hardiker, P. (1977), 'Social work ideologies in the probation service', *British Journal of Social Work*, vol. 7, no. 2.

Harris, J. R. (1980), 'A changing service: the case for separating "care" and "control" in probation practice', *British Journal of Social Work*, vol. 10, no. 2, pp. 163–84.

Lipton, D., Martinson, R., and Wilks, J. (1975), *The Effectiveness of Correctional Treatment. A Survey of Treatment Evaluation Studies* (New York: Praeger).

McKay, A., Goldberg, E. M., and Fruin, D. J. (1973), 'Consumers and a social services department, *Social Work Today*, vol. 4, no. 16, pp. 486–91.

Martinson, R. (1974), 'What works. 2 – Questions and answers about prison reform', *The Public Interest*, spring issue, no. 23.

Mullen, E. J. (1968), 'Differences in worker style in casework', *Social Casework*, vol. 50, pp. 546–51.

Mullen, E. J., Chazin, R. M., and Feldsteing, D. H. (1970), *Preventing Chronic Dependency* (New York: Community Service Society).

Parsloe, P. (1979), 'Issues of social control', in J. F. S. King (ed.), *Pressures and Change in the Probation Service* (Cambridge: Institute of Criminology).

Phillpotts, G. J. O., and Lancucki, L. B. (1979), *Previous Convictions, Sentence and Reconviction* (London: HMSO).

Reid, W. J. (1967), 'Characteristics of casework intervention', *Welfare in Review*, vol. 5, no. 8, pp. 11–19.

Reid, W. J. (1978), *The Task-Centred System* (New York: Columbia University Press).

Reid, W. J., and Epstein, L. (1972), *Task-Centred Casework* (New York: Columbia University Press).

Reid, W. J., and Shyne, A. W. (1969), *Brief and Extended Casework* (New York: Columbia University Press).

Shaw, M. J. (1974), *Social Work in Prison*, Home Office Research Study No. 22 (London: HMSO).

Sinclair, I. A. C. (1971), *Hostels for Probationers*, Home Office Research Study No. 6 (London: HMSO).

Sinclair, I. A. C., Shaw, M. J., and Troop, J. (1974), 'The relationship between introversion and response to casework in a prison setting', *British Journal of Social and Clinical Psychology*, vol. 13, no. 1, pp. 57–60.

West, D. J. (1982), *Delinquency: Its Roots, Careers and Prospects* (London: Heinemann Educational Books).

West, D. J., and Farrington, D. P. (1973), *Who Becomes Delinquent?* (London: Heinemann Educational Books).

PART III

TASK-CENTRED SOCIAL WORK
AFTER PARASUICIDE

By Jane Gibbons, Irene Bow and Janet Butler

ACKNOWLEDGEMENTS: PART III

This project was supported by the Department of Health and Social Security and Wessex Regional Health Authority and was administered by Professor J. L. Gibbons. The reseach assessors were Dr J. Elliott, Dr P. Urwin, Mrs C. Foster, Mrs G. Glastonbury and Mrs J. Powell. Janet Butler (Mrs J. Wilson) died in 1979.

Chapter 17

PARASUICIDE: TRENDS AND CHARACTERISTICS

Social work methods are not, we believe, techniques or recipes that can be described, learnt and then applied to a variety of problems. Rather, social work intervention in problems at any level is particular, developed out of the perceptions of that problem achieved by those involved, including the social worker. The social worker should differ from others involved in having more relevant knowledge which can be brought to bear on the problem. Thus the starting point for discussion of social work intervention in the problems of people who have deliberately harmed themselves must be a consideration of the phenomenon of deliberate self-harm itself. Before presuming to intervene in problems we need to find out what is already known about them. We shall therefore begin our account of an experiment to test the effectiveness of task-centred casework with people who had deliberately poisoned themselves with a general consideration of parasuicide.

People who deliberately harm themselves were formerly usually described as having attempted suicide. As it became clear that only a small proportion said they wanted to die, or had in fact endangered their lives by their behaviour, this term was generally abandoned as unsatisfactory. However, deliberate self-harm remains an action that has a connection with suicide – in the minds of the actor and those close to him or her, and in reality, since people who have harmed themselves deliberately are in one of the highest risk groups for suicide, 1–2 per cent killing themselves in the subsequent year. We therefore prefer the term parasuicide, 'referring to any act deliberately undertaken – which *mimics* the act of suicide but which does not result in a fatal outcome' (Kreitman, 1973, p. 49).

Parasuicide is used both for the act, and for the actor. Parasuicides, therefore, include people who intended to commit suicide but failed; people who did not intend to die but deliberately poisoned or injured themselves for some other reason; and people who 'by accident' took a harmful amount of a substance or injured themselves (drug

experimenter, confused old person, for instance). By far the most common means of self-harm is self-poisoning with drugs (over 90 per cent).

It is well known that the rates of parasuicide have risen sharply in
the last thirty years (Jones, 1977). Parasuicide is most often performed by young people, especially young women. Although found in
all social classes, among men it is most often performed by the
unemployed and those from semi-skilled and unskilled manual
occupations, although this pattern is less clear for women. Parasuicides tend to be divorced and separated and less often in stable
marriages. Studies of motivation (for example, Bancroft *et al.*, 1977)
agree on the importance of unhappy personal relationships, with the
act often provoked by a quarrel: one of the partners impulsively takes
an overdose of drugs which are available in the house, usually because
they have been prescribed by the family doctor. Parasuicides consult
their general practitioners more frequently than does the general
population; they tend to be well known and recognised as having
emotional difficulties for which psychotropic drugs are prescribed
(Gibbons *et al.*, 1980). Although about a third of parasuicides coming
to hospital are likely to have had some previous contact with a
psychiatrist, there is some dispute about the importance of mental
illness as a factor in this form of behaviour. Recent studies which have
used standardised instruments to study psychiatric symptoms in representative samples, show that the great majority of self-poisoning
patients experience painful and distressing symptoms, usually of a
depressive kind, at the time of their act (Urwin and Gibbons, 1979;
Newson-Smith and Hirsch, 1979). In as many as 70 per cent, these
symptoms are at a level of severity which normally leads to a clinical
psychiatric diagnosis. However, this clinical syndrome is usually
short-lived: one week after self-poisoning it will have disappeared in
about a quarter, and three months later in 40 per cent. Only very small
proportions of self-poisoners suffer from psychotic disorders, but
about a quarter are likely to have serious alcohol, drug, or personality
problems.

Helpful clinical insights are suggested by epidemological studies of
parasuicide carried out in several local areas, most notably in
Edinburgh over the past twenty years. Kreitman and Schreiber (1980)
directed attention particularly to young women aged 15–19 (and, to a
lesser extent, 20–24) as being the group who have shown most increase
in parasuicide: by 1974–5, almost 1 per cent of girls in Edinburgh aged
15–19 could be expected to be treated at hospital for parasuicide in a
year (and about 0.6 per cent of girls aged 20–24). Married girl
teenagers showed a particularly marked increase in parasuicide over
the period studied. Unhappy marital relations, debts and violence
were common stresses which had increased disproportionately among

these young married girls. Studies in other local areas agree that para-suicide was increasing most among young women in the 1970s and it may be that this trend in parasuicide was reflected in the suicide rate. An official report found that the estimated suicide rate for girls aged 15–19 had doubled in the twenty years 1951–4 to 1971–4, and the rate for women aged 20–24 also rose, though less steadily (OPCS, 1978).

There is no one identifiable cause for the 'epidemic' increase in parasuicide. Many social and cultural factors appear to be implicated. General explanations may be sought at a general level: for example, in the trend towards marriage at earlier ages, the increase in alcohol consumption (linked with suicidal behaviour and violence) and, above all, the 'medicalisation' of problems formerly defined as social or personal, so that sufferers are brought into contact with doctors and prescribed psychotropic drugs. Means to 'mimic' suicide in a relatively safe way are readily available to increasing numbers of people.

PREVENTION

The problem is a serious one from the public health point of view, as parasuicides make heavy demands on health service resources. Approximately one in seven of all acute medical admissions is for deliberate self-poisoning, and parasuicide patients make greater than average demands on psychiatrists and general practitioners in the long term. A growing literature exists on efforts towards primary and secondary prevention of parasuicide. Primary prevention is extremely difficult since the level of parasuicide is probably a product of much more general social and cultural forces. However, there is evidence to suggest that reducing the availability of the means of self-harm leads to a reduction in completed suicide. It may well be that easy availability of a method of killing oneself increases the total number of suicides, not just the proportion committed by that particular method. Suicide by coal gas poisoning is the clearest example. In the early twentieth century coal gas started to be used for domestic heating and cooking and suicidal gassing rose sharply after this. In the early 1960s a decline in suicidal gassing coincided with the introduction of non-toxic gas for domestic purposes. There was no evidence that substitution (potential suicides switching to other methods) occurred. It has been forcefully argued that the introduction of non-toxic domestic gas was responsible for the fall in suicide mortality during this period (Kreitman, 1976). It might, therefore, be thought that restricting the availability of the commonest means of parasuicide (prescribed psychotropic drugs) could lead to a decline in the overall level of parasuicide, not merely to a switch to other means of self-harm. So far this hypothesis has not been systematically tested.

Because of the difficulties in the way of primary prevention, more effort has been directed towards people who have already deliberately harmed themselves, to prevent repetition of the act or death by suicide in the future. The risk of repetition is high: various studies report between 20 and 30 per cent of patients repeating their act within twelve months (WHO, 1968).

The risk of repetition is increased by a history of previous para-suicide and psychiatric illness, by problems with alcohol and the law, and by living apart from a family (Buglass and Horton, 1974). Pointers to subsequent suicide are different: in general, parasuicides who most closely resemble completed suicides (male, older, mentally ill, living alone, with a recent history of loss) are more at risk. Special programmes to bring help to suicidal individuals have been set up and evaluated in different countries and centres.

(1)   Samaritans and Suicide Prevention Centres
As we have seen, parasuicide is often an impulsive response to personal and inter-personal crises. It has been thought that if help were immediately available at the time of crisis without any formal barriers, a person contemplating suicide or parasuicide would have an alternative to it. Thus, the Samaritan Organisation in this country provides trained volunteer counsellors available at the end of a telephone, and similar organisations have been set up in the United States and Europe. The Samaritan Organisation attracts some 200,000 new clients in a year and is succeeding in reaching the potentially suicidal. However, although the majority of parasuicides admit to knowing of the organisation's existence, few of them actually seek help, and the evidence suggests that suicide prevention centres, including the Samaritans, are not effective in preventing suicide or parasuicide (Holding, 1975; Jennings and Barraclough, 1980).

(2)   Specially Designed Services for Parasuicides
Experimental intervention programmes have been set up and evaluated in several centres. Although some positive effects have generally been found, no definite evidence of the efficacy of such programmes in preventing repetition of parasuicide or subsequent suicide has been produced. Greer and Bagley (1971) and Kennedy (1972) found that compliance with psychiatric treatment, or treatment in a specialised unit, following parasuicide was associated with lower repetition rates. In Canada an intensive domiciliary after-care scheme produced lowered repetition (Ternansen and Bywater, 1975). However, later larger-scale and more carefully designed studies have generally been negative. Ettlinger (1975) compared over 600 patients admitted to hospital in Stockholm before the introduction of a

planned (but not crisis-oriented) after-care service, with a similar number admitted afterwards. There were no positive effects on suicide mortality or repetition. Chowdhury *et al.* (1973) compared medium-risk parasuicides in Edinburgh receiving intensive after-care with those who received only routine after-care. A random allocation experimental design was used so that the two groups did not differ. No positive effects on repetition were observed, although the experimental service succeeded in relieving some of the patients' social problems. In Oxford, Hawton (1980) compared a flexible domiciliary service with a weekly out-patient regime, also using an experimental design. Although twice as many patients in the domiciliary group completed their planned treatment, their results in terms of repetition, social adjustment and improvement in target problems were no better. Although Hawton does not draw this conclusion, his findings, with those of Chowdhury, suggest pessimism about the effectiveness of special services for parasuicide patients. The study which we shall report here has no better results to offer in terms of prevention of repeated suicidal behaviour, though there were other positive results.

From the social work point of view it should perhaps be noted that, with training, social workers or nurses are as effective as psychiatrists in treatment roles (Hawton, 1980). After training, social workers, or junior doctors on medical wards, can also be as effective as psychiatrists in assessing the problems of parasuicides and their need for help (Newson-Smith, 1980; Gardner *et al.*, 1978). If special services are to be offered to parasuicides therefore, there is no particular reason why they should be run by psychiatrists.

PARASUICIDE IN A SOUTH COAST CITY: THE SETTING OF THE EXPERIMENT

The city at the time of this study (1975–7) had an estimated population of some 210,000. It was a prosperous south coast city, with a population rather younger and more mobile than average, and comparatively low unemployment. Housing problems of overcrowding and lack of facilities, with other social problems, tended to be concentrated in an inner city area which was also the area where New Commonwealth immigrants clustered.

As background for the study, data were collected on all cases of deliberate self-poisoning (defined as 'the deliberate taking of a substance believed to be pharmacologically active in a quantity which exceeded the therapeutic dose (if any) or the habitual level of consumption') from an address in the city, who attended the Accident and Emergency Department in 1972, 1975–6 and 1976–7. Data were collected by searches of the casualty book and medical records and, in 1975–6, by personal interviews with patients. (Methods are fully described in Gibbons *et al.*, 1978). The results showed that rates of deliberate self-poisoning in the city approximated to those found in other recent surveys of parasuicide in British towns with, in 1972, a male rate of 213 and a female rate of 355 per 100,000 population. The overall male:female ratio was 1:1·82; while rates for older males and females were similar, the rate for females aged 15–24 was double that for males. Female rates peaked at this age, while for males the peak was 25–34. The trend over the period 1972–7 showed a steady increase for males (from 168 cases in 1972 to 193 in 1976–7, a rise of nearly 15 per cent). There was a 12 per cent increase for women over the first four years, which then levelled off.

The social characteristics of parasuicides in the city in 1975–6 on whom detailed information was collected, were also similar to those of other British samples. They were more often divorced and less often married than the local population; they were more often unemployed or, if working, from semi-skilled and unskilled manual or personal service occupations; they were less often living in private households and more often at the two extremes of living alone or being over-crowded. Inner city areas characterised as 'rooming house reception' (with a large number of hostels, privately rented and shared accommodation and a high proportion of mobile adults); and 'immigrant reception' (with a high proportion of foreign-born residents, especially from the New Commonwealth) had particularly high rates of parasuicide throughout the period studied. (It should be emphasised, however, that although social problems, such as unemployment and bad housing conditions, occurred more among parasuicides than in the local population, only a minority were affected and the majority of parasuicides did not suffer from unemployment, poor housing, or poverty.) In summary, there is every reason to think that parasuicides in the city during the period of our study were no different from samples studied in other parts of Britain, and were a reasonably representative group.

The city's Accident and Emergency Department, serving the whole catchment area, was at one of the two general hospitals. People who had poisoned or deliberately injured themselves came initially to this department for necessary emergency treatment and were then, in 85 per cent of cases, admitted to a medical ward where they usually stayed overnight. There was little change in preferred methods of self-poisoning between 1972 and 1975–6. Over 80 per cent of the cases in both periods had used one or more psychotropic drugs to poison themselves, the most common being anxiolytics (benzodiazepines) and non-barbiturate hypnotics. Less than a third used proprietary drugs such as aspirin or paracetamol. Sixty-nine per cent used prescribed drugs in their self-poisoning, the drug having been prescribed for themselves in 90 per cent of these cases. Seventeen per cent bought drugs over the counter. Kessel (1965) has shown how easy it is to buy a large quantity of aspirin from a chemist: even when the customer is looking distraught and behaving in a disturbed manner questions are unlikely to be asked. In nearly half the cases the self-poisoning occurred when the patient was drinking alcohol. The danger to life posed by the self-poisoning act was slight in the great majority. Only 5 per cent were rated in the Accident and Emergency Department as likely to have died if no treatment had been given – however, even this would have meant thirty-three unnecessary deaths in the city in 1975.

The Hill Report (1968) recommended that in all cases of deliberate self-poisoning patients should be referred to designated treatment centres and assessed by psychiatrists. Although arrangements varied in different areas, in the main this guidance was heeded and the majority of parasuicides were routinely seen by a psychiatrist before being discharged from hospital. In the city, self-poisoners were routinely managed by a consultation on the medical ward with a duty psychiatrist who referred the patient on to more specialised services where necessary. In 1972, under this routine service, more than twenty different psychiatrists took part in the duty rota and so there seemed to be no consistent or unified management policy. In that year 43 per cent of patients assessed were thought by the psychiatrists to have a problem needing further psychiatric treatment; 15 per cent of the total were admitted to a psychiatric hospital and 28 per cent referred for out-patient treatment. Only 6 per cent, however, were referred to social agencies for further help. Thus under the routine service, patients were rather likely to be seen as suffering from a psychiatric illness and in need of further, hospital-based treatment; if this was not offered they were usually referred back to the general practitioner with an explanatory letter. Only a small minority were offered help with social and inter-personal problems in a non-medical setting.

Chapter 18

SOCIAL WORK METHODS
AND PARASUICIDE

We have argued that deliberate self-poisoning can frequently best be understood as an episode, or climax, in a turbulent period of a person's life. This period of turmoil is marked by an increase in stressful life events, some of which the person has brought upon himself, others of which are out of his control. Other people are likely to be closely involved and a quarrel is frequently the precipitant of parasuicide, especially for women. Although outsiders observing this inter-personal context tend to interpret the act of deliberate self-poisoning as, in some sense, aimed at other people – a cry for help or an expression of hostility – the actors themselves usually fail to acknowledge this motivation and seem instead to seek relief from unbearable tension in a period of unconsciousness. Thus preventive help – talking to a doctor or Samaritan – may be ineffective in the sufferer's eyes as a way of resolving the personal crisis: the closed circle has to be broken by a dramatic action which secures temporary oblivion and also removes him or her physically from the scene. Some have argued that, on the whole, parasuicide achieves the results hoped for and so is a functional act for the performer. However, this is not borne out by the high repetition rate and, in general, although parasuicide often seems to succeed in reducing the unbearably high levels of emotional tension and distress experienced by the individual, he or she usually returns to an inter-personal and social situation that shows little change as a result of such an action.

Certain principles to guide intervention by helpers after the act – whether those are to be social workers or others – follow from this evidence. First, the response needs to be rapid: help should be available as soon as the patient has recovered from the physical effects of the overdose, and there should not be lengthy assessment procedures or organisational barriers. Secondly, help should not usually be offered to the individual in isolation, but as a partner in a disturbed relationship or member of a family in conflict: the other parties in the disturbed inter-personal relationship need to be drawn in from the first. Thirdly, because the problems are likely to be complex, confusing and often chronically persistent, there is a need for clarity of focus and clear limits. From the social work point of view, therefore, there is most to be learnt from the principles outlined by writers on crisis intervention and by recent work on contracting. The task-centred approach provides a means of putting these principles into operation.

CRISIS INTERVENTION

The basic propositions (developed out of the work of Erich Lindemann, and subsequently Gerald Caplan, at Harvard in the 1940s and 1950s) of crisis theory are that emotional crises, initiated by one or more hazardous life events may occur during the life-span of individuals, families and possibly larger groups (see, for example, Rapoport, 1970). An individual, normally in a state of emotional equilibrium, is rendered vulnerable by the impact of a hazardous event and then uses his or her customary problem-solving repertoire to try to regain equilibrium. If this is unsuccessful in dealing with the event, tension increases and a relatively small precipitating factor can trigger a state of disorganisation and active crisis. This state is self-limiting, normally lasting no more than four to six weeks, and is a critical period during which a small amount of help, appropriately focused, can be much more effective because of the individual's weakened defences than more extensive help offered at a time when the individual is less open to it. Thus the crisis may be resolved by the individual's rising to the challenge and developing new and more adaptive ways of coping, but regression and a permanently lowered capacity to cope may also be the result. If the period following deliberate self-poisoning can be seen as a time when the patient and those closest to him or her are in crisis, it may be said that it is a particularly favourable time for intervention.

The goals for intervention in crisis situations are limited to alleviating the immediate impact of the disruptive life event, and helping those involved to mobilise their resources to cope adaptively with it. Thus the approach can be seen as suitable, on the one hand, for normally well-functioning people faced with an unusual amount of stress that is particularly threatening to them (bereavement, birth of a handicapped child, for example); and to people whose personalities seem vulnerable and whose life-style is precarious. Crisis intervention, for the first group, restores the normal ability to cope successfully and independently; for the second group it is confined to alleviating the acute problem without attempting to change long-established modes of functioning. In either case, it has been argued that crisis

Table 18.1 *Problem Classification*

Reid (1978)	Present Project
(1) *Inter-personal conflict* For this category to apply, the persons affected must define the problem in terms of their interaction – 'We fight all the time'. Subtypes include marital, parent/child, sibling, peer and teacher/student conflict.	**(1)** *Problems in significant personal relationships* Difficulties in getting on with someone important to the client with whom (s)he is in a continuing personal relationship. 'Difficulties' are rows and arguments, other ways of showing upset, e.g., walking out; difficulty in talking to each other.
(2) *Dissatisfaction in social relations* The client is dissatisfied with some aspect of his or her relations with others or with some particular person...the client may centre the problem in himself or herself (I don't have enough friends)...or on the behaviour of others towards him or her ('other kids pick on me', 'my wife nags me all the time').	**(2)** *Social transitions* Recent changes in the client's situation or environment that cause problems now; changes about to happen that the client expects to cause problems; difficulty in deciding to make a change.
(3) *Problems with formal organisations* Difficulties in the client's relations with such organisations as agencies, hospitals, residential institutions and schools.	**(3)** *Difficulties in social relations* The client feels that his or her social life is unsatisfying; (s)he has difficulties in mixing with the opposite sex; (s)he has insufficient friends; (s)he feels lonely.
(4) *Difficulty in role performance* The client's main concern is his or her difficulty in carrying out an ascribed social role to his or her satisfaction. Subtypes are differentiated according to the role involved; such as, parent, spouse, employee, student.	**(4)** *Difficulties with formal organisations* Difficulty in reaching agreement with an organisation or official; client is not getting needed services from some organisation; client is in trouble with the law.
(5) *Decision problems* Problems in reaching particular decisions usually involving contemplated change in a role or social situation.	**(5)** *Reactive emotional distress* The client describes his or her feelings of being upset in relation to some stress as a main problem.
(6) *Reactive emotional distress* Problems centred on emotional upsets precipitated by some event or situation.	**(6)** *Practical difficulties* The client has housing problems (overcrowded, repairs, homeless); financial problems (debts, low income, irregular income); work problems (unemployed, not coping with the job as well as (s)he would like, not doing the job (s)he would prefer); other practical problems.
(7) *Inadequate resources* Lack of money, food, housing, transportation, child care, job, or other tangible resource.	**(7)** *Domestic difficulties* The client has problems in role performance as a housewife (shopping, washing, cooking); or as a parent (being affectionate to the children, spending time with the children, discipline, worry over the children).
(8) Psychological or behavioural problems not elsewhere classified.	**(8)** Other not classified.

intervention is preventive of further disintegration and clinical mental illness.

The techniques and actual processes of crisis intervention are not very clearly described in the literature, but four principles are always stressed: intervention should take place as early as possible; it should be brief, usually lasting less than three months; significant people in the patient's environment should be included in the work; the focus of work should not be on unravelling the past roots of present difficulties but on the person's coping efforts now. Thus, people involved in the crisis should be helped to keep the problem in consciousness, rather than denying or avoiding it, and seek new knowledge and information about it; they should be encouraged to relieve tension, for example, by talking; they need to be helped to mobilise themselves to make use of all available resources and actively try out new ways of coping. Golan (1978) suggests that the concept of 'task' can be used in planning and carrying out crisis intervention. Within the broad framework of crisis theory, the practitioner may turn to the structure and techniques which have been developed in task-centred practice.

MAKING CONTRACTS IN SOCIAL WORK

The general principles developed in recent social work writing on the use of contracts are also helpful in relation to social work with self-poisoning patients. The legal term, 'contract', is used only loosely when applied to agreements between social workers and their clients, nevertheless, it does allow emphasis to be placed on important principles (Maluccio and Marlow, 1974). These are (1) mutuality: both worker and client must share in making the agreement; (2) specificity: the agreement is not vague and general but is about definite purposes and actions; (3) explicitness: the agreement is put into clear words and can, if necessary, be written down; (4) accountability: although legal penalties do not apply to breaches of the agreement by any party to it, the worker and client must feel that it has a binding force and they are accountable to each other for its performance. Corden (1980) has argued that the legal paradigm has a more specific relevance to the use of contracts in social work practice. He also pointed out that a contractual approach is not justified by its effectiveness, but is rather an expression of the value of reciprocity, whereby each party recognises the differing needs and goals of the other and enables the other to meet his or her goals. These principles are wholly compatible with task-centred practice whose processes provide a means of putting them into action. In Chapter 22 we shall illustrate the importance of reaching clear mutual agreements at every stage of task-centred work.

THE TASK-CENTRED APPROACH

The development and essential features of task-centred practice have been described in the Introduction (pp. 7–9). Here we point out some of the features of the method which seem to make it particularly suitable to help people who have deliberately poisoned themselves. The essential principles of the task-centred approach can be briefly summarised as follows:

(1) The purpose of intervention using this method is to help people solve or reduce problems. It is a problem-solving activity rather than one whose purpose is personality change, personal growth, or cure.
(2) Problems are those which are acknowledged by the person concerned, not attributed to him or her by someone else. Explicit agreements on the nature of the problem and the desired intervention are essential.
(3) Intervention is planned to be brief, with explicit agreement from an early stage on the time limit.
(4) The problems to be tackled are focused and specific, not global or general.
(5) The emphasis is on planned actions carried out by worker and clients (tasks), rather than on internal processes.

In all these ways, the task-centred method is in accord with principles derived from crisis intervention and 'contract' in social work. Its great advantage is that the actual processes of intervention have been successively described, tested and refined in different settings and by different workers, many of whom have published their evaluations (Reid and Epstein, eds, 1977). Thus the task-centred approach provides a model for practice, drawing on empirical evidence and open to change and improvement. Practitioners can profit from the inventiveness of other workers and also hope to contribute to the method's further development.

Problems, in this model, are sets of conditions the client wants to change. A wide range of problems is considered suitable to be tackled using task-centred methods and these are grouped into a number of broad areas. Reid (1978, p. 35) has summarised the latest version of this problem-classification system. However, in the study to be described here we deviated slightly from this system. Table 18.1 sets out the problem typologies. The main differences are due to Reid's fourth category, 'Difficulty in role performance'. We found reliability poor in assigning problems to this category when the problem was to do with domestic role performance. Because of this, for our research purposes job problems were grouped with other practical difficulties and domestic role performance problems were placed separately. We also found difficulties in reliably classifying marital problems using Reid's typology, where they may be placed under 'Inter-personal conflict', 'Dissatisfaction in social relations' or 'Difficulty in role performance'. We found it easier to assign all personal relationship problems to a single category: 'Significant personal relationships'.

The task-centred model is structured into successive phases of work which may overlap and have been described in the introduction. We attempted to adhere to these stages.

A further advantage of the careful development of the task-centred model of practice is the existence of recording forms to describe workers' activities which have been used in British settings (Goldberg *et al.*, 1977; Goldberg and Stanley, 1979). We were able to use these recording instruments, with some adaptations.

Chapter 19

THE EXPERIMENT

AIMS

As we have seen, the routine service in the city for people coming to hospital after deliberately poisoning themselves was considered to be not well suited to the task of intervening in crisis situations. Too many different psychiatrists were involved in the assessment of patients and they had few sources of social help to which they could refer patients immediately. Our aim was to set up a social work service for self-poisoning patients which would be carefully evaluated against the performance of the routine after-care service. Task-centred methods were to be used in the experimental service, while the routine service would resemble as closely as possible the existing pattern. We hoped to test the effectiveness of a task-centred social work service in a representative sample of parasuicide patients, using an experimental method.

In an experimental design, cases are randomly allocated between an experimental group (receiving the new treatment or drug to be evaluated) and one or more control groups (receiving some other treatment or, if ethical, no treatment). Over the past thirty years many experiments have been carried out within social work to test the efficacy of various forms of casework and group work intervention. Fischer (1976) has comprehensively reviewed the American literature. More recently, experimental studies seem to have become unpopular, perhaps because of their tendency to produce negative results which were usually explained away by practising social workers as due to defects in the research method. We believed, however, that a randomly controlled trial was the only way to produce convincing evidence of the efficacy of a proposed new service which, if generally introduced, would need administrative changes and possibly extra funds. Also, task-centred methods were capable of being defined and instruments already existed for describing them. This had not been true of many earlier social work experiments in which the nature of the social work 'input' remained unclear.

METHODS

The population consisted of all patients aged at least 17 who attended the designated Accident and Emergency Department for a defined geographical area during one year (April 1975 to March 1976) after deliberate self-poisoning – 626 patients attended at least once during the year.

One of the two research psychiatrists carried out assessments of patients as soon as possible after they had recovered consciousness. The assessors used structured instruments (see Appendix) to obtain information about:

(1) The circumstances of the self-poisoning (medical seriousness and suicidal intent).
(2) The patient's psychiatric state (present state examination, depression scale).
(3) The extent and severity of perceived social problems (Social Problem Questionnaire).
(4) The risk of repetition of parasuicide.
(5) Socio-demographic information.

Of the 626 patients eligible, 87 were not assessed by the research psychiatrist at the time of self-poisoning. Seven were unavailable because they died in casualty or were in police custody and 80 (13 per cent) refused or could not be contacted. The assessed sample therefore consisted of 539 patients, 86 per cent of the 'eligible' population. The missing cases were similar to those assessed in age distribution, marital status and areas of residence, but men were significantly over-represented in the non-interviewed group: half of them were men compared with a third of the assessed sample. The main reason for missing cases was that they were not admitted to a medical ward. The non-interviewed group were significantly more often fully conscious on arrival at hospital, less likely to receive any emergency treatment or to be admitted. The medical seriousness of their self-poisoning was less than the assessed sample's.

After all assessment procedures were completed the psychiatrist decided on whether a patient was eligible to take part in the trial of task-centred social work. Patients were excluded, if they had a formal psychiatric illness requiring immediate treatment, usually as an in-patient (6 per cent of the total were so diagnosed); if they were judged from scores on a predetermined scale measuring suicidal intent to be an immediate suicidal risk (2 per cent of the total); or if, though otherwise suitable, they were in continuing treatment with a psychiatrist or social worker whom they had seen within two weeks

(18 per cent of the total). Table 19.1 sets out the reasons for exclusion. Having made his decision about eligibility, the psychiatrist opened a sealed envelope which informed him whether the patient, now in the trial, was to be allocated to the experimental (E) or control (C) group. The allocation was made randomly, using a table of random numbers, and could not be influenced by the assessing psychiatrist's opinion about the patient's needs or suitability.

If a patient was allocated to the experimental group, the psychiatrist explained that a special service was available to help people who took overdoses and that he would be referring the patient to it, although it was up to the patient whether to accept or reject the help offered. E patients were directly referred to one of the two special social workers and 44 per cent were first seen before leaving hospital, the remainder at home, usually the following day. Control patients received the routine service, modelled on what had existed before the project started: 54 per cent were referred back to the general practitioner, 33 per cent were offered an out-patient appointment in one or two weeks' time, and 13 per cent were referred to social agencies. The experimental service was provided by two qualified and experienced women social workers who were based in the university department of psychiatry, with honorary appointments to the social services department. Consultation was provided by the senior author, based in the university social work studies department, who also directed the social work trial. The overall project director was the professor of psychiatry. Thus the two social workers had support from psychiatric and social work colleagues in a multi-disciplinary environment. The strain of this work was considerable, because of the risk of repeats and fatalities, and provision of support was essential. None of the three social workers involved had previous experience with task-centred methods, so that our work may have deviated from the 'pure' task-centred model.

Table 19.1   *Reasons for Exclusion from the Trial*

	N	% exclusions	% total sample
Major psychiatric disorder	34	24·5	6·3
Immediate suicide risk	9	6·5	1·7
Current psychiatric treatment, otherwise suitable	61	43·8	11·3
Current social work treatment, otherwise suitable	35	25·2	6·5
Included in trial	400	—	74·2
Total	539	100	100

Outcome Criteria

In evaluating service effectiveness neither clients' problems nor successful outcomes can be easily defined. Both are likely to have different meanings depending on whether they are viewed from the clients' or the service providers' perspectives. We believed that objective, 'hard' criteria of outcome were important in evaluating the success of the experimental service, but that it was equally important to devise outcome measures that were closely related to the declared aims of workers and clients in individual cases. We therefore developed a range of outcome measures, summarised in Table 19.2.

Repetition of self-poisoning This was defined as documented re-admission (including casualty treatment) at any hospital during the year following the index overdose. General practitioners' records were searched, the records of the local and neighbouring general hospital were monitored and records of patients who had moved were obtained.

Use of services In addition to the search of general practitioners' records, searches were made at three psychiatric hospitals in the region and the records of patients who obtained treatment elsewhere were obtained.

Change in depressive mood A self-report depression scale (the Beck Depression Inventory) was administered immediately after the self-poisoning and then to half the trial sample four months later, to the remainder eighteen months later.

Change in social problems A random half of the trial sample was interviewed four months after the index self-poisoning, the remainder eighteen months after it. There were three experienced interviewers, independent of the project and with no prior knowledge of the patients. They had a short preliminary training. Changes in social problems were assessed by a semi-structured questionnaire

Table 19.2 *Criteria of Outcome and Sources of Information*

Criterion	Follow-up period	Source of Data
Repetition of self-poisoning	1 year	GP and hospital records
Use of GP and psychiatric services	1 year	GP and hospital records
Change in mood	4 and 18 months	Beck Depression Inventory
Change in social problems	4 and 18 months	Interview questionnaire
Satisfaction with service	4 and 18 months	Interview questionnaire

administered immediately after self-poisoning and at the two follow-up stages. Detailed information was gathered about problems in seven life areas that followed the problem typology developed by Reid (Table 18.1). Reliability studies were carried out on twenty cases at the baseline and follow-up stages. Inter-interviewer agreement was better than 90 per cent for all sections except 'domestic difficulties' where agreement was less than 70 per cent. This section was therefore omitted as a change measure. After detailed questioning subjects were asked to rate the severity of difficulties mentioned under each of the headings on a scale ranging from 0 (no problem) to 4 (very considerable problem). The scales were added to make a total problem score. Scores of experimental and control groups were compared at baseline and four and eighteen months later.

Satisfaction with service   This was assessed by a short structured questionnaire given to half the sample at four months and to the remainder at eighteen months follow-up.

Our hypotheses were that:

(1) Experimental patients would repeat self-poisoning less in the following year.
(2) Experimental patients would become psychiatric patients less often in the following year.
(3) Experimental patients would have less treatment with psychotropic drugs from general practitioners in the following year.
(4) Experimental patients would show more improvement in depressed mood at short and longer-term follow-up.
(5) Experimental patients would show more improvement in social problems at short and longer-term follow-up.
(6) Experimental patients would feel more satisfied with their service.

Table 19.3   *Age Distribution of Experimental, Control and Treatment Groups*

	E	C	T	Total N
Under 25	61	59	41	161
25–34	66	64	35	165
35–44	37	38	27	102
45–54	22	18	19	59
55–64	6	17	7	30
65 and over	8	4	10	22
Total N	200	200	139	539

DESCRIPTION OF THE SAMPLE

The trial sample consisted of 400 self-poisoning patients randomly allocated between experimental (E) and control (C) groups. One hundred and thirty-nine self-poisoning patients were assessed but excluded from the trial, because they were in need of urgent psychiatric treatment or they were already in treatment with another psychiatrist or social worker. This group will be called treatment (T) group. We now describe the characteristics of these three groups at the time of their self-poisoning.

Age and Sex
Women made up 69 per cent of E and 73 per cent of C cases, compared with 60 per cent of T cases. Men were thus over-represented among the excluded cases. Table 19.3 sets out the age distribution of the three groups. There was no significant difference between them.

Marital Status and Children
44 per cent of E and C groups were currently married, but only 33 per cent of T cases. A high proportion in all groups had experienced marriages broken by death, separation, or divorce, but the number was higher in the T group: 37 per cent of T cases had a broken marriage compared with 29 per cent of E and 26 per cent of C cases. The numbers who had experienced a separation at some time during their current marriage were also very high: 39 per cent of E, 43 per cent of C and 45 per cent of T cases had separated for a time from their current spouses. Forty-four per cent of E and C cases, but only 29 per cent of T cases, were living with school-age children. Seventeen per cent of E, 14 per cent of C and 11 per cent of T cases were single parents looking after children. Only a few had a child in the care of the social services department at the time of self-poisoning – six E, one C and five T cases.

Households
The main difference between E and C cases on the one hand, and T cases, on the other, was the high proportion of the latter – nearly a quarter – who were not living in private households but in hostels and other communal living arrangements. (The city had hostels run by the 'Y', the Church Army and Salvation Army, as well as a reception centre.) The differences between the E and C groups were not significant. Approximately 10 per cent of all three groups lived alone in private households and a similar proportion lived in large households of six or more people. Overcrowding, as measured by there being over one person to a room, affected 10 per cent of E, 8 per

Table 19.4   *Psychiatric Diagnosis: Experimental,*
Control and Treatment Groups

	E	C	T	Total N
Psychosis	2	3	24	29
Neurosis	63	58	36	157
Alcohol and drug abuse	16	12	29	57
Personality disorder	27	29	35	91
No psychiatric illness	92	98	15	205
Total N	200	200	139	539

cent of C and T groups. Only small proportions lived in households that lacked exclusive use of basic amenities, such as running hot water, a bath and inside toilet: 8 per cent of E and C groups, 6 per cent of T cases. Approximately 20 per cent of E and C cases were in households dependent on social security at the time of self-poisoning, but twice as many T cases (a significant difference).

A third of E and C cases and 38 per cent of T cases had lived at their present address for less than a year. In all three groups there was a minority of extremely mobile people who had moved more than five times in the five years preceding the self-poisoning: 12 per cent of E and C cases, compared with 21 per cent of T cases.

Economic Activity
There were no differences between E and C groups in economic activity, but great differences between the trial sample as a whole and the excluded T cases. Forty per cent of the trial cases were in full-time work, compared with only 20 per cent of T cases. Correspondingly, 42 per cent of the T cases were sick or unemployed, compared with 17 per cent of the trial sample. Again, E and C groups did not differ significantly from each other in socio-economic status, but differed significantly from the T group, having more foremen and skilled manual workers and fewer unskilled manual workers. (However, these social class categories may be regarded as somewhat unsatisfactory in a sample that includes so many women, who have to be assigned to a category on the basis of their husbands' or fathers' occupations.)

Clinical Characteristics
The research psychiatrists who interviewed patients on recovery of consciousness made a clinical diagnosis in each case and gathered information about the previous psychiatric history from the patients themselves and from medical records. Table 19.4 shows the numbers

in broad clinical categories in the E, C and T groups. There was no difference between E and C groups but very marked differences between them and the T group. Whereas nearly half the trial sample were considered to have no formal psychiatric illness, only 11 per cent of the excluded cases had none, and more of them were psychotic, addicted to alcohol or drugs, or considered to have personality disorders. Neurotic disorders were more common in the trial sample. Twenty-three per cent of the trial sample had had previous out-patient psychiatric treatment, a fifth having been previously in psychiatric hospitals, but almost 60 per cent of the excluded cases had had previous in-patient psychiatric treatment. Nearly 20 per cent of the trial sample had committed offences for which they were taken to court, compared with 29 per cent of excluded cases. While 27 per cent of the trial sample had been admitted to hospital for parasuicide at least once before, this proportion rose to 52 per cent of the excluded cases, 15 per cent of whom had taken more than four previous overdoses.

A standardised scale which has been shown to predict the risk of repetition was given to patients at the time of self-poisoning. Six factors are included: previous parasuicide, in-patient and out-patient psychiatric treatment, sociopathic personality, problems with alcohol and not living with relatives. One point is given for each item positively scored. Table 19.5 shows the numbers of cases in E, C and T groups in different risk categories. Whereas 42 per cent of E and C groups scored 0 (lowest risk of repetition, according to the scale) only 10 per cent of T cases scored 0. Only 6 per cent of the trial sample scored four or more, compared with 29 per cent of T cases. Thus there were no differences between E and C cases in their predicted risk of repeating parasuicide, but the excluded cases had a significantly higher risk of repetition.

Differences between the Groups
The random allocation procedure used to assign cases to experimental or control groups should have worked to ensure that the two groups did not differ significantly from each other. As we have seen, the procedure was very successful as there were, in fact, no differences between E and C groups on any baseline measure. If any differences were to be found between the two groups after a period of treatment, we should feel more confidence in attributing them to the effects of different treatments, rather than to characteristics already present before treatment started. However, the trial sample was less representative of the total population of self-poisoners than we had hoped. While it was necessary on ethical grounds to exclude people from the trial who clearly needed some other form of treatment

Table 19.5   *Risk of Repetition of Self-Poisoning: Experimental, Control and Treatment Groups*

Buglass Score	E	C	T	Total N
0	85	82	14	181
1	56	62	22	140
2	36	28	21	85
3	14	13	39	66
4	5	10	28	43
5	4	4	6	14
6	0	1	6	7
Total N	200	200	136*	536

* 3 T cases were missing.

urgently, these 'ethical' exclusions numbered only forty-three cases. The remaining ninety-six cases, whom we should have included were it not for the practical and professional impossibility of removing them from their current treatment with another worker, proved in fact to be more socially deprived and psychiatrically disturbed than the trial cases. This fact showed the success of the existing local psychiatric and social services in picking the most needy people for their treatment, but it meant that the trial of task-centred casework included a smaller number of high-risk cases than we had hoped. The cases in the trial sample differed from the local population in expected ways in terms of socio-demographic composition, the prevalence of social problems such as unemployment and the extent of psychiatric disturbance. However, they were closer to the population, a more 'normal' group, than the T cases who were the most deviant and disadvantaged self-poisoners. Table 19.6 summarises the differences between the groups at the time of self-poisoning. Henceforward, we shall be concerned only with the trial sample.

Social Problems Experienced by Experimental and Control Groups at Self-Poisoning
We shall now describe in more detail the personal and social problems which the 400 experimental and control cases described in their assessment interview at the time of self-poisoning. Information about the nature and extent of social problems in life areas specified as suitable for task-centred help was gathered by means of a semi-structured questionnaire. Definitions of these social problem areas have already been given (Table 18.1, p. 178). The problem areas will now be described in order of their magnitude in E and C groups.

Reactive emotional distress   Patients were asked: 'Would you say at

Table 19.6 *Differences between Trial and Treatment Groups*

Differences: Social	E v. C	Trial v. T	Differences: Clinical	E v. C	Trial v. T
Age	—	—	Diagnosis	—	***
Sex	—	*	Previous psychiatric		
Marital status	—	—	treatment	—	***
Children	—	—	Drugs/alcohol		
Household	—	—	problem	—	***
Crowding/			Previous parasuicide	—	**
amenities	—	—	Previous offences	—	**
Tenure category	—	***	Psychiatric family		
Time at address	—	*	history	—	**
Economic activity	—	***	Risk of repetition	—	***
Social class	—	*	Circumstances of		
Socio-economic			self-poisoning	—	—
group	—	*			
Income source	—	***			

χ^2 was used to determine whether differences were statistically significant:
$* = p < ·05$, $** = p < ·01$, $*** = p < ·001$.

the moment that one of the main problems you have is feelings of being upset?' Events causing these feelings, the frequency with which they occurred and the problems they created for the patient were elicited, and the patient then rated the severity of distress on a five-point scale. There were no significant differences between E and C groups, some 30 per cent rating the problem as none or a little, while about 60 per cent rated it as considerable or very considerable. Reactive emotional distress was the problem most commonly admitted to and rated as considerable (a finding that is consistent with the function of self-poisoning in putting an end to unbearable feelings of tension, as well as with the psychiatric diagnoses of these patients). There were no significant differences in the proportions of men and women, older and younger, married and unmarried cases or cases in different social classes who admitted to problems of reactive emotional distress, suggesting the universal importance of this problem in parasuicidal behaviour. However, cases who were given a psychiatric diagnosis were significantly more likely to have a problem in this area.

Example 1 illustrates a case where reactive emotional distress was rated as a very considerable problem.

A married woman of 26. Sexual difficulties were making her second marriage tense and unhappy and there were problems with her 7-year-old son by her first marriage, who was soiling, as well as financial difficulties. She rated feelings of emotional distress as a very considerable problem. 'I feel all the time I want to cry – it never quite comes out. I get the shakes a lot, usually only for a little while but sometimes all afternoon. I can't stand noise.'

In comparison, Example 2 illustrates a case where reactive emotional distress was not rated a problem.

A single girl of 18 who took an overdose of aspirin in her lunch hour at work with other people present. She had quarrelled with her boyfriend on the previous night and when she telephoned him at lunch time on the day of the overdose he refused to speak to her. She suddenly felt angry and upset and impulsively took the aspirin. She had not felt like this before.

Social transition Patients were asked, 'Have there been any recent changes in your life that are causing problems for you now?', and were also questioned about impending changes expected to cause problems, and difficulties in deciding whether to make a change. There was no significant difference between E and C groups, and patients' age, sex, marital status and social class positions had no influence on their ratings. Eleven per cent had experienced a recent bereavement; 16 per cent had moved house and 13 per cent had changed jobs. The commonest recent event, however, was the break-up of a love relationship which had affected 39 per cent. In over a third of these the rupture, usually in the form of a final quarrel, had come in the week before the overdose. Imminent changes, or anxiety about deciding on a change, were less important than recent changes, affecting only about 16 per cent.

Example 3 is of a case where problems of social transition were rated as very considerable.

A 27-year-old married man took a large overdose of mixed prescribed drugs, having locked himself in the lavatory at home. He immediately opened the door and informed his mother what he had done. A few months previously his house in another part of the country had been repossessed by the building society on his failure to keep up mortgage repayments, and his wife had been forced to take the children back to her mother's. He lost his job. A few weeks previously he had come to his mother's to find that his father had just died, leaving large debts which would force his mother's house to be sold also.

Example 4 illustrates a case who rated problems of social transition as only slight.

A 17-year-old girl took an impulsive overdose of barbiturates belonging to a friend after a quarrel. Two months previously she had moved away from home for the first time to live with her boyfriend in a house belonging to friends of his. Since her parents disapproved of the move she could no longer turn to them for support. However, she rated this change as only a little problem compared with others.

Significant personal relationships Patients were asked, 'Are you worried about how you are getting along with any important person in your life?' and were questioned in detail about arguments, other ways of showing upset and difficulties in talking to the other person. Nearly half of both E and C groups reported a considerable or very considerable problem and about a third had no or only a little problem. Younger patients were significantly more likely to report a problem in significant personal relationships. Sixty-nine per cent of those under 34, 63 per cent of those aged 34–55, but only 56 per cent of those over 55 rated at least 'some' problem in this area. Personal relationship problems affected women significantly more often than men: 53 per cent of men, but 66 per cent of women reported them as at least 'some' problem. The married were significantly more often affected than the single or those whose marriage had ended: while nearly three-quarters of the married had at least 'some' problem of significant personal relationships, 57 per cent of those whose marriage had ended and half the single did. The difficulties were most often with a spouse (56 per cent), then with a boy- or girl-friend (23 per cent) and with a parent (11 per cent). Rows and arguments occurred at least weekly in 36 per cent and there had been at least one violent episode in 39 per cent. Example 5 illustrates a case who rated problems of significant personal relationships as very considerable.

A 21-year-old married woman took an overdose of painkillers at home when her husband was present. She rated her relationship with him as a very considerable problem. There were arguments two or three times a month normally when the husband had been drinking. 'He calls me a whore, tells me I'm no good and I've been unfaithful.' He shouted at her, but didn't hit her. They had had no sexual relations for eight months because she couldn't bear him now and she was considering separation.

Example 6 illustrates a case who did not have personal relationship problems.

A 49-year-old divorced woman took an overdose of prescribed

tranquillisers in her daughter's house. She had no problems with individuals, but complained of loneliness, lack of friends and social contacts, and financial worries. She lived alone in her flat which felt like a prison.

Practical difficulties   Patients were asked if they had financial worries, problems with housing, were unemployed, or were having other job problems. Twenty-eight per cent of E and C patients reported considerable or very considerable problems under this heading, while about half had no or slight problems. While older and younger patients were equally likely to have practical difficulties, married patients had them less often than the single or those with broken marriages (45 per cent *v.* 55 per cent); and women had them significantly less often than men (42 per cent *v.* 71 per cent). Example 7 illustrates a patient who rated practical difficulties as a very considerable problem.

A 38-year-old married woman who took an impulsive overdose of phenobarbitone prescribed for her epilepsy after a row with her husband. The husband was unemployed, debts had built up and they were two months behind on their rent.

Example 8 is of a case who rated practical difficulties as a slight problem.

A single man of 37 who took an overdose of diazepam in front of some friends. He had lost his labouring job a month earlier and due to the circumstances was not getting unemployment benefit. He also had an unpaid fine of £25. However, he rated these practical difficulties as only a little problem, saying he had had far worse in the past, and he was much more concerned about a number of recent deaths in his family and the belief that he might have a serious illness himself.

Social relations   Patients were asked, 'Do you feel your social life is as satisfying as you would like?' Further questions were asked about difficulties in mixing, whether the patient had close friends, when he or she last went out socially and whether he or she felt lonely. A fifth of E and C groups had considerable problems in this area, while 63 per cent had none or little. Social isolation itself, in the sense of having no friends or never seeing them, or seldom going out socially, was not very important: subjective feelings of loneliness and boredom were often expressed, even though the patient had seen several people she called friends in the previous week and had gone out socially at least

once. Younger and older, male and female, and married and unmarried patients were equally likely to complain of problems in social
relations. Example 6 illustrated a case with considerable problems in
this area.

Example 9 illustrates a slight problem.

A married woman of 55 who took a small overdose of prescribed
anti-depressants after a row with her husband. She felt her social
life was unsatisfying since she had made few friends since moving to
the city five years previously. She felt she had no close friends and
wanted more. However, she went out with her husband once a week
which she felt was enough. She sometimes felt lonely. She rated this
as a little problem in comparison with her jealousy of her husband.

Formal organisations   Patients were asked whether they were having
difficulty in reaching agreement with any organisation, such as social
security, school, whether they were in trouble with any organisation,
such as the police; and whether there were any organisations from
which they were not getting services they needed. Only a small
minority of E and C cases complained of such problems (about 14 per
cent). Younger people were significantly more likely to have problems
with organisations (25 per cent of those under 35 as opposed to 13 per
cent of those over 35). Men had these problems significantly more
than women (22 per cent *v*. 10 per cent). Marital status and social class
had no effect on problems with organisations.

Example 10 illustrates a case who had very considerable problems
with formal organisations.

A single man of 22 took an overdose of valium tablets prescribed
for his father after a row with his girl-friend. A warrant was out for
his arrest for non-payment of a fine of £98 imposed for assault. He
believed he would get an automatic ninety days in prison since his
offer to pay the fine in small amounts, all he could afford, had been
refused.

Example 11 illustrates a case who rated problems with formal
organisations as slight.

A 34-year-old married woman who took an overdose of prescribed
sleeping tablets when at home with her husband. She felt she was
not getting the services she wanted from the social services since she
was unable to get information from the social worker about the progress of her daughter, who was in care and with foster parents. She
had heard rumours that her daughter had been drunk at school but

the social worker 'didn't want to know'. However, the problem with social services was a slight one in comparison with the bad relationship with her daughter, which led to arguments with her husband.

Domestic difficulties   Patients were asked whether there were any problems in coping with things they had to do at home, such as coping with housework or with being a parent. Only a small minority (about 12 per cent) of E and C cases, nearly all of whom were women, rated this as a problem. Example 12 is of a very considerable problem.

A married woman of 25 took an overdose of nembutal when at home with her children, but immediately 'phoned the GP to inform him. She had two children under 5 and felt she could not cope with them. 'I feel I am a rotten mother. They would be better off with someone else. I feel I have failed. I don't do enough for them. I'm more interested in keeping the house tidy.' She felt she could not be affectionate to the children and did not like cuddling them.

Example 13 is of a slight problem in this area.

A 26-year-old married woman took an overdose of paracetamol and librium when alone at home. However, she straight away told a neighbour what she had done. She rated domestic role performance as a little problem – 'I can't be bothered with housework. I don't do it at all. He complains that the house is a mess and I'm a mess.' Much more serious was her unhappy relationship with her husband to, whom she had recently confessed having an affair with someone else.

In summary, the experimental and control groups did not significantly differ from each other in their perception of social problems at the time of self-poisoning, any more than they did in demographic or clinical characteristics. The problem areas that were most important for both groups were unpleasant feelings of emotional distress; recent changes and life events, especially the break-up of a love relationship; unhappy and conflictful personal relationships, especially with a spouse, boy- or girl-friend; and practical difficulties to do with money, work, or housing. Difficulties in social relations, problems with formal organisations and domestic role performance difficulties affected only a minority. Women in both groups were more often affected by personal relationship problems and domestic role performance difficulties. Men more often had practical problems and problems with formal organisations. The illustrations were drawn at random from the various categories and are not necessarily the most outstanding or 'best' examples, but give a representative picture. They show that the patients' own ratings of the severity of a problem are subjective and personal to them: while they would sometimes co-incide with a common-sense external standard of severity (for example, cases 3 and 5) at other times they probably would not (for example, case 9). In our view, the impact of a problem upon the person experiencing it and its meaning to him or her must be subjective. It is impossible to devise an objective, value-free standard of problem severity that does not distort the person's own experience of the problem. However, patients' subjective ratings of their problems did generally conform to what would be expected from more objective studies of self-poisoners. We are left with a picture of vulnerable people usually experiencing acutely painful feelings of tension, depression and anxiety, faced with disturbing life events and often caught up in conflictful personal relationships. Drugs are readily available to provide a means of action seen as a temporary solution.

Chapter 20

THE RESULTS OF THE TRIAL

We shall first briefly describe the outcomes of the experimental and control groups (E and C groups) and then look in more detail at the task-centred service and how clients evaluated it.

OUTCOMES OF THE EXPERIMENTAL AND CONTROL GROUPS

(1) Repetition of Self-Poisoning in the Following Year

We had hypothesised that fewer E clients would repeat self-poisoning. In fact, there was no overall difference between E and C cases, with 13·5 per cent of the former, compared with 14·5 per cent of the latter repeating.

(2) Use of Psychiatric Services during the Following Year

We wished to test whether the task-centred service could provide a substitute for psychiatric treatment during the following year, not merely an addition to it. We compared E and C groups as to whether they had any psychiatric contact in the following year, and whether it was brief or continuing. 'Brief' was defined as less than five out-patient visits, and/or less than seven in-patient days and/or a week or less as a day patient. 'Continuing' was defined as five or more out-patient visits, and/or more than a week as an in-patient or day patient. Seventy-eight per cent of E cases compared with 66 per cent of C cases had no contact with psychiatric services; 10 per cent of E cases compared with 17 per cent of C cases had brief contact; and 11 per cent of E cases compared with 16 per cent of C cases had continuing contact. Thus significantly fewer E cases used psychiatric services in the year following overdose. Sex and the level of psychiatric pathology made a difference to service use. Although fewer experimental than control men used psychiatric services overall, actually more of them had continuing psychiatric treatment; while for women, the task-centred service appeared better able to substitute for psychiatric treatment. When the level of psychiatric pathology was low (the patient did not have a formal psychiatric disorder and had no previous psychiatric history) neither E nor C cases were likely to use psychiatric services (only 4 per cent of E cases and 7 per cent of C cases did so). Where psychiatric pathology was moderate (either a formal psychiatric disorder or a previous psychiatric history) of high (both a formal psychiatric disorder and a previous history) the experimental service made more of a difference (Table 20.1).

Sixty-two per cent of E cases with high psychiatric pathology avoided using psychiatric services and 81 per cent of E cases with moderate pathology, while only 48 per cent and 61 per cent of C cases in these categories did so. The task-centred service, therefore, did prevent recourse to psychiatric treatment in the following year, especially for women and cases of moderate psychiatric pathology.

(3)   Treatment with Psychotropic Drugs by General Practitioners
There was no difference in the proportions of E and C cases prescribed psychotropic drugs by general practitioners for 'psychiatric' problems in the year following self-poisoning – 59 per cent of E cases and 61 per cent of C cases were prescribed such drugs. The task-centred social workers contacted all general practitioners about their clients, but did not try to influence their prescribing habits. Clearly, the mere knowledge that a patient was being offered counselling and practical help from a social worker was insufficient to make doctors reconsider their use of drugs, and they did not perceive experimental patients as any less in need of medication than controls.

(4)   Change in Depressive Mood
Table 20.2 shows that both E and C groups had improved markedly by the four months' follow-up, and that improvement was maintained at long-term follow-up. E cases had improved somewhat more at four months and considerably more at eighteen months' follow-up.

Table 20.1   *Use of Psychiatric Services in the Year following Overdose: Experimental and Control Groups by Levels of Psychiatric Pathology*

Psychiatric services:	High pathology E		C		Moderate pathology E		C		Low pathology E		C	
	N	%	N	%	N	%	N	%	N	%	N	%
Use	25	38	30	52	17	19	33	39	2	4	4	7
No use	40	62	28	48	73	81	52	61	43	96	53	93
Total	65	100	58	100	90	100	85	100	45	100	57	100

$\chi^2 = 2 \cdot 18$; df $= 1$; NS. $\chi^2 = 8 \cdot 51$; df $= 1$; p $< \cdot 01$.

Table 20.2   *Mean Scores on Beck Depression Inventory after Self-Poisoning and at Four and Eighteen Months After Follow-Up*

	E	C	E	C
	4 Months		*18 Months*	
	N = 74	*N = 72*	*N = 69*	*N = 71**
Time 1	17·61	19·63	20·54	19·31
Time 2	11·15	13·49	10·57	12·62
Difference	−6·46	−6·14	−9·97	−6·69

* Numbers are reduced since some patients refused the Beck Depression Inventory at the time of self-poisoning. The missing cases did not differ from the others in age, sex, or level of pathology.

However, the difference between the groups just failed to reach statistical significance.

(5) Changes in Social Problems

At the four months' follow-up, 81 per cent of E cases and 78 per cent of C cases were reinterviewed by the three independent assessors (using the same social problem questionnaire as at the baseline assessment). At the eighteen months' follow-up, 78 per cent of E cases and 75 per cent of C cases were reinterviewed, so that altogether 312 cases were reinterviewed and 88 (12 per cent) could not be traced or refused. Reinterviewed and missing cases were compared in terms of their age and sex distribution and no differences were found.

Four months after the overdose, 81 per cent of E cases as compared with 67 per cent of C cases showed overall improvement in social problems – a statistically significant difference. At longer-term follow-up, however, this difference had largely disappeared, with 66 per cent of E and 63 per cent of C cases showing overall improvement. A rather different pattern of results emerged in the different problem areas, five of which we shall discuss in more detail.

Reactive emotional distress   There was little difference between the four months' and eighteen months' follow-up periods. About 40 per cent of E cases and a third of C cases improved. Fewer E cases were worse at short-term and at long-term follow-up.

Social transitions   A very similar pattern occurred in problems of social transition. Slightly under half of both groups had improved four months after self-poisoning, and 56 per cent had improved eighteen months afterwards. There was no significant difference between the groups but the problems of C cases were somewhat more likely to worsen.

Significant personal relationships In this area there were differences between E and C groups at follow-up. Forty-five per cent of E cases had improved after four months compared with 37 per cent of C cases; and 64 per cent compared with 40 per cent after eighteen months. Fewer E cases had unchanged or worse problems in personal relationships after eighteen months. The task-centred service thus was more successful than the routine service in reducing problems between clients and their spouses or other significant people in their lives in the longer term (Table 20.3)

Practical difficulties Problems in this area showed disappointingly little improvement in either E or C groups, and in over a third the problems actually grew worse during the eighteen months following overdose. There was no difference between the groups (Table 20.4).

The task-centred service therefore seemed to have little effect on inadequate housing, lack of money, or unemployment. The causes of these difficulties are often outside the control of individual workers and clients, particularly when (as was the case at this period) unemployment was rising and national policies restricted the number of council houses being built and let.

Social relations By contrast, it is possible for individuals and families to alter their behaviour in order to lead a more stimulating and satisfying social life, and in this problem area the task-centred service appeared more successful than the routine one. More E cases improved and fewer deteriorated at both short- and long-term follow-up (Table 20.5).

Table 20.3 *Significant Personal Relationships: Improvement at Follow-Up in Experimental and Control Groups*

| | 4 Months | | | | 18 Months | | | |
| | E | | C | | E | | C | |
	N	%	N	%	N	%	N	%
Improved	36	45	28	37	41	64	29	40
Not improved/worse	27	33	31	41	10	14	25	34
No problem either time	18	22	17	22	16	22	19	26
Total	81	100	76	100	73	100	73	100
	$\chi^2 = 1 \cdot 15$; df = 2; NS.				$\chi^2 = 10 \cdot 95$; df = 2; $p < 0.1$.			

Table 20.4   *Practical Difficulties: Improvement of Follow-Up in Experimental and Control Groups*

| | 4 Months | | | | 18 Months | | | |
| | E | | C | | E | | C | |
	N	%	N	%	N	%	N	%
Improved	18	23	18	24	21	29	17	23
Not improved/worse	36	44	35	46	40	55	36	49
No problem either time	27	33	23	30	12	16	20	28
Total answering	81	100	76	100	73	100	73	100

Table 20.5   *Social Relations: Improvement at Follow-Up in Experimental and Control Groups*

| | 4 Months | | | | 18 Months | | | |
| | E | | C | | E | | C | |
	N	%	N	%	N	%	N	%
Improved	20	25	13	17	26	36	19	26
Not improved/worse	25	31	37	49	17	23	29	40
No problem either time	36	44	26	34	30	41	25	34
Total answering	81	100	76	100	73	100	73	100

$$x^2 = 5.27; \ df = 2; \quad\quad\quad x^2 = 4.67; \ df = 2;$$
$$p < .10. \quad\quad\quad\quad\quad\quad p < .10.$$

In summary therefore, the task-centred service was significantly more effective in reducing the overall severity of clients' social problems in the short term; but the difference gradually disappeared in the long term. The task-centred service was, however, more effective in reducing problems of significant personal relationships and of social relations.

Who Had the Best Outcome with the Task-Centred Service?

We have described earlier (p. 189) the predictive scale which was used to divide the sample into low-, moderate- and high-risk groups. Patients who scored three or more on this scale were nearly three times as likely to repeat self-poisoning within a year as patients who scored two or less, and four times as likely to do so as those scoring one or less. We had hoped that the task-centred service could help those in the higher-risk categories, the most disturbed and problem-burdened people. However, when we compared E and C groups within high-, medium- and low-risk categories the results showed that E cases did significantly better than controls only in the low- and moderate-risk categories. In the high-risk category slightly more E cases repeated parasuicide and slightly fewer improved their social problems. In the moderate- and low-risk categories, fewer E cases repeated and significantly more avoided subsequent psychiatric treatment and improved their social problems (Table 20.6).

Sex also had some influence on outcome. Women experimental cases did significantly better than women controls, while men experimental cases did only slightly better than men controls.

In summary, there were modest but real differences between the outcomes of the experimental and control cases on the outcome criteria we had selected. There were no differences in the proportions repeating parasuicide nor in those receiving psychotropic drugs from the general practitioner. However, experimental cases tended to show more improvement in depressed mood and made significantly less use of psychiatric services. They showed more short-term improvement in social problems, and improved more in respect of two problem areas, in particular: social relations and significant personal relationships, where the improvement was maintained eighteen months after self-poisoning.

USE OF THE TASK-CENTRED SERVICE

We shall first examine the extent to which clients used the task-centred service in the planned way. Did they agree target problems, work at tasks and finish within an agreed time limit of not more than three months? Table 20.7 sets out the pattern of service.

Only eleven cases refused any contact with the social workers. We classified the remainder as:

(1) *Task-centred* (recorded agreement on target problems, work on tasks, case closed within time limit).

Table 20.6 *Effects of Risk Category on Outcomes*

Outcome	Low/moderate risk (0–2)		High risk (3+)	
	E	C	E	C
% Repeating	10·7	12·3	34·8	24·2
	(177)	(171)	(23)	(29)
% Psychiatric treatment	16·9	26·9	56·5	72·4
	(177)	(171)	(23)	(29)
% Improved social problems (short term)	85·9	68·2	50	55·5
	(71)	(67)	(10)	(9)

Note: Totals in brackets.

PROBLEMS, TASKS AND OUTCOMES

Table 20.7 *Use of Task-Centred Service (N = 200)*

	N	%	Mean interviews	Mean weeks	Mean social agencies	Mean significant others	Mean target problems
Task-centred	105	56	8·9	9·9	2·7	1·1	1·3
Task-centred, overran time limit	33	17	24·2	25·9	5·1	2·3	2·1
Problem search only	49	26	2·5	3·7	1·1	0·6	—
Planned long-term	2	1	75	50	8	2	4·5
Total	189	100	10·6	11·5	2·8	1·2	1·53

(2) *Attempt at task-centred work, but overran* (agreement on target problems and work on tasks, but time limit not kept).

(3) *Problem search only* (no agreement on target problem, or no work on tasks).

(4) *Planned long-term* (no apparent attempt to use the method)

One hundred and five cases (55·5 per cent) were classified as task-centred. They had a mean number of 8·9 interviews in 9·9 weeks. The number of target problems per case averaged 1·3. On average, the social worker contacted 2·7 other agencies and 1·1 significant other people per case. Thirty-three cases (17 per cent) were in category 2 and could not be contained within a time limit, although the social workers had attempted to use a task-centred approach. They had a mean number of 24·2 interviews in 25·9 weeks. They had an average of 2·1 target problems and, on average, the social worker contacted 5·1 other social agencies and 2·3 significant others on their behalf. Forty-nine cases (25·9 per cent) ended because no agreement on a problem or on tasks could be made, the clients not wanting to proceed further after the problem search. They had a mean number of 2·5 interviews in 3·7 weeks. In only two cases, both of whom had severe, long-standing psychiatric problems, was there no recorded attempt to apply a time-limited method. These cases had 75 interviews in 50 weeks and were transferred to long-term care. In summary, initial take-up of the task-centred service was very high (95 per cent). Over half the clients used the method in he prescribed way and were classified as 'task-centred'. About a quarter ended after the problem search; social worker and client usually concurring that there was no need for further work. The 18 per cent who became long-term project cases had a wider range of problems, usually of great complexity, and were resistant to the limited focus of the task-centred approach.

Satisfaction with Service

How did experimental and control cases evaluate their respective services? Were there any differences in their experiences of the help offered? The attitudes of E and C cases to the help they had received were explored in a short, structured questionnaire at the time of follow-up. They were asked how much help they felt that they had received following their overdose, and how much help in each of the seven problem areas. E cases felt that they had received significantly more help overall. In particular, E cases reported receiving more help in leading a more satisfying social life; in feeling less upset and disturbed in themselves; in getting along better with someone important to them; in coping better with various jobs; in getting needed services; and with practical problems. Both groups felt equally helped in coping with some change or upheaval. E cases were significantly more satisfied with the service they had received: about three times as many E cases were very satisfied and twice as many C cases unsatisfied (Table 20.8). E clients were also significantly more likely to report their problems subjectively as 'much better' or 'better' at follow-up.

We were interested in whether task-centred clients were in fact aware of the limited focus and time-limited nature of the method. It was reassuring to find that E and C cases perceived their respective services as differently organised. Half the E cases, but only 18 per cent of C cases, said help had been concentrated on one or two limited problems. Sixty-two per cent of E cases but only 12 per cent of C cases said there had been agreement on a time limit. There was no evidence that E cases disliked the time limit: 81 per cent of them, compared with 75 per cent of C cases, felt the length of contact had been about right.

The evidence, we felt, was overwhelming that clients much preferred the experimental task-centred service to the routine service. They correctly perceived its limited focus and approved this,

Table 20.8   *Satisfaction with Service Received after Self-Poisoning*

| | At 4 Months | | At 18 Months | |
	E	C	E	C
Very satisfied	43%	10%	39%	14%
Satisfied	22%	22%	19%	20%
Fairly satisfied	19%	14%	27%	19%
Unsatisfied	6%	13%	5%	12%
No service acknowledged	10%	41%	10%	35%
Total N answering	81	78	77	75

welcoming the method's concentration on problem-solving while seeing the workers as understanding, good listeners who were able to give them a new insight into themselves and their difficulties (Gibbons *et al*. 1979). Our hypothesis that E cases would feel more satisfied with their service had received convincing support.

Good and Poor Outcomes within the Experimental Group

We were interested in whether, within the experimental group, outcome was associated with characteristics of the clients, with variations in the service input, or with personal differences between the two task-centred workers. In order to examine possible relationships we took only the experimental follow-up sample and divided it into outcome groups based on a combination of our main objective outcome criteria.

(1)   Good outcome   We defined 'good outcome' as occuring when: (a) the person did not repeat parasuicide within twelve months, (b) the person had no psychiatric treatment within twelve months, (c) the person had an improved social problem score at the time of follow-up. (This measure thus combines scores at short- and long-term follow-up into one outcome criterion.) All three of the above had to be present for a good outcome, which was achieved by ninety cases (58 per cent of the follow-up sample).

(2)   Fairly good outcome   We defined this as occurring when two of the three outcome criteria were positive. A 'fairly good' outcome was achieved by forty-six cases (29 per cent of the follow-up sample).

(3)   Poor outcome   This occurred when a positive result was achieved on one or none of the three criteria. Twenty cases (13 per cent) had a poor outcome.

Outcome and Client Characteristics

There was no association between outcome within the E group and the clients' sex, marital status, or social class. However, older cases had poorer outcome: the mean age of good outcome cases was 30·89, compared with 38·0 and 35·85 for fairly good and poor outcome cases, a difference that would have occurred by chance less than five times in a hundred. The clients' total problem score at the time of self-poisoning had no influence on outcome. However, clients with high scores on the scale measuring their risk of repetition had significantly worse outcomes. Just as when we compared E and C groups and found that high-risk cases were not helped by task-centred work, so within the E group itself the high-risk cases did badly. While 65 per

Table 20.9 *Experimental Cases' Outcome and Degree of Task-Centredness*

Outcome	Fully task-centred N	%	Problem search N	%	Extended N	%
Good	59	63	24	67	7	27
Fairly good	27	28	9	25	10	38
Poor	8	8	3	8	9	35
Total	94	100	36	100	26	100

χ^2 (Extended v. Other) = 12·19; df = 1; p < ·001.

Table 20.10 *Outcome and Amount of Service Received*

Outcome	Mean interviews	Mean types practical help	Mean types counselling help
Good	8·11	1·10	2·11
Fairly good	11·43	1·93	2·55
Poor	21·60	2·55	2·91

cent of low-risk cases in the E follow-up sample had a good outcome, 48 per cent of moderate-risk cases and only 21 per cent of high-risk cases did so. Over 40 per cent of high-risk cases had a poor outcome, compared with only 8 per cent of low-risk cases.

Outcome was significantly associated with a number of features of the task-centred method. We first looked to see whether the degree of task-centredness – that is to say, whether the client was in Group A (fully task-centred), B (failed to adhere to the time limit) or C (ended after problem search) – made a difference to outcome. Table 20.9 shows that clients who failed to keep to a time limit and had their period of service extended had a significantly worse outcome than the other two groups: only 27 per cent had a good outcome, and 35 per cent had a poor outcome.

The results for the fully task-centred cases were very similar to those for cases who ended after the problem search (Table 20.9): about 8 per cent having a poor outcome and some two-thirds a good outcome. The finding that cases who overran did worst of all is supported by further evidence. Outcome was negatively associated with number of interviews and with number of different kinds of practical and counselling help received (Table 20.10).

Thus cases who had more interviews and more practical and counselling help did worse. We were unable to find associations between other aspects of the task-centred method and outcome. Whether or not the client was first seen immediately (before leaving hospital) or a few days later at home made no difference. The time taken to reach agreement on a target problem or tasks, the amount of initiative taken by the client in selecting a task, and who was involved in working at the tasks (the client only, the client and significant others, or others only) had no effect on outcome. The nature of the target problem related to overcome only for cases with a target problem of significant personal relationships, who more often had a good outcome: 66 per cent had a good outcome and only 7 per cent a bad one. This is consistent with the independent assessment of change in social problems as between E and C groups, where problems of significant personal relationships were more often improved by the task-centred service than by the routine service. However, problems of social relations, which also discriminated between E and C groups, did not show the same relationship with outcome within the E group, perhaps because there were only nineteen cases in the follow-up sample where social relations was the target problem. Good outcome cases had fewer target problems (mean 1·16) than poor outcome cases (mean 1·85), but this result was not statistically significant.

The social workers rated the task-achievement of cases who worked on tasks on a five-point scale ranging from 0 (no achievement) to 4 (task completely achieved). Good outcome cases had higher task achievement, but not significantly so. (The mean score for good-outcome cases was 2·21, for fairly-good-outcome cases: 2·13, and for poor-outcome cases: 1·41).

Outcome and Social Worker
Only two social workers were involved and they worked closely together with regular joint consultation designed to help them adhere to a task-centred framework. It is not surprising therefore that outcome was very similar for the two workers (Table 20.11).

The social workers made overall ratings of how easy it had been to maintain a task focus, and of the suitability of the method at the close of their cases. Both these ratings were strongly associated with outcome, so that cases where the social workers had difficulties in maintaining a focus on the task and cases for which they rated the method as unsuitable had the worst outcomes.

There is, therefore, strong evidence that cases who failed to use the method – by overrunning time limits and demanding many interviews and items of service – and with whom the workers were conscious of difficulty in applying the method, were those who also had the poorest

Table 20.11 *Outcome of the Experimental Social Workers*

Outcome	Social worker 1		Social worker 2	
	N	%	N	%
Good	43	56	47	59
Fairly good	23	30	23	29
Poor	11	14	9	11
Total	77	100	79	100

outcomes. It would be wrong to conclude from this that extra interviews and help from the social workers actually caused the poor outcome. It was more likely that the high-risk category of some cases accounted both for their receiving extra help and for their poor outcome. We therefore reanalysed the data, controlling for risk category, to test this explanation. We compared the outcomes of cases who had extended service (not adhering to a time limit) with the remaining cases at two levels of risk: low (0–1 on the predictive scale) and high (2–5 on the scale). In the higher-risk group 40 per cent of extended service cases compared with 21 per cent of non-extended had a poor outcome. In the low-risk group 28 per cent of extended service cases compared with only 4 per cent of non-extended cases had a poor outcome – an even bigger difference. Thus, controlling for risk category did not cause the relationship between poor outcome and failure to adhere to the task-centred structure to disappear. Over-running the time limit was most strongly associated with poor outcome in low-risk cases. By yielding to their clients' demands for prolonged contact and more services, the social workers did not improve their outcome but rather the reverse.

THE TASK-CENTRED PRACTICE

At this point, we shall pause to take stock of our research methods and findings. We shall then see if further light can be thrown on the practice of task-centred casework by examining our material from a clinical point of view, using the social workers' own records of their work and the clients' views, as expressed in the final interview with the social worker and in the follow-up interviews with the independent assessors.

We adopted an experimental design in order to test the efficacy of task-centred casework with people who had deliberately poisoned themselves. In our view, the task-centred method differed from much other social work practice in that its procedures had been systemati-cally described and a comparatively large amount of previous descriptive research on it had been carried out. It therefore seemed justified at this stage to subject the approach to experimental evaluation, in a real-life setting. If no positive findings in favour of the task-centred sample emerged we might, given sufficient confidence in our methodology, conclude that further attempts to apply a task-centred approach to parasuicide patients were very unlikely to produce desired results and decide not to invest further resources or effort. If positive findings could be demonstrated, on the other hand, we might conclude at the very least that further, more refined practice and subsequent evaluation was a needed and worthwhile investment.

Our research design resulted in 400 self-poisoning patients aged at least 17 from a defined geographical area being randomly allocated to experimental (task-centred casework) or control (routine) services. These 400 patients were not a representative group, but we were able to describe their differences from the total population of self-poisoners in the area. The most important difference was the under-representation of the highest-risk cases in the trial sample. Any findings from the experiment, therefore, cannot be applied to unselected parasuicide samples. We predicted that experimental cases would have a better outcome, both in terms of a reduction in the kinds of social problem that the task-centred method was designed to relieve and that the clients complained of, and presumably wished to relieve, and in terms or problem behaviour (self-poisoning) that the clients may not have particularly wished to give up, but which other people – the DHSS, the local hospital service, the research team and usually family members – *did* wish to abolish for various reasons. The findings were that the task-centred service was no more successful than the routine service in inducing clients to give up self-poisoning. However, experimental cases did have a better outcome on some other measures. Their social problems improved more, particularly in the short term; with problems of significant personal relationships they showed long-term improvement as well; they showed more improvement in depressed mood and needed less psychiatric treatment; and they were notably more satisfied with their service, described themselves as receiving more help and more often (subjectively) rated their problems as better. In the next section we shall consider in more detail why, if task-centred casework could achieve these positive gains, there was no effect on repetition of self-poisoning.

When we considered which clients did best with task-centred help we found that the most important distinguishing factor seemed to be the client's risk category. High-risk clients – those who had previous psychiatric treatment as in- and out-patients, who had made previous suicide attempts, were sociopathic, had drinking problems and were not living in a family setting – seemed to do no better, or even slightly worse, with task-centred help than with the routine service. On the other hand, moderate- and low-risk clients and, in particular, younger people, women and those with relationship difficulties had significantly better outcomes with the task-centred than with the routine service. Within the experimental group itself, these client characteristics continued to be associated with outcome. In addition, certain features of the task-centred service (though not individual characteristics of the workers) seemed to have an independent importance. Independently of the client's risk category, adherence to the task-centred structure seemed significantly associated with outcome. Whereas clients who decided not to proceed after the problem search had as good an outcome as the fully task-centred group, clients who had a broader range of target problems, receiving more services from the workers and overrunning the time limit appeared to do worse. This finding points to questions about task-centred practice which will be discussed further in the next chapter.

Our findings demonstrate yet again how extremely unlikely it is that casework methods of whatever school will succeed in changing people's behaviour in dramatic ways. Disappointingly, in our hands task-centred methods did not seem effective in relieving serious practical problems of poverty, lack of adequate housing and unemployment. However, it may be that in combination with social policy measures and structural changes in the availability of resources to different groups in our society, task-centred methods directed towards helping individuals tackle such problems could have more relevance. It may also be that since the social workers in our study had no resources at their own disposal they were not as well placed or as expert in tackling practical problems as workers in area teams or probation settings. Our results, however, do suggest that task-centred help does produce encouraging improvements in clients' immediate social situations, in their personal relationships and their morale. The method seems to make sense to clients and is much appreciated by them. These findings seem reason enough to examine the workers' task-centred practice more closely in the hope of elucidating rather more clearly what it was about it that was experienced as useful, and where difficulties in applying the method arose.

Chapter 21

TASK-CENTRED WORK WITH CLIENTS WHO REPEATED OVERDOSE

In this chapter we shall look more closely at the experimental clients who took another overdose in the year following their admission to the trial. We shall explore the reasons why task-centred casework failed to prevent these overdoses and consider whether these clients were helped or showed improvement in other ways in spite of their repeats.

There was a small group who took another overdose almost at once, after the first or second interview. In spite of this, task-centred work was able to take place successfully and subsequent outcome was good.

Mrs Rogers, a married woman of 30, took an overdose when depressed after the sudden death of her mother. A year previously she had had in-patient psychiatric treatment for depression after childbirth. After the first interview with the social worker, Mrs Rogers took another overdose and had to be readmitted to hospital. However, task-centred work continued as planned on her discharge the next day. The target problem was expressed as: 'Mainly the way I feel – very low since John's birth.' The goal was to alleviate feelings of depression. The first tasks – to make efforts to visit friends and to visit a particular friend during the week – were agreed in the fourth interview. Mrs Rogers worked successively at tasks which were aimed at reducing the factors that made her worry and feel depressed: thus, she carried out suggestions to help her son be less anxious about separating from her; she tried to 'switch off' if she started worrying about her elderly father (who, in fact, was coping well); she took steps to obtain all the welfare benefits she was entitled to; she found out about a mothers' group and then joined it. The work seemed to go smoothly and tasks were rated as substantially achieved when contact ended as planned after twelve interviews. At follow-up eighteen months later Mrs Rogers described her problems as better. There had been no further overdose or recourse to psychiatric treatment.

In another group of cases the repeat occurred later during the period of task-centred work. The original overdose had usually failed to improve the client's situation and a period of extreme distress followed when the client could not engage in task-centred work, but needed the social worker as an understanding listener. At some point during this period another overdose would happen, after which there might be acceptance of the loss or change and a readiness for tasks.

Mrs Johnson, a married woman of 39, took a serious overdose of high suicidal intent when her husband, who was working abroad, unexpectedly wrote asking for a divorce. Mrs Johnson continued for a long time in a state of despair in which she wished to die and she accepted visits from the social worker only as a chance to ventilate her feelings. The target problem was formulated in the first interview – 'She has received a letter from husband saying he wants a divorce after twenty years of marriage. There have been some sexual problems and also their child's death some years ago made Mrs Johnson retreat within herself. She can't be angry with husband. She wants him back.' In the sixth interview the first task was formulated: to contact husband on the phone to discuss the problem and persuade him to come home and talk it over. A good deal of rehearsal and planning in interviews preceded the accomplishment of this difficult task. Mr Johnson did agree to return, but on his arrival he made it clear his decision was not to be altered. At this point Mrs Johnson took another overdose (of tablets she had been hoarding to take on her wedding anniversary). However, this proved a turning point in her ability to accept that the marriage was over. In the twenty-fourth interview she accepted a new target problem of social transition – to reorganise her life by looking for a job and moving to another house. This was essentially a new contract and task-centred work proper could now start. Subtasks were set and Mrs Johnson went for job interviews. In the final (thirtieth) interview Mrs Johnson said: 'I've actually begun to face up to the fact that he is going off with this woman. I have begun to do things about it. I'm going to get what I can out of him.' She felt tasks for the future were to keep on with the job search and arrange the move and get as much money as possible from her husband. The social worker felt that task-centred work could only begin near the end of contact.

At the eighteen months' follow-up Mrs Johnson felt her problems were much better. She was very satisfied with social work help. She had a part-time job, had moved house and divorced her husband. She had not repeated overdose again or needed psychiatric treatment.

The two groups of cases so far discussed were made up of repeaters with a fairly good outcome. Although task-centred intervention did not prevent one repeat, these clients nevertheless used the method, as planned or after a delay, and achieved good results. However, the majority of the twenty-seven repeaters did not fall into these two groups. We shall look more closely at these remaining failures.

There were five cases where repeating clients quickly rejected contact with the social workers. Two were single men in their thirties with long-standing drinking problems, living in hostels or sleeping rough, and drifting from place to place. In the first case, Mr Mackilroy left hospital before seeing the social worker and although he subsequently phoned her asking for money, he did not keep an offered appointment the same afternoon. When the social worker called at his lodgings she found he had left without paying the rent and he could not be found. Mr James was living rough after leaving prison and saw the social worker once in hospital, stating his problems as: 'No accommodation, no job, no friends. Drinking gets me into trouble with the law – thieving to get money for drink.' The target problem was 'I haven't got anywhere to stay – I haven't a clue where to go.' The social worker got him a bed in a charitable hostel. She saw him once more in the hostel, where she found he antagonised the warden by drinking and having barbiturates (prescribed by the general practitioner) in his possession. The social worker feared Mr James would not comply with the hostel's rules, as shortly proved to be the case when he left for an unknown destination. Four months later Mr James was interviewed for the follow-up in prison where he was serving his eighth short sentence for stealing. His problems were exactly the same – he was due to be discharged with nowhere to go, no money and no friends. He stammered badly and so felt out of place in company and tried to avoid meeting people. The social worker again tried to contact Mr James on learning his whereabouts but he left for another city. The task-centred approach was clearly inappropriate for these repeaters and had nothing to offer them.

The remaining three cases in this 'rejecting contact' group were women who had less than three interviews. Mrs Knutson was involved in a difficult homosexual relationship, but found it too painful to continue work on the problems having succeeded with the social worker's help in moving out of the house. The social worker had to agree to terminate despite feeling 'unhappy about the situation'. The other two clients were never really willing to accept any social work involvement, one preferring to seek group psychotherapy instead.

In a second group of failures, a period of task-centred work was attempted but both client and social worker seemed to be paying lip-service only to the method. Sometimes the client's problems were unsuitable for this method – unacknowledged drinking, for example, or hypochondria – or the problems frequently shifted.

Mr Cutworth was a 45-year-old divorced man with a serious drinking problem which, however, he did not admit to the research psychiatrist nor to the social worker. He easily agreed a target problem in the first interview: 'I feel so useless not working but I can't find work because I take so much time off with headaches.' The goal was to find a job. At the second interview Mr Cutworth came smelling of drink and talked in a rambling way. However, tasks were agreed: he was to phone for an advertised job interview and explore a further offer of work from a friend. At the third interview he had phoned but the job had gone. The social worker found it hard to focus on tasks. Mr Cutworth wanted to talk of his feelings of not belonging and loss of contact with his children. At the fourth interview he was again smelling strongly of drink, and had a new problem: a notice from court about his ex-wife's application for maintenance. He accepted a task of going to a solicitor, the social worker having rung during the interview to make the appointment for him. The social worker was now beginning to feel that the target problem should have been difficulties in social relations – his loneliness and feeling of not belonging – and she gave him information about a club. Soon after Mr Cutworth took another overdose. In hospital, where the social worker visited him, he was 'dwelling on the injustice of the maintenance hearing in a paranoid way'. There were four more interviews, but the social worker recorded: 'In the light of the overdose and previous failure to get anywhere with tasks I felt it important to allow him to talk freely.' In the final interview Mr Cutworth said it had been helpful 'to talk and unburden himself'. However, when asked what had been particularly helpful he mentioned drug treatment from the GP which had helped him sleep. At the follow-up Mr Cutworth did not recall seeing the social worker and felt his problems were 'the same'. The social worker felt the method had failed to help. 'He hadn't included drink as a problem and so it wasn't possible to tackle this. The target problem and tasks kept changing and it was hard not to go along with changing preoccupations as I felt the preceding tasks wouldn't work.'

Mr Cutworth's case illustrates a common feature of this group of failures – premature agreement on a target problem without sufficient exploration of the client's motivation to reduce it. The social worker needed to be more honest about her own perceptions of the problem.

This might well have resulted in Mr Cutworth's terminating after the problem search, but this might have been preferable to the fruitless period of contact that did occur.

The next group consisted of eight long-term cases who between them had a mean of thirty-two interviews. In one of these cases it was decided at the outset that long-term work was appropriate. The others represented a continuation of planned brief treatment. These eight cases were all women. The planned long-term case was a borderline mentally handicapped woman with a child in care, rejected by her family, who had taken many previous overdoses to get herself admitted to the psychiatric hospital. Once in, she behaved in a dramatic and destructive way to get attention. We decided to make a serious effort over the year to help her establish another way of life, and the social worker persisted heroically and was rewarded, in so far as, at the end of the year the client was in lodgings and no longer wanting to get readmitted. Task-centred principles were useful in providing direction and goals to aim at in the course of this type of long-term work. However, the other extended cases seemed to represent rather more often a yielding to the demands of dependent people and task-centred principles sometimes seemed neglected by the social workers. The possibility of repeated overdoses and even of a fatal outcome made it difficult to resist pressures in some of these cases.

In the final group of repeaters who also seemed to the social workers to have gained little from their social work, task-centred work had been carried out but seemed to make little impact on a chaotic life-style, except in the very short term.

Mr Philpot, a 22-year-old divorced man, was living with his girl-friend (still married to another man) and her child by yet another relationship. He had taken several previous overdoses in circumstances suggestive of emotional blackmail, had a drinking problem and was clinically anxious and depressed. The problem search took place in two sessions, the first with Mr Philpot alone, when significant personal relationships emerged as the target area and he accepted the task of arranging a joint appointment with his girl-friend; the second with Mr Philpot and Mrs Tippet. A large number of problems was listed:

(1) The couple's bad relationship: they are both moody and Colin gets violent especially after drinking.
(2) Colin's parents are threatening divorce.
(3) Colin feels low and no good and worried about his sexual adequacy.

(4) There are money problems due to sorting out maintenance for Colin's ex-wife.
(5) Although Colin is divorced there are still problems with the ex-wife as she lived next door.
(6) They are dissatisfied with the flat and want to move.

Two target problems were agreed in the second interview. In the area of significant personal relationships: 'We don't talk about things. Colin drinks and gets irritable. Janice bottles things up. We don't talk for days and then get angry over silly little things.' In the practical area: 'They don't like living in the flat because the ex-wife spreads gossip.' The goals were, to talk more to each other; and to get a council exchange. The tasks agreed at the end of the second interview were:

To think why it is difficult to talk.
To note what it is difficult to talk about.
To note how decisions are made.
Colin to go to Housing Department about transfer.
Social worker to write in support.

The social worker noted, 'Contract formulation stimulated mainly by me. Target problems readily agreed as they were the ones they were most aware of. Initial tasks suggested mainly by me and agreed on without much exploration or questioning. I mentioned a time limit which was again passively agreed on. I made it clear that I was there to help them find ways of sorting things out for themselves and could not provide any complete solution to problems.'

The third interview started with a review of task progress. Colin had been to the Housing Department and filled in the appropriate form. They were also making inquiries about a private transfer. They had discussed the problem of talking and decided that it occurs when both are feeling 'moody' and withdrawn. In a recent incident, instead of withdrawing Janice had asked Colin what was upsetting him. He was relieved and they talked about their feelings. They had also talked about Colin's jealousy and, as a result, Janice had thrown away her former wedding photos. They had decided in future they would do everything together. The social worker encouraged their efforts but also explored the reasons for this decision. It appeared that it was mainly Colin's and Janice said she felt he wanted to smother and control her. Colin was resistant to further discussion. When the social worker asked about progress on task two (noting what was difficult to talk about) Janice brought out that she was afraid Colin would 'blackmail' her again by taking another overdose, but she couldn't discuss this with him. It was decided to continue the same tasks.

The next interview began with Janice saying, 'now confess'. At the weekend there had been an incident where Janice walked out 'to cool off' despite Colin trying to talk to her. Colin then set up a situation to look as though he'd taken an overdose, summoning an ambulance and the police, though in fact he hadn't taken anything. Both felt despondent and angry. The social worker helped them look at opportunities that were lost to talk about it, and to examine ways in which they were provocative to each other. There had been progress on the practical tasks which she encouraged. However, a further problem emerged as the ex-wife's solicitor was pursuing Colin for maintenance. A task was set to consult a solicitor. They also agreed: to continue to try to talk before things explode; to try to explain to each other (a) how they feel as tension builds up, (b) how they would like the other person to respond to them.

At the fifth interview there had been no task progress. There had been another explosion about decision-making with both wanting the other to give in completely. Colin had not been to the solicitor and intended going to court unrepresented. During a stormy session in which the social worker rebuked Colin for 'pig-headedness', a further problem emerged – his bad relations with Janice's parents – which caused some of the tension between them. The social worker decided not to pursue this for fear of losing focus. At the sixth interview Colin had gone to the maintenance hearing, put his case, unaided by solicitor, and won. There had been some progress on the other tasks with examples of successful talking things over. The time limit was again discussed and the next interview set for two weeks' time.

In the next interview a new problem emerged as Colin had been drinking heavily and was charged with an offence committed while under the influence. The interview focused on this with new tasks set to get help in cutting down his drinking. At the eighth interview there had been good progress on the tasks, with Colin cutting his drinking and several incidents where mutual tension was aborted by recognition and discussion. However Colin had received a summons in respect of his offence. New tasks were set: Colin was to go to an agency concerned with drinking problems; the social worker was to write a court report on his behalf.

At the ninth interview there had been renewed conflict and no task progress. Shortly after this Colin rang the social worker to tell her he had taken another overdose after hearing Janice criticising him to a friend. She later saw him on the medical ward and agreed to go home with him to try and talk things out with Janice. On reaching home they found Janice not there, but she phoned asking Colin to pack his bags and leave. He again felt suicidal. After a discussion of alternatives he agreed to leave a note for Janice and go to his parents, in the hope this would be the least destructive way of dealing with the situation.

There were two further interviews with Colin at his parents' house. He and Janice were again going out together but had decided not to live together for the present. At the final interview Colin said: 'I've been talking a lot about myself, can't get everything I want. I'm more aware of that now. I'm coping with things a bit calmer.' He thought the target problem had been, 'arguments – me wanting my own way and wanting to be shown affection'. He said the problem was 'solved' – 'I'm able to accept compromise.' On the time limit he felt 'three months seemed a long time – would have liked to end when things began to go better'. Tasks for the future were 'being more reliable at work' and 'getting retrained for a more interesting job'. Soon after termination Colin spent the night in prison after breaking Janice's parents' windows. The social worker was contacted by his father and wrote a further court report at Colin's request. Colin did not ask for a further meeting. The social worker was left feeling task-centred work was 'not relevant' to the couple.

However, at the four months' follow-up Mr Philpot felt his problems were 'much better' and was 'very satisfied' with social work help. He felt he had had 'a lot of help' in getting on better with someone important to him and with practical problems. In the following year he did not take a further overdose nor receive psychiatric treatment.

We have described the process of this case at some length, since it well illustrates the difficulty of using task-centred methods with impulsive clients who are not good at sustaining relationships on an even keel nor at persisting with agreed courses of action. Such clients also tend to be buffeted by practical problems and unforeseen events.

However, although the social worker at the end of the contact was left feeling that the method had achieved nothing and was irrelevant, we might argue, from a greater distance, that her ability to maintain much of the essential framework of task-centred work and to end at the agreed time actually achieved modest gains for Mr Philpot. In this case the social worker was not blackmailed into abandoning the agreed contract and continuing a 'supportive' but unproductive relationship. In the next chapter we shall consider further the importance of making clear and realistic agreements at every stage of task-centred work.

In conclusion, the reasons why task-centred work failed to prevent repeat self-poisoning appeared complex. First, nearly a fifth of the repeaters had very limited contact with the social workers, rejecting social work involvement as not relevant to their problems. Secondly, there was a group where task-centred help seemed successful in reducing target problems and producing a good long-term outcome, but where repeat overdose was not prevented. In some cases, this was because the repeat occurred in the very early stages of contact, before any impact had been made on the problems. In other cases, the repeat, occurring later in the contact, represented a turning point in the clients' ability to give up unrealistic solutions and involve themselves more fully in task work. However, in a third of the cases there were repeats and also a generally poor outcome. In these cases the social workers had often felt forced to give up the task-centred framework and to involve themselves in long-term supportive work which tended to drift along without clear goals. In general, the characteristics of repeating clients (their high risk in terms of a previous history of self-poisoning, psychiatric illness, alcohol problems and loss of contact with family) differentiated them from clients with a good outcome. They were less likely to have the problems of personal relationships with which task-centred work was particularly successful. A planned long-term approach, using task-centred methods to agree problems and tasks to guide the work, might have been more satisfactory in some cases, though no more likely to prevent repeats.

Chapter 22

MAKING CONTRACTS IN TASK-CENTRED WORK

We have earlier (p. 179) discussed the increasing use of contracts between practitioners and clients in social work. As Reid (1978, p. 133) has pointed out, contracts vary in form, but they have one essential purpose: to set forth explicit agreements between practitioner and client on what is to be done and how. In task-centred practice an initial contract is developed after tentative accord has been reached on the target problems. The initial contract must specify at least one explicitly stated, acknowledged problem the social worker and client agree to work on. Contracts in task-centred work may be oral or written. The drawbacks of the written contract are that it can be very time-consuming and result in a loss of momentum which is crucial to maintain in time-limited work. It can also be experienced by clients as demonstrating the worker's power and control rather than as formalising their joint agreement (Smith and Corden, 1981). The written agreement has advantages of clarity and the avoidance of misunderstanding. The project social workers rarely drew up formal written agreements, although they always noted what the agreement was on the target problem, the tasks and the time limit.

Target problem specification arises out of the work done in the problem search: problem areas are identified and then the client is helped to break these down into more detailed and specific problems. This process, however, needs to be brief, since Reid states it is important to arrive at agreement on a problem as early as possible, preferably in the first interview. If agreement on a target problem cannot be reached, even after efforts to modify the original definition into something both worker and client agree is a workable problem, the case may be closed at that point, the client may be referred to a more suitable agency or, in certain unusual circumstances, the worker may continue using other methods. We shall now look at the reasons why clients in the study did not proceed beyond the problem search to agree an initial contract.

CLIENTS WHO ENDED AFTER THE PROBLEM SEARCH

We have already seen that the clients who did not enter into a contract to work on a target problem but ended their contract with the social worker at the problem search stage, tended, with some exceptions, to be low-risk cases in comparison with the rest of the sample. Their overall outcome was as good as the task-centred group and better than those who worked on tasks but overran the time limit. In these cases the usefulness of the task-centred approach often lay in clarifying quickly that the client did not wish for or need prolonged social work help. Apart from a small group who accepted an interview but did not trust the social worker enough to make any real use of it, these clients usually wanted one or two interviews in which to review their problems and 'make sense' of the overdose.

Mrs Andrews was a 29-year-old divorced woman who agreed with the social worker to have two interviews which she would use to discuss her feelings over the breakdown of her marriage and her much younger boy-friend's wish to marry her. She had other legal, financial and housing problems. After the two planned interviews she declined entering a contract to work on tasks in any of these areas. Although her outcome, objectively, was good, at follow-up she felt subjectively that her problems were still there and seemed to regret this decision. She said 'the social worker listened to me, understood and tried to put her point of view. I didn't accept it at the time, but thought about what she said. I decided not to continue. It was my decision, but I sometimes regret breaking off contact.'

Cases like this suggest that some clients may need longer to consider the implications of entering a contract to work at problems. It was right to accept her decision to terminate, but if she had been offered a later opportunity to agree a plan of work she might have accepted. If these cases are recognised by the social worker, it might be helpful to send a follow-up letter a month later, offering task-centred help again. In other cases, however, it seemed clear that the decision to terminate was the right one. These clients often had other sources of help – friends and extended family – whom they preferred to the social worker.

Mrs Acres, a 26-year-old married woman, took an overdose when her husband, who was living apart from her and the children, failed to visit as he had promised. The social worker recorded, 'Mrs Acres was uncertain about seeing a social worker but agreed to a problem search. She minimised her problems, especially as husband returned after the overdose which she felt had opened up communication.' The social worker suggested another interview to explore the difficulties further and discuss seeing husband. Mrs Acres reluctantly agreed but the case was closed after three home visits by appointment found her not at home. At follow-up, Mrs Acres had moved and was living apart from her husband. She now felt better off without him. She felt that the most helpful thing had been talking to friends who 'knew both sides and could see what was happening – social worker had to start from the beginning'.

Joan Lee, an 18-year-old girl, took an overdose when her relationship with her boy-friend ended. She had two interviews in which she reviewed her problems, and did not want another appointment. At follow-up, when her problems were much better, Joan saw her friend as the most important source of help, 'I could talk to her about intimate things because she was a friend. She made me go out and helped to occupy me. I could talk to her about things I couldn't to the social worker.'

There were, however, some clients whom the social workers saw as having major problems that were suited to task-centred help, but where it proved impossible to form a contract because of the opposition of another key person in the situation.

Mrs Barton, a 40-year-old married woman, took an overdose in the context of marital and financial problems caused by her husband's gambling. In the first interview she talked despairingly about these problems but did not think the social worker could help her because of her husband's suspicions. The social worker had one further interview with her and a joint session including the husband and recorded, 'there was a gradual covering up of the situation revealed in hospital. Mrs Barton had decided that the marital situation was as it was and the answer was to get a job. She also received much help from her family which contributed to her withdrawal.' At follow-up, Mrs Barton's problems had been improved by a serious accident to her husband which curtailed his gambling and drinking. She felt that the social worker had tried to help her but her husband didn't think problems should be aired in public and so they hadn't co-operated with her.

Gillian Singleton, aged 17, also withdrew when faced with a choice, as she saw it, of siding with her mother or the social worker. After four interviews, during which Gillian's serious problems with her mother and divorced father were discussed, and her problems over whether to leave home and school, she withdrew without entering into a contract. At follow-up, she criticised the social worker for seeing things too much 'from the younger person's point of view'.

Gillian perhaps also illustrates another reason why work did not progress beyond the problem search: the client's resistance to structured work and decided preference for a more informal and loosely supportive short period of contact. In only one case was the social worker willing to agree, probably because of the client's age and high risk for suicide.

Mr Orton was a widower of 80 who lived alone and had taken an overdose after his only remaining family tie, with a nephew, was ruptured when he became convinced his nephew was after his money. The social worker and he had eleven interviews but no target problem was ever mutually agreed. Instead, it was agreed in the third interview that contact should go on for three months 'to enable him to talk things over' (an extended problem search). The social worker, with Mr Orton's approval, met his supportive neighbours, and also the nephew, failing however to heal the rift. She discussed voluntary visitors and old people's homes with Mr Orton but accepted his rejection of these. He did accept her efforts to get him better medical care and a more intensive follow-up from the health visitor when social work contact ended. At follow-up, Mr Orton praised the social worker for the friendly, informal atmosphere she had created, which was what he wanted, and felt he had no further problems since he was no longer concerned about his nephew.

AGREEMENT ON TARGET PROBLEMS

One hundred and forty-six cases (73 per cent of the total E sample) made an initial contract after a problem search. Six of these dropped out without agreeing any tasks and have been grouped with the cases that ended after the problem search. One hundred and five were fully task-centred, in the sense of their having agreed target problems, worked on tasks and ended within an agreed time limit. Thirty-five were extended cases, overrunning the time limit. Table 22.1 shows the target problems agreed by social workers and clients for cases entering a contract. There was some difference between the fully task-centred and the extended cases in respect of target problem areas. 'Significant personal relationships' tended to be the target problem area more often in the task-centred than in the extended cases. There were also some differences from the distribution of problem areas found by the independent assessors at the time of self-poisoning. 'Reactive emotional distress' was the problem area occurring most frequently at baseline, but was only the fifth largest area among the target problems. The social workers may have felt less confident in tackling

Table 22.1   *Target Problem Areas*

	Fully task-centred *N = 105*	*Extended* *N = 35*
Significant personal relationships	32	14
Social transitions	31	16
Social relations	10	12
Role performance	19	18
Reactive emotional distress	19	14
Formal organisations	7	7
Inadequate resources	20	18
Other	2	0
Mean target problems	1·33	2·1

emotional distress as a target, seeing it as more suitable for a medical or strictly behavioural approach.

Reid (1978) has stated that in task-centred work agreement on some specified target problem is essential before problem-solving activities can begin. However, although an effort to specify the problem *must* take place at the very beginning, it is likely that further specification and modification will take place during the case, as worker and client develop their understanding of the problem. In the project cases the first interview usually produced a listing of the main problems perceived by the client. During the second interview, when worker and client were trying to describe the main problem more precisely, there was sometimes quite a marked change in the way the problem was understood and in the relative importance of different problems. This change following negotiation between worker and client could represent a genuine shift in the client's perception or, in some cases, a mere acceptance of what the worker considered a workable problem. Sometimes, however, the client remained firm in his or her own definition of the problem and the social worker shifted ground. We shall illustrate this process of negotiation with case examples.

Miss Jones was a single woman in her late twenties who lived with her parents. She took an overdose of high suicidal intent following a period of in-patient treatment for depression. Miss Jones was articulate, insightful and keen for social work help after initial hesitation. In the first interview she described two problems – feelings of depression, loss of energy, poor sleep and wishing she were dead and needing to return to work at once in spite of difficulties with her job as an under-manager in a store, which she attributed to the manager's interference. She attributed her depression partly to worries about her grandfather's serious illness and partly to loneliness and having no friends. In the second interview these problems were analysed in much more detail. It emerged that Miss Jones felt a tremendous pressure to succeed and do well and not to disappoint her parents – she was forcing herself back into a job she disliked for fear of letting them down. She demanded a great deal of herself and had always been unable to 'let up' and go out and enjoy herself. The social worker and Miss Jones agreed that four of the five problems so far listed – unhappy in job; feeling depressed and tense; tendency to push herself to achieve but not sure what she really wants to achieve; feeling friendless – were in fact related to one another. They felt that the need for a job should be shelved until she had been able to let up and enjoy herself. Thus, in the second interview the target problem area was listed as: 'Forcing herself to achievements and hard work, unable to let up and relax and see value of enjoying herself. Also tends to seek perfection in her work and drives herself too hard.' (Problem of 'social relations')

A similar process of negotiation to define the target problem, with the social worker this time needing to draw in others, occurred with Mr Saunders.

Mr Saunders, a porter in his twenties, took an overdose of high suicidal intent after his wife left him. The social worker had three interviews with Mr Saunders and one with his wife in the week following the overdose to carry out the problem search. Initially, he expressed his problem as 'wanting my wife back'. The social worker explored with him his dependence on his wife, finding that he had very little confidence and needed his wife to do all manner of things for him, especially filling in forms as Mr Saunders could barely read. When the social worker met Mrs Saunders she found her adamant that she would not return and that she had rushed into marriage for the wrong reasons. The social worker and Mr Saunders together faced the fact that the marriage appeared to have ended. The target problem was now expressed as, 'Marjorie has left me, I feel so lost without her, I've got to get on without her. I depended on her too much. I want to try and get by by myself' – this was broken down into 'overcoming problems of the separation – (a) managing household tasks in the flat; (b) starting an illiteracy project.' (Problem of social transition)

In the previous examples the clients shifted their initial view of their problem to one that was more in conformity with the social worker's view of a workable target problem. Sometimes the client was not willing to make this shift.

Mrs Morris, aged about thirty, had taken an overdose in the context of pressing marital, family and financial difficulties. She was anxious about social work intervention and found looking at problems painful and upsetting. She tended to deny problems and try to reassure herself that all would be well. However, in the first two interviews, she and the social worker listed a number of problems to do with the marriage which the social worker saw as the crucial area. Mrs Morris, however, was only willing to consider a limited problem: financial difficulties which may cause husband to go bankrupt. The target problem was, 'anxiety about bankruptcy, what will be taken, will husband be charged with fraud because he didn't use loans for agreed purpose', and this led to limited tasks concerned with clarifying bankruptcy proceedings (Problem of formal organisations). When her mood did not improve as a result of completing these, the social worker reopened negotiations on the target and a quite different problem emerged: her relationship with her mother, which had not previously been mentioned but proved, in fact, very important.

Mrs Tannar, in her twenties, had been married to an Indian bus conductor for four years. She herself had come from Ireland in adolescence. They had three children under 4, and she also had a part-time factory job. She took an impulsive overdose in the middle of a violent row with her husband. The problem search was carried out in the first interview and the following problems listed: (1) She and her husband were having several rows a week since husband's brother and his family had moved in with them two months previously. (2) Husband did little with the children and preferred his nephew to his own daughters, since boys were more valued than girls in his culture. (3) The house was overcrowded – there were nine people and only three bedrooms – and her household routine was disrupted. The social worker saw the main problem as a marital one, partly due to cultural differences between the couple, and suggested this to the client and that she should meet the husband as well. The client very firmly disagreed. In the second interview the target problem was formulated as follows: 'There aren't any problems between husband and me that I can't handle when we're on our own. The problem has arisen since (brother-in-law) came. It all comes from overcrowding.' With a target problem of overcrowding, the goal was specified as being to find alternative accomodation for the in-laws and persuade them to move. The client proved quite capable of carrying out tasks in this area and the goal was achieved within the period of contact without any other problems becoming a focus of work.

The last example illustrates particularly clearly the value of explicit agreement on a target problem before further work is undertaken. This can pinpoint the areas where clients are prepared to invest energy and work, and exclude areas which, for whatever reason, they are not prepared to open up. Where social worker and client disagree about what the target problem should be, and further exploration and specification of the problem does not modify this disagreement (as in the case of Mrs Tannar), the client's view of the problem has to prevail. The only clear exceptions to this rule would come if the client is incapable of forming a judgement (because of age or serious illness) or where he or she wants to achieve something that is against the law. When the client wants to achieve a goal that might injure someone else, or which seems totally impracticable, the task-centred worker is in a difficult position if he or she cannot, by convincing argument, change the client's mind and help him or her to reformulate the problem. However, as Reid (1978, p. 117) has said, 'in rejecting an applicant's definition of the problem, the "burden of proof" is clearly on the practitioner. He should have a clear reason for his decision. He should be reluctant to write off an applicant-stated problem as unsolvable simply because the means of solution may not be clear or because of his doubts about the applicant's capacity to solve it.'

The process of negotiating a target problem may be even more arduous when the problem is inter-personal, involving aspects of a relationship between two people. Since the problem belongs not to an individual but to the interaction between two people, it is clearly important to involve both parties in the problem search and problem specification. But the search for clarity and specificity is difficult to pursue in the emotional, conflictful and sometimes explosive atmosphere of most early marital cases.

Professor Reid's interesting discussion of conjoint task-centred work suggests that, in understanding problems of marital interaction, the system of rules governing the interaction is highly significant. Two such rules may have a general applicability: 'the rule of mutual devotion', under which partners should be sensitive to each other's needs and self-sacrificing in trying to meet them; and 'the norm of reciprocity', concerned with what each gives to and gets from each other. Exchanges should achieve a fair balance in the long run. Both these rules have probably broken down when couples have to seek marital help. Each partner will probably feel unloved and cheated by the other, and 'negative reciprocation' – paying each other back – may dominate their interaction, if they are still communicating at all. To help couples resolve acknowledged problems in their interaction, ideally the rules contributing to the difficulties should be clarified and new rules worked out. Tasks would then help to put these new rules into operation. In practice, it often seemed very difficult for the social workers to retain enough control to help clients stand back from their angry, mutually blaming and provocative ways of interacting in order to clarify or work out anything.

In specifying target problems in the area of marital interaction the social worker had to start with the partner who had taken an overdose and find a way of involving the other party as quickly as possible, before the situation had hardened and she was seen as on the side of the first partner. Sometimes the situation was even more complicated, and the problem had to be clarified with three parties.

Mrs Binns took an impulsive overdose after the break-up of a twelve-year affair with her employer. During the social worker's first interview with Mrs Binns, the problem was described as, 'she has decided to end relationship with boss/boy-friend. She is unhappy about this but must stay with husband for fear of hurting him and of his helplessness without her.' During the problem search the social worker met separately with Mr Binns and with Mr Goat, the 'other man'. Mrs Binns gradually revealed that she had no feelings for her husband and was only staying out of a sense of duty which proved not to be strong enough. Mr Goat, in turn, decided that he must break with his own spouse and live openly with Mrs Binns. The social worker was left forming a new contract with Mr Binns, to help him deal with the separation.

However, usually the social worker was involved only with the couple concerned. The strategy was to move into joint interviews as soon as possible and to specify the target problem jointly. The couples could often agree with the social worker that conflict in the marriage was their major problem and the one they most wanted to reduce. Difficulty arose in specifying the problem in a constructive way, rather than engaging in an exercise to find out who was to blame.

Mr and Mrs O'Halloran, for example, were a couple in their early twenties with three small children. Mrs O'Halloran's overdose was provoked by her husband's behaviour at Christmas; on Christmas Eve he returned home drunk and shouting abuse at her, and he slept for most of Christmas Day. In the problem search carried out with both partners at home it was difficult to move from their separate problem definitions in which each blamed the other. Mrs O'Halloran said the problem was her husband's coming home

Table 22.2　*Interview at which Tasks First Formulated*

Interview	N	%
One	11	8
Two	46	33
Three	28	20
Four	29	21
Five	12	8
Six	7	5
Seven	2	1
Eight	5	4
Total formulating tasks	140	100

drunk two or three times a month when he abused her, called her whore, etc. Mr O'Halloran accused his wife of frigidity. The social worker reformulated the target problem as: 'Mr O'Halloran feels left out, Mrs O'Halloran feels he is not involved – Mr O'Halloran drinks and becomes abusive and this drives them apart as does Mrs O'Halloran not showing any affection.' However, she noted that although it was easy to involve Mr O'Halloran in work using this definition of the problem, Mrs O'Halloran really did not accept her part in the situation.

A similar strategy of redefining the problem in a way that minimised mutual criticism and the search for someone to put in the dock was used with Mr and Mrs Simons. The problem search was conducted with them both over several interviews. Initially, Mrs Simons, who had taken the overdose, complained that her husband was cold, selfish and neglectful while Mr Simons complained that his wife was an inefficient housewife and mother who did not want to please any of them. They both found it so painful to express these thoughts about each other that the problem search had to be interrupted. When they were ready to resume it was possible to formulate the problem as more of a joint one: 'Mrs Simons feels Mr Simons is inattentive and she feels she lacks interest in the house partly as a result of this. Mr Simons is aware that he takes a lot for granted and is not as attentive as she would like.'

The target problems, as written down by the social worker at the time the inital contract was made, tended to be fairly general as these examples show. The problem was rarely specified in precise behavioural or quantitative terms and the social worker sometimes regretted this at a later stage in the work. There seemed to be two dangers at this stage of task-centred work: premature acceptance of a target problem without sufficient effort to explore and specify it; or, less often, getting bogged down in descriptions of the problems and losing the client's impetus and hope of any solution. The second course probably had the worst consequences, as a vague initial agreement could be developed into a more precise problem specification as work proceeded and clients engaged in tasks.

In this method a 'task' is defined as one of a series of actions that the client, in discussion with the worker, agrees to carry out when the worker is not present. Tasks may be discussed, planned and prepared for within the interview but their actual performance takes place outside it. This applies also to actions the worker agrees to carry out ('practitioner tasks'). The contract between client and worker includes explicit statements of the tasks each will undertake within a certain period of time. (This contract may be written down, but it does not have to be.) There is nothing particularly therapeutic about performing tasks, which are merely sensible small-scale steps taken to reduce particular identified problems. However, successfully accomplishing an agreed action is likely to increase both clients' and workers' confidence and produce more energy for further work. Thus it is important that tasks should be selected which have the greatest possible chance of success, and which also, when completed, will have a significant impact on the problem.

Once clients in the present study had entered into an initial contract and agreed a target problem they were unlikely to drop out without agreeing and working on tasks. Only six did so. This suggests that once the problem had been formulated tasks were relatively easy to generate.

Table 22.2 shows that 61 per cent of all those formulating any tasks had formulated at least one in the first three interviews, and over 80 per cent had done so in the first four interviews. A task was usually first formulated in the same interview as the target problem. We shall illustrate the process of task selection in two of the cases previously discussed (see pp. 225–6 and 229)

Miss Jones had agreed a target problem of 'forcing herself to achievements and hard work, unable to let up and relax and see value of enjoying herself ... drives herself too hard'. The goal was 'to take life more easily'. In the fourth interview Miss Jones was eager for problem-solving activity to begin and initially (forgetting the agreed target problem) suggested tasks to do with finding a more suitable job. The social worker 'tried to hold her back' and eventually it was agreed that the first general task should be 'to get out more'. Miss Jones agreed to operational tasks of finding out about clubs and activities available to her. The social worker 'in order to relieve the pressure of achievement a bit set the tasks low' and also 'raised the idea that if she found them very hard she should not pursue them' until after further discussion. By the following week Miss Jones had obtained details of a badminton club. Worker and client were able to agree new tasks of going to the club and going out with a friend from church, which were accomplished the following week. Miss Jones now began to go further than her agreed task, joining another social club where she met a young man who asked her out. In the seventh interview she felt she was overcoming her loneliness and anxiety about mixing and she wanted to change her target problem to the job area, which the social worker now accepted. The new target problem was 'not sure what job she would like to do, now off sick and needs to look around'. The general task 'to look at possibilities for other jobs' was immediately agreed and Miss Jones very rapidly completed several operational tasks in this area. By the ninth interview she had started a secretarial course, and the final agreed task – harking back to the first target problem – was 'to limit the hours spent studying at the weekend'.

Tasks set when the target problem is one of significant personal relationships might be *individual*, like Miss Jones's task, but were more often *joint*, with both husband and wife co-operating in some planned action, or *reciprocal*, with one partner performing a task that is separate from, but inter-related or in exchange for, a task performed by the other.

Mr and Mrs O'Halloran had reluctantly agreed a target problem involving them both: 'Mr O'Halloran drinks and becomes abusive and this drives them apart as does Mrs O'Halloran not showing any affection.' The goal was a very general one, 'to bring them closer together'. In the fourth interview Mr O'Halloran agreed to a general task of stopping heavy drinking, apparently 'accepting all the blame for what's been wrong'. He succeeded in cutting his drinking back over the following two months, which had a dramatic effect in improving the relationship. The social worker made efforts to involve Mrs O'Halloran in a reciprocal task – 'letting husband do things with the children if he's not drinking' – and the couple in joint tasks of going out together. The couple were successively able to do things together in the house and talk regularly to each other.

Sometimes the agreement to work on limited and specific tasks brought renewed hope and movement to a situation that had seemed hopeless.

Mrs Masters, in her thirties with two children, took an overdose which she attributed to their unhappy marriage and her suspicions that her husband was having an affair with someone else. In the problem search many other difficulties emerged of a practical kind, but the marital problem was clearly the most serious one, plainly manifest to the extent of open violence in interviews. Neither partner, however, would agree to enter a contract and the social worker was hanging on by the skin of her teeth until, in the eighth interview she suddenly changed her approach and suggested they should tackle the practical affairs. For the first time Mr Masters joined in the interview work and tasks were immediately set for each of them and for the social worker to contact the Housing Department (over unpaid rent) and the Department of Employment (over Mr Masters's suspended employment benefit). They also worked out debt repayment schedules. Contact ended as planned in the twelfth week with the financial problems largely under control. These successes appeared to have improved their relationship which in the final interview was reported as 'much better' although no tasks had been carried out in this area. However, by the follow-up, the marriage was again a major problem area so that the improvement was very short lived.

In a similar way, tasks seemed to enable some clients who felt unwilling to share very much with the social worker and needed to keep her at a distance, to accept help.

Mrs Barker was a widow in her fifties who had lived alone since the death of her husband four years previously. She took a serious overdose but later denied all suicidal intent, claiming she merely wanted a good sleep. She had very mixed feelings about seeing the social worker, but in the first two interviews described a number of problems: a month ago she had been made redundant, partly through her own choice; she was lonely and had nothing to do all day; she was sleeping badly and could not get to sleep at all in her own house so she had to stay with her daughter; she found herself constantly brooding over her husband's loss and blaming the doctor who had failed to make an early-enough diagnosis. The target problem was agreed as her fear of being in her own house, which Mrs Barker connected with this brooding. Tasks were agreed: to spend some time each day in the house and to sleep there once during the week. After a week she had moved back entirely to her

Table 22.3   *Interview when Time Limit First Discussed*

Interview	N	%
One	43	31
Two	43	31
Three	16	11
Four	16	11
Five	8	6
Six	5	4
Seven	2	1
Eight	7	5
Total agreeing time limit	140	100

own house and new tasks were agreed: to structure the day with activities, first painting the bathroom; to investigate Women's Institute groups and, later, to go to a particular group. Contact was ended after seven weeks. Mrs Barker commented that what had helped most was 'getting on and doing things'.

It was important to judge the client's commitment to a particular task and not to impose unwanted tasks upon clients. Sometimes the social worker became overenthusiastic in generating ideas and tasks and was brought back to reality by the client.

Vashi Singh was an 18-year-old who took an overdose in the midst of a family row about her wish for independence and the freedom of the English teenagers. Her parents spoke little English and work was therefore only with Vashi. The target problem was Vashi's not getting opportunities to meet people of her own age and have interests outside the home. In particular, she wanted to go to discos and have boy-friends. However, the social worker, perhaps trying to placate the parents, suggested that opportunities might be found by doing voluntary work and joining sports clubs, and set tasks for herself and Vashi in pursuit of these aims. Vashi did follow up one or two but, independently, she joined an evening class and, after a confrontation with parents, gained permission to go to a weekly disco. Thus she had achieved her goal and to the social worker's disappointment was no longer interested in tasks.

By the time work was begun on tasks, client and worker were likely to have developed an agreed definition of the problem and to have some knowledge of, and confidence in, each other. The client, by this time, usually had some understanding of task-centred methods. In a sense, conditions of work were easier than in earlier stages when worker and client were trying to negotiate a workable problem. However, in our view, the stage of task selection and working at tasks made the greatest demands on the workers' imagination, energy and skill. It was, perhaps, the hardest stage of work because it was the one which differed most from ordinary casework practice. Our practice at this stage might have gained from more systematic planning and rehearsal of tasks with clients in the interview on lines recommended in the task-centred literature (Reid, 1975), but this often proved difficult with clients who frequently lacked strong motivation for change. It was all too easy to become diverted from task planning into discussions of the clients' feelings and relationships at a more general level, and this was often what clients wanted. The frequently chaotic and incident-filled lives of our clients also produced 'obstacles' to work on tasks, and temporary diversions had to be accepted.

AGREEMENT ON ENDINGS

There is comparatively little social work literature on closing cases and ending relationships with clients. This might be because termination is a straightforward affair arousing little casework interest, or because, on the contrary, it is a somewhat painful event which is avoided. The fact that some social services clients are left uncertain about whether their case is open or closed (McKay *et al.*, 1973) lends support to the second view. In the task-centred method an explicit statement about the time contact will end has to be made as part of the contract. Both sides are clear about the approaching end of the contract, which is formalised in a structured final interview. This consists of a review of the problems the client had at the beginning; of how these have changed and of what the client has done about them; a critique of the social work method from the client's point of view, and a discussion of jobs to be tackled in the future. The social worker makes an assessment of task achievement on a predetermined scale.

We found that this stage of work did not always run smoothly. The social workers' usual practice was to mention in the first interview that the maximum period of contact would be three months, and then to discuss an actual time limit at a later interview when the contract was formulated. Table 22.3 shows the interview when the time limit was first discussed, in this contractual sense.

Although about three-quarters had discussed the time limit in the first three interviews, there was a minority where the topic was delayed until the sixth interview or even later. As we have seen, a larger minority (thirty-five cases) could not adhere to a time limit and we shall consider the reasons for this in more detail later.

The majority of cases did finish contact within an agreed time limit.

Was this really termination, or were they referred to some other agency for longer-term help? Only a small proportion of the total E sample (17 per cent) were referred to another agency at closure and the proportion among the task-centred group was even smaller. Twenty-two (11 per cent) of the total E sample made some further contact with the social workers after case closure, a small minority. On the whole, therefore, apart from the thirty-five extended cases, termination itself did not cause particular problems.

There was some evidence, however, that the final 'review' interview could be perceived as an ordeal which clients preferred to avoid. Twenty-eight cases (20 per cent of those working on tasks) managed to avoid this final interview, by persistent cancellations or by telling the social worker openly that they would find it a strain. Miss Jones, for example (see pp. 225–6), asked the social worker in their second-to-last meeting if that could be the last session. She said she felt prepared for the break and would be worried about the final session and would rather not have this build-up of anxiety. In some cases clients did find the ending of a valued relationship to be painful, even though they were prepared for the break and did not wish contact to continue. In these circumstances, the structure of the final interview could be felt as burdensome and irrelevant. Perhaps the last interview should be a time of leave-taking and is not the best moment to stand back and review progress in the dispassionate manner required. The review might be more appropriately conducted in a routine follow-up some weeks later. However, further research would be needed to clarify this.

·We shall now look more closely at the thirty-five 'extended' cases, two of which were planned to be long term. We have shown earlier that overrunning the time limit, receiving more interviews and more counselling and practical services from the social workers, tended to be associated with a poor outcome. The extended cases also tended to be those with higher-risk scores, whose outcome in any case was likely to be less good. There was, however, a minority (about a quarter) whose outcome was good in spite of their failure to adhere to the time limit – these cases had an average of twenty interviews (compared with twenty-six for poor-outcome cases who overran). It is of interest that the extended cases with a good outcome were in a higher-risk category than extended cases with a poorer outcome: their mean score on the Risk of Repetition scale was 1·5; compared with 0·91 for poorer-outcome extended cases. Thus the good outcome of the minority of extended cases was not explained by their being in a lower-risk category. When we examined the social workers' records of their work with these extended cases, there was a striking difference in the practice recorded. In the minority of good-outcome cases an extension of the time limit for a specific purpose had nearly always been agreed with the clients and was clearly recorded as part of the contract. However, in most of the poorer-outcome cases this not the case, and the time limit appeared to have been almost overlooked in the need to offer a continuing supportive relationship. It is possible that adherence to the task-centred approach (which permits an extension of a contract in certain circumstances) produced a better outcome. It may be, however, that there were differences between the good- and poorer-outcome cases, other than their level of risk, which made it impossible to maintain a contractual approach with the latter and which also caused their poorer outcome.

We shall describe a case to illustrate how a negotiated extension of an agreed time limit could be useful. Mrs Davies is particularly interesting because of her high risk for repetition (score of 4 on the predictive scale) and her good outcome.

Mrs Davies was an Italian lady in her forties who had been deserted by her British husband a year previously. She had become extremely depressed, needing in-patient psychiatric treatment for a time. She took an overdose of fairly high suicidal intent on the same day that she learnt by telegram that her mother was very ill in Italy. Mrs Davies agreed a target problem of social transition in the second interview with the social worker: 'How to cope with my husband's separation, my feelings about it and the isolation and loneliness.' She wanted to set about this by meeting more people and finding a more suitable job. The social worker agreed to find out information about suitable clubs in her area while Mrs Davies pursued tasks to do with sorting out her benefits since she lost her job after the overdose. Much of the interview time was devoted to talking of her relationship with her ex-husband and with her mother – Mrs Davies eventually decided to visit her mother in Italy. Task work resumed on her return but was punctuated by dramatic events (such as Mrs Davies being attacked in the street, her being falsely accused by the police) which the social worker was able to contain as diversions and obstacles to their work together. Mrs Davies had succeeded in finding a job and was using interviews to discuss her fears of joining a club when, in the tenth interview, she suffered a major set-back when her mother died. She was plunged back into feelings of overwhelming loss and loneliness and her tension brought difficulties in the new job. In the eleventh interview the social worker and she negotiated a further period of work with a new two-month time limit. The tasks were now to improve the situation at work. Mrs Davies eventually decided to change jobs, found new and more suitable work and joined the social club. The case was closed in the nineteenth interview, by which time she felt settled and that she could cope alone. The social worker had been very conscious of the danger of drifting into an endless supportive relationship with this dependent client but felt that the task-centred structure had prevented this.

In summary, three-quarters of cases entering a contract were able to end within the agreed time limit. There was no evidence from the follow-up that the time limit caused difficulties. The final evaluative interview itself, however, did appear to cause problems to some clients since a fifth avoided it altogether. A quarter of the cases making a contract failed to adhere to the time limit. While most of these cases had a poor outcome, a minority (eight cases) had a good outcome in spite of their relatively higher risk. In these cases the social workers appeared to have renegotiated the contract as the agreed time limit approached and to have agreed a further time-limited period of work, either to complete tasks or to undertake new tasks. In the other cases the initial contract had more often faded from view and supportive work of a more general kind was being undertaken.

Chapter 23

IMPLICATIONS OF THE RESEARCH

It will be remembered that the major aim of the project was to evaluate, using an experimental method, the feasibility and effectiveness of a task-centred social work service for people who had deliberately poisoned themselves. In the first half we attempted to describe our research methods and findings as objectively as possible. In the second half we came much closer to our material, trying to see the social workers' practice through their own eyes and those of their clients. How far have we come towards answers to our original questions? Our findings suggested that the provision of a task-centred service was feasible in the setting of a multi-disciplinary research project based in a university department of psychiatry for cases not already in psychiatric treatment. Ninety-five per cent accepted the offer of service. Less than 20 per cent developed into long-term cases. Two hundred cases could be managed during the year by only two full-time social workers who, because of the planned short-term nature of the work, carried caseloads of only twenty at any one time.

However, 'demonstration' services, which it is feasible to organise for a limited time as part of a research project, cannot always be transplanted into ordinary service settings. It seems clear that social workers in area teams of the social services department would not be in a position to provide the rapid response necessary for patients and their families after self-poisoning. In any case, only a minority of self-poisoning patients fall within statutory definitions of the agency's functions. Medical social workers who have ready access to general medical wards where self-poisoning patients are treated would be in a more favourable position to develop planned, short-term services operating on task-centred lines. Social work departments in general hospitals provide a setting where social workers are used to collaborating with doctors and nurses on the wards – who are likely to become increasingly responsible for the routine assessment of parasuicide patients – and to the necessity for short-term work organised rapidly to meet tight deadlines. The role of the psychiatrist is already changing. There is growing agreement that the psychiatrist does not need to see all self-poisoning patients if, instead, there is effective training of junior medical staff to carry out assessments, and continuing psychiatric consultation and liaison (Gardner, 1980). Social work departments in hospitals seem well placed, therefore, to collaborate in training of junior medical staff carrying out assessments; to offer a service organised on task-centred lines to a proportion of self-poisoning patients; and to obtain and co-ordinate other more appropriate services for a further proportion. Even social workers in general practice settings, still comparatively rare, are in a less strategic position than hospital social workers to intervene after parasuicide in a planned and systematic way.

We have argued that a task-centred service could *feasibly* be organised by hospital social work departments, in collaboration with medical and nursing staff and with psychiatric liaison. Does the evidence on the likely *effectiveness* of the service justify such an effort? Our own research showed that the experimental task-centred service was no more effective than the routine service in preventing repetition of parasuicide. We considered the reasons for this failure in Chapter 21. The most important reason was that people who repeated an overdose tended to have personal and social characteristics which prevented them from using the task-centred service in the planned way. There was a minority who were substantially helped to improve their social position by a period of task-centred work in spite of the fact that they took another overdose, but for the remainder the task-centred service either failed to engage them at all, or could not be operated as a time-limited, focused, problem-solving method. Repeaters tended to be people with previous psychiatric illness and parasuicide, with drinking problems and broken family ties. The task-centred service proved unable to help them, but there is no convincing evidence, as yet, of any form of service which can achieve the prevention of repetition. At present, therefore, this aim appears an unrealistic one for services to self-poisoning patients to adopt.

We therefore should admit in advance that the provision of a social work service for parasuicides and their families is unlikely to reduce the repetition rate. Our work suggested that a task-centred service, in fact, should rarely be offered to the people at most risk of repeating self-poisoning since it is very unlikely to benefit them. The highest-risk group is made up very largely of people who are already well known to medical, social and legal agencies and especially to the psychiatric services. It is probably to specialised psychiatric and mental-health social work services that we should look to devise new ways of caring in the community for these vulnerable people (Wing and Olsen, eds, 1979).

On the other hand, there was evidence to suggest that task-centred social work help offered selectively to medium-risk patients and to younger women, especially with problems of personal relationships, would be worthwhile. We concluded that the task-centred service was more effective than the routine service in preventing subsequent recourse to continuing psychiatric treatment, in reducing clients' social problems in the short term, and their personal relationship difficulties in the longer term as well. It was more acceptable to its users who felt more satisfied and that they had received more help. These benefits may be considered modest ones by those who argue that social work intervention should change the structure of society or the personality of an individual, or should enable clients permanently to manage without help in the future. We would argue that 'effective' helping in social work consists of co-operating with clients to achieve improvements in their immediate social situation, in accordance with their own priorities, and in a relationship where each party respects and values the other. In this sense, the task-centred service was significantly more effective than the routine service and we would argue that the evidence justifies additional investment of social work resources, in hospital settings, in work with patients who have deliberately poisoned themselves and with their families.

The task-centred method used in this project provided the structure for 'helping'. This structure proved valuable in a number of ways. The problem search stage was the equivalent to diagnosis or assessment in other casework methods. It differed in that the role of the worker was largely confined to helping the client(s) express problems as clearly as possible and sort out priorities. The social worker rarely collected information about the client from other sources, explored early histories, or indeed made any independent assessment of the clients' personality and situation. However, the social workers were encouraged to make use of the predictive scales to assess risk of completed suicide and risk of repetition of parasuicide used in the baseline research assessment. Validated objective measures of this sort were useful, first, in preventing unnecessary anxiety about closing low-risk cases after a short problem search. As we have seen, the majority of cases who ended at the problem search stage were low risk, without particular problems they wished to work on, and the task-centred structure enabled rapid clarification of this and an agreed parting. Secondly, the use of objective predictive instruments enabled the social workers to make better judgements about the need to maintain contact in high-risk cases. Thus extended problem searches or extensions of the contract were sometimes appropriately negotiated for high-risk cases. (More systematic use of the predictive scales might, in fact, have prevented some unnecessarily prolonged and unproductive work with lower-risk cases.) When social workers are engaged with clients in dangerous situations, where there is a risk of injury to themself or others, instruments which help to define the level of risk can be helpful to them in controlling anxiety and tolerating uncertainly. However, within a task-centred structure, the decisions about whether to acknowledge and work at problems must remain with the client. A knowledge of high risk incurred may spur the social worker to negotiate harder and argue more convincingly for a particular course of action.

The need for agreement on a specified target problem was helpful in providing a focus for subsequent work and preventing both social worker and client from becoming overwhelmed by a mass of changing problems. Systematic work at one difficulty could produce a feeling of achievement and mastery, generating energy for further work. However, the actual *classification* of the target problem remained an area of some difficulty for the social workers. The tasks agreed with the client often applied to other problem areas in addition to the target one. For instance, the most common tasks agreed when the target was in the area of 'reactive emotional distress' were to do with renewing or creating social contacts ('social relations'). Thus, any improvement would not necessarily be specific to the target problem area.

The time limit, which is an essential part of the contract in task-centred work, caused problems only with a minority who could not adhere to it. Further work seemed needed to identify earlier those people who could make use of some of the elements of task-centred work (agreements on problems and tasks) but within a longer time span. Further research also might investigate the use of the final evaluative interview. In this project it was often avoided and its formal structure sometimes seemed to cause anxiety and propitiatory responses intended to please the social worker.

Further research on the task-centred method should investigate further its usefulness as a means of reducing marital problems. Recent work (Mattinson and Sinclair, 1979) suggested that a small number of married cases with severe marital problems consumed a disproportionate amount of the social services department's resources. However, marital problems were rarely the focus of work with clients in the department. Task-centred intervention might be undertaken, and evaluated, with clients of the social services department acknowledging marital problems. It might be hypothesised that the task-centred structure should, first, enable marital problems to be identified and described during the problem search; secondly, enable them to be explicitly agreed on as the target for work (if they are so central in the lives of clients as previous research suggested); thirdly, be more successful in reducing identified areas of difficulty than long-term supportive work.

In this project no differences were found between the two social workers in the proportions of clients who became task-centred, nor in clients' outcomes. With only two workers it is impossible to conclude that individual workers' personalities and styles are unimportant. However, it may be that the importance of individual differences can be reduced by joint training of workers and, thereafter, by their functioning as a work group developing a common goal of applying and evaluating the method.

REFERENCES: PART III

Bancroft, J., Skrimshire, A., Casson, J., Harvard-Watts, O., and Reynolds, F. (1977), 'People who deliberately poison or injure themselves: their problems and their contacts with helping agencies', *Psychological Medicine*, vol. 7, no. 2, pp. 289–304.

Beck, A. T., Hermann, I., and Schuyler, D. 'Development of suicidal intent scales', in A. T. Beck, H. L. P. Resnik and D. Lettieri (eds), *The Prediction of Suicide* (Bowie, Md: Charles Press).

Beck, A. T., Ward, C. H., and Mendelson, M. (1961), 'An inventory for measuring depression', *Archives of General Psychiatry*, vol. 4, no. 6, pp. 561–71.

Buglass, D., and Horton, J. (1974), 'A scale for predicting subsequent suicidal behaviour', *British Journal of Psychiatry*, vol. 124, pp. 573–8.

Chowdhury, N. L., Hicks, R. C., and Kreitman, N. (1973), 'Evaluation of an aftercare service for parasuicide (attempted suicide) patients', *Social Psychiatry*, vol. 8, no. 2, pp. 67–81.

Corden, J. (1980), 'Contracts in social work practice', *British Journal of Social Work*, vol. 10, no. 2, pp. 143–61.

Ettlinger, R. (1975), 'Evaluation of suicide prevention after attempted suicide', *Acta Psychiatrica Scandinavia*, Supplement 260.

Fischer, J. (1976), *The Effectiveness of Social Casework* (Springfield, Ill.: Charles C. Thomas).

Gardner, R. (1980), 'Medical-psychiatric consultation and liaison: an evaluation of its effectiveness', in R. D. T. Farmer and S. R. Hirsch (eds), *The Suicide Syndrome*, (London: Croom Helm), pp. 226–34.

Gardner, R., Hanka, R., Evison, B., Mountford, P. M., O'Brien, V. C., and Roberts, S. R. (1978), 'Consultation-liaison scheme for self-poisoned patients in a general hospital', *British Medical Journal*, vol. 2, pp. 1392–4.

Gibbons, J. S., Butler, J., and Gibbons, J. L. (1980), 'Treatment by general practitioners and psychiatrists of patients who deliberately poison themselves', in *Symposium on the Role of Chemotherapeutic Agents in Self-Poisoning and Suicide* (Crawley, Sussex: Crawley Postgraduate Medical Centre), pp. 48–58.

Gibbons, J. S., Elliot, J., Urwin, P., and Gibbons, J. L. (1978), 'The urban environment and deliberate self-poisoning', *Social Psychiatry*, vol. 13, no. 3, pp. 159–66.

Gibbons, J. S., Bow, I., Butler, J., and Powell, J. (1979), 'Clients' reactions to task-centred casework: a follow-up study', *British Journal of Social Work*, vol. 9, no. 2, pp. 203–15.

Golan, N. (1978), *Treatment in Crisis Situations* (New York and London: The Free Press and Macmillan).

Goldberg, E. M., Walker, D., and Robinson, J. (1977), 'Exploring the task-centred casework method', *Social Work Today*, vol. 9, no. 2, pp. 9–14.

Goldberg, E. M., and Stanley, S. J. (1979), 'A task-centred approach to probation', in J. F. S. King (ed.), *Pressures and Change in the Probation Service*, Cropwood Conference Series No. 11 (Cambridge: Cambridge University Press).

Greer, S., and Bagley, C. (1971), 'Effect of psychiatric intervention in attempted suicide: a controlled study', *British Medical Journal*, vol. 1, pp. 301–12.

Hawton, K. (1980), 'Domiciliary and out-patient treatment following deliberate self-poisoning', in R. D. T. Farmer and S. R. Hirsch (eds), *The Suicide Syndrome* (London: Croom Helm), pp. 246–58.

Hill Report (1968), *Hospital Treatment of Acute Poisoning* (London: HMSO).

Holding, T. A. (1975), 'Suicide and the befrienders', *British Medical Journal*, vol. 3, no. 11, pp. 751–2.

Jennings, C., and Barraclough, B. M. (1980), 'The effectiveness of the Samaritans in the prevention of suicide', in R. D. T. Farmer and S. R. Hirsch (eds), *The Suicide Syndrome* (London: Croom Helm), pp. 194–200.

Jones, D. I. R. (1977), 'Self-poisoning with drugs: the past 20 years in Sheffield', *British Medical Journal*, vol. 1, pp. 28–9.

Kennedy, P. (1972), 'Efficacy of a regional poisoning treatment centre in preventing further suicidal behaviour', *British Medical Journal*, vol. 4, pp. 255–7.

Kessel, N. (1965), 'Self-poisoning: part 1', *British Medical Journal*, vol. 2, pp. 1265–70.

Kreitman, N. (1983), 'Social and clinical aspects of suicide and parasuicide', in R. E. Kendell and A. K. Zealley (eds), *Companion to Psychiatric Studies*, (Edinburgh: Churchill Livingstone), pp. 396–411.

Kreitman, N. (1976), 'The coal gas story: United Kingdom suicide rates 1960–71', *British Journal of Preventive and Social Medicine*, vol. 30, no. 2, pp. 86–93.

Kreitman, N., and Schreiber, M. (1980), 'Parasuicide in young Edinburgh women', in R. D. T. Farmer and S. R. Hirsch (eds), *The Suicide Syndrome* (London: Croom Helm), pp. 54–72.

McKay, A., Goldberg, E. M., and Fruin, D. J. (1973), 'Consumers and a social services department', *Social Work Today*, vol. 4, no. 16, pp. 486–91.

Maluccio, A., and Marlow, W. D. (1974), 'The case for the contract', *Social Work* (USA), vol. 19, no. 1, pp. 28–37.

Mattinson, J., and Sinclair, I. A. C. (1979), *Mate and Stalemate: Working with Marital Problems in a Social Services Department* (Oxford: Blackwell).

Newson-Smith, J. G. B. (1980), 'The use of social workers as alternatives to psychiatrists in assessing parasuicide', in R. D. T. Farmer and S. R. Hirsch (eds), *The Suicide Syndrome* (London: Croom Helm), pp. 215–25.

Newson-Smith, J. G. B., and Hirsch, S. R. (1979), 'Psychiatric symptoms in self-poisoning patients', *Psychological Medicine*, vol. 9, no. 3, pp. 493–500.

OPCS (1978), *Trends in Mortality 1951–1975* (London: HMSO).

Rapoport, L. (1970), 'Crisis intervention as a mode of brief treatment', in R. W. Roberts and R. H. Nee (eds), *Theories of Social Casework* (Chicago: University of Chicago Press) pp. 267–311.

Reid, W. J. (1975), 'A test of a task-centred approach', *Social Work* (USA), vol. 20, no. 1, pp. 3–9.

Reid, W. J. (1978), *The Task-Centered System* (New York: Columbia University Press).

Reid, W.J., and Epstein, L. (1972), *Task-Centered Casework* (New York: Columbia University Press).

Reid, W. J., and Epstein, L. (eds) (1977), *Task-Centered Practice* (New York: Columbia University Press).

Smith, G., and Corden, J. (1981), 'The introduction of contracts in a family service unit', *British Journal of Social Work*, vol. 11, no. 3, pp. 289–313.

Ternansen, P. E., and Bywater, C. (1975), 'S.A.F.E.R.: a follow-up service for attempted suicide in Vancouver', *Canadian Psychiatric Association Journal*, vol. 20, no. 1, pp. 29–34.

Urwin, P., and Gibbons, J. L. (1979), 'Psychiatric diagnosis in self-poisoning patients', *Psychological Medicine*, vol. 9, no. 3, pp. 501–7.

Wing, J. K., Cooper, J. E., and Sartorius, N. (1974), *The Description and Classification of Psychiatric Symptoms* (Cambridge: Cambridge University Press).

Wing, J. K., and Olsen, R. (eds) (1979), *Community Care for the Mentally Disabled* (Oxford: Oxford University Press).

World Health Organisation (WHO) (1968), *Prevention of Suicide*, Public Health Papers No. 38 (Geneva: WHO).

CONCLUSION

This book has described how task-centred casework was introduced, and its effectiveness evaluated, in three different English social work settings. We shall now compare the findings from these projects, and consider what meaning they may have for task-centred practice and social work in general. We begin by comparing the projects in terms of their different agency bases, research methods and client groups. If, despite their differences, the projects produced similar results, we can be more confident in drawing out the implications and considering them of general relevance.

Of the three projects, the one in the social services department had a setting nearest to that of ordinary social work practice. It took place in two intake teams in an inner London social services department. The teams received no extra resources, but workers gave one and a half hours a week to the project. By contrast, in the probation project the team of six officers had been established as an experimental unit for a previous research project, were expected to innovate, and had developed an interest in short-term methods of work. The parasuicide project created a special research team of two social workers based in a university department of psychiatry. Thus these workers operated in a research setting, freed from the constraints but also lacking the resources of ordinary social work practice.

All three projects were similar in that the researchers introduced and supervised a method of social work which, although well established in the United States and tried out in England, had not yet been fully evaluated in this country. However, for reasons discussed earlier in this book, different methods of research were adopted. The probation and social services projects used 'before and after' designs. Clients were described at the point of entry to the study, their progress was monitored, and the final outcome was assessed by the clients in collaboration, first, with their social worker and then with an independent assessor. The parasuicide project used a random allocation experimental design, and this made it possible to compare similar groups of task-centred and control cases not receiving task-centred casework on the various outcome measures.

These differences in research design were associated with different ways of measuring effectiveness. In the probation and social services projects, a case was designated 'successful' if the client completed all the stages of the task-centred process and reported that the tasks agreed upon had been achieved and that the relevant problem had been substantially or completely reduced. In addition, the probation project used reconvictions as an independent outcome criterion. In the parasuicide project, clients were said to have a good outcome if they did not repeat an overdose or need psychiatric treatment in the following year and if, at an independent follow-up interview, they showed evidence of problem reduction in a variety of problem areas, not necessarily those which had been selected as the targets of task-centred casework.

The client groups naturally differed considerably in the three settings. The social services sample consisted of 133 referrals allocated to the project's social workers (simple requests for practical services and aids were excluded). They were mainly women responsible for dependants and troubled by problems of family relationships, housing, or debt. The probation sample consisted of 100 probationers on short-term (one year) orders, drawn from a much larger group of offenders on whom social enquiry reports (SERs) had been prepared. The parasuicide sample consisted of 200 project and 200 control cases, all of whom had come to a hospital casualty department in the course of one year after deliberately poisoning themselves. The 400 cases were not a representative sample of all parasuicides, and included a disproportionate number of people who had a low risk of poisoning themselves again. The social services clients and the parasuicide sample were broadly similar in terms of age, sex and marital status. Both groups consisted predominantly of married or divorced women who were living with their families. By contrast, the probation clients were younger and much more likely to be single and male.

Not surprisingly, these differences were reflected in the target problems selected as the focus for task-centred work. In all three settings, clients and workers were commonly concerned with problems of inadequate resources, role performance and reactive emotional distress. The probation clients, many of them young men at odds with society and with disturbed relationships, were more likely to focus on dissatisfaction in social relations; the social services and parasuicide groups, whose marriages were often breaking up, on problems of social transition. The inter-personal difficulties of the parasuicide group were marked by the fact that for this group 'significant personal relationships' represented the second most common target problem.

Bearing these differences in setting, client group and research strategy in mind, we shall now consider the findings of the three projects. Results which hold for all three settings and client groups will be of particular interest.

THE EFFECTIVENESS OF TASK-CENTRED WORK

The three settings differed in the degree to which the clients progressed through the various stages of task-centred work. In the social services 42 per cent of the cases ended after the problem search, since no target problem could be agreed. The corresponding proportion in the psychiatric setting was 30 per cent, while agreement on a target problem was a condition of entry to the probation sample. Fifty-seven per cent of the social services clients, 64 per cent of the probationers and 67 per cent of the parasuicide clients at least started to work on tasks. In all settings most clients were able to agree on a target problem, work on tasks and finish within a three months' time limit (or six months in the probation setting). In this rather restricted sense, the task-centred model proved applicable to between a half and two-thirds of cases in all three projects.

Again in each project, most of the clients who were followed-up were pleased with the results of task-centred work. Fifty-eight per cent of those interviewed in the social services project and 60 per cent of those discharged at six months and interviewed in the probation project said that their problems were no longer present or a lot better. In these projects, problem reduction was assessed after clients had been asked to identify the problems that most concerned them at the beginning of task-centred work. It will be remembered that the parasuicide clients were asked if their problems were better or worse in a number of specified areas. At four-month follow-up, 81 per cent of the parasuicide clients were assessed as showing improvement on these measures. A comparable figure at eighteen months was 66 per cent.

In the parasuicide project it was possible to compare outcomes for the clients offered task-centred casework with those of their controls. The two groups did not differ in terms of further suicide attempts, or in overall problem reduction at eighteen months. At four months, however, the experimental group did have better problem reduction scores. Moreover, the experimental group made less subsequent use of psychiatric services, were less depressed and were more satisfied with their treatment. The disappointing results in relation to further suicide attempts should not obscure these more positive findings.

Rather similar findings were reported from the probation project, which did not have a special control group. From available comparative data, it seems likely that on the objective criterion of 'reconviction' the task-centred group differed little from apparently comparable groups of probationers receiving traditional long-term probation casework. Many of the task-centred probation group, however, appeared to gain in confidence and to have a sense of achievement and they were, on average, on the books of their probation officers for much shorter periods of time than would have been the case with probationers receiving traditional probation supervision. It seems, therefore, that a more widespread use of time-limited task-centred casework should prove satisfactory to clients and also, since there is no evidence this would bring increased recidivism, acceptable to magistrates.

In summary, these projects suggest that there is considerable scope for task-centred work. All the studies found that task-centred methods could be applied with a sizeable number of clients, and that clients who completed an episode of task-centred work were likely to report that their problems had been reduced. It is unlikely that the method can reduce the chances of a client being reconvicted (except possibly in the medium-risk groups), or making a further suicide attempt, but then no other social work methods are known to be more effective in this respect. On the positive side, the method can almost certainly help people to tackle some of their problems and, to a certain extent, resolve them. It can also lead to a lower level of expenditure on long-term casework through probation supervision or on psychiatric services.

THE LIMITS OF TASK-CENTRED CASEWORK

Despite these achievements, task-centred casework obviously could not help all the clients. In some cases this was because the clients were well able to help themselves. In the social services study, for example, it appeared that a number of clients resolved their own problems without the benefit of social work, while in other cases circumstances changed so that the original problem no longer existed. In the parasuicide project, drop-out at the end of the problem search was not associated with a poor objective outcome. The majority of clients who withdrew after the problem search had a low risk of making a further suicide attempt and rightly assessed their own need of further help as small. Their outcome was no worse than that of the fully task-centred cases. By contrast, clients who overran the time limit and could not adhere to the task-centred structure did significantly worse. Similarly, probation clients whose order ran for a full year did apparently worse, on both task-centred outcome criteria and reconviction rates.

In none of the three settings did task-centred casework appear to have much success with the minority of clients who caused the greatest difficulties, for themselves and other people. In the probation project, those for whom the time-limited task-centred method did not work out seemed to have more unfavourable characteristics – they were more often unemployed, had longer criminal records and were less likely to be living as a member of a family. Rather similar findings were obtained in the parasuicide project, in which greater age and the relatively high risk of attempting suicide again were both associated with poor outcomes. Age was also associated with outcome in the social services projects, in which case studies also suggested that clients who had difficulties in many areas of their lives were unlikely to make successful use of task-centred work, a result which confirms earlier work in Buckinghamshire (Goldberg, *el al*. 1977).

The task-centred approach may also be difficult to adopt with those clients who disagree with the social worker about what should be done. Agreement between client and worker is central to the theory of task-centred casework (Reid, 1978) and, it seems from the social services study, to its actual success. Particular skill may therefore be required in adapting its practice to work which has an element of control – for example, the supervision of probationers or parents who are likely to batter their children. Nevertheless, such an adaptation seems to be possible. The probation project raised the question of whether the method could be applied within the context of a court order, and answered with a qualified 'yes'.

Agreement on the nature of a problem is not in itself enough to ensure success. The client and worker must also agree on a feasible objective or task. In the parasuicide project it was found that the experimental group were particularly likely to report improvement in relation to loneliness and personal relationships. However, both this project and the probation research suggested that the resolution of one of the client's problems will only affect other problems in which the worker may be even more interested (for example reconviction, or repetition of suicide attempts) if the two types of problems are related. For example, in the probation project, the problems on which clients and workers agreed to work were not necessarily directly associated with the clients' delinquency. In the social services study, some clients distinguished between help with specific practical problems (for example, over a particular debt) and help with major strategic problems (for example, how to leave their husband). It may well be that major changes in the clients' lives and behaviour can only be achieved in a small number of cases where worker and client agree to concentrate on strategic problems.

Clearly, more research needs to be done on the question of which clients are likely to benefit from task-centred methods. In particular, we need to know what part the approach can play with the chronic 'problem families' whose endless emergencies take up so much of the time and energies of trained social workers and in other chronic situations where 'support' is provided by others and intervention of the social worker is only required at specific points. In the meantime, the findings suggest that task-centred casework, like other forms of social work and social therapy, is best suited to the 'middle-range' clients – those whose problems are neither pervasive and deep-seated, nor easily resolved by the clients' own efforts or the passing of time. By itself, a limited episode of task-centred casework is unlikely to have a major impact on life-long difficulties.

SKILLS REQUIRED IN TASK-CENTRED CASEWORK

A further requirement for the success of task-centred casework is that the worker has the necessary personal and professional qualities. The social services project, and to a lesser extent the probation project, provided evidence of the importance of workers' characteristics in influencing outcomes. Other, more qualitative evidence for variations in workers' effectiveness may be provided by a comparison of the kinds of work undertaken by different workers in the various projects. For example, two workers in the social services study seemed to have very particular skills, one in arranging short-term placements for children and one in enabling battered wives to leave their husbands. Both seemed to understand the feelings of women in these different situations and to have a good grasp of the resources which could be brought to bear upon them. Neither of these workers seemed to have much success with couples in marital difficulties who wished to stay together. By contrast, workers in the parasuicide project seemed to develop particular skills in applying the task-centred model to marital casework.

These examples bring out the point that the task-centred approach provides a framework within which a variety of techniques, for example, family therapy or behavioural therapy, may find their place. Thus, training in task-centred casework or in other forms of casework needs to take into account both general principles and the way these principles can be applied to specific kinds of problems.

Nevertheless, the general principles of the task-centred approach remain important. Taken together, the projects may help to define these principles and provide examples of their use. The skills required seemed to include:

(1) *The ability to listen to the clients* – The research interviews brought out clearly the degree to which the clients valued this, and the unfortunate consequences of a failure by the worker to grasp what the client was bothered about. The ability to listen is a prerequisite of all forms of casework. In task-centred casework it is essential that the social worker should listen in a purposeful way.

(2) *Ability in timing* – Workers using the task-centred model were

not apparently tempted to indulge in endless explorations of the past while the client became increasingly bemused by the purpose of the encounters. However, a few depressed clients seemed to feel hounded by irrelevant suggestions and trapped into irrelevant actions by workers who were keen to get results. The probation officers developed a useful technique whereby clients were allowed a limited number of sessions to talk about their past lives without endlessly putting off the hour when something was decided. This method was used when some aspect of the past was 'bugging' the client and had to be discussed before progress could be made in the task.

(3) *The ability to negotiate* – Clients cannot always have what they want, and sometimes they can only achieve their aims at an unacceptable cost to others. For these reasons, genuine agreement between the client and worker often involves the worker in negotiating with the client as well as listening. The marital work undertaken in the parasuicide project is a particularly elegant example of such negotiations. A number of examples show that worker and client can sometimes renegotiate a definition of tasks and problems and that the worker must therefore have skill in knowing when to encourage persistence in the original plans and when to urge flexibility.

(4) *Ability to act as a partner* – Social workers must be able to allow the client to choose without signifying indifference to the choice made or to its outcome. As the client's ally, the social worker may need to break down a complex problem into manageable pieces, clarify who is doing what about the problem and demonstrate commitment in acquiring resources, encouraging the client's efforts, redirecting them if necessary and acknowledging failure if things do not work out. Examples of successful 'partnerships' are provided by all three studies.

(5) *Closure* – Task-centred casework encourages explicitness about time limits and closure. The studies reported in this book certainly suggest that this was a difficult, if important, area of work. More thought must be given to the conditions under which time limits are helpful, and to the questions of whether leave-taking and formal review of work appropriately combine in a final interview.

As can be seen from the above, task-centred casework is not easy. On the one hand, social workers must allow their clients freedom and choice, listening, encouraging and demonstrating concern; on the other hand, they must provide direction, intervening to prevent too much digression, leaving as much as possible to their clients, not taking them beyond their capabilities, clarifying what has to be done and by whom, and perhaps seeking to close the case when clients may wish to go on. This complex task no doubt requires the worker to have a clear grasp of the method, intervene firmly but yet with tact and, if appropriate, with humour, and time his or her interventions to the client's emotional state. And all this must be done in such a way as to encourage the client to contribute as much as possible to the solution and redirection of his or her problem and to remain as far as possible in control of his or her own situation.

IMPLICATIONS FOR RESEARCH

The findings reported in this book may help to explain the alleged failure of many experiments in social casework, and hence provide ideas for future research. As has been seen, success in task-centred casework is associated with a number of conditions:

(1) The client's difficulty should be of a medium level, that is neither too trivial nor too severe.
(2) The problems selected for attention should be of a kind which the client and the social worker together can resolve or reduce.
(3) The client should attach importance to this problem and wish to resolve it.
(4) The social worker should agree with the client on strategy and on specific tasks that ought to help to resolve the problem.
(5) The problem and tasks should be *relevant* to the criteria of ultimate success (for example, absence of reconviction) if these are different from the reduction of immediate problems in living. The resolution of some problems (for example, those which predispose to suicide or chronic delinquency) may be too ambitious a goal for short-term work.
(6) The social worker should have the necessary skill.
(7) Client or social worker should have access to the necessary resources or be able to create them.

It may be that these seven conditions coincide quite rarely. If so, this would explain the fact that in these studies the social workers failed to reduce parasuicide and were probably not particularly effective in achieving other forms of social control. In the past, experiments in casework have generally been concerned with general criteria, defined by policy-makers, and not with specific problems as the client defines them. These experiments have usually failed to demonstrate that casework has an effect. Future experiments in this area might do better to concentrate on the degree to which social work can help to resolve or reduce problems with which a client is concerned and which are commonly accepted as the proper concerns of social work.

Social workers, as well as researchers, may take heart from these results. Success, it seems, is possible provided the goals are limited and the aim is to help the clients to achieve their aims rather than change them in pre-determined ways. Accountants no doubt draw satisfaction from helping their clients sort out *financial* difficulties, and psychotherapists are pleased if they enable patients to get over a bad patch. Why should not social workers draw satisfaction from similar outcomes?

This does not mean that social workers should have nothing to do with reluctant clients. The social worker is in a position to take the key decisions which determine whether a child is received into care or discharged from it, and decisions of this kind can be taken skilfully, sensitively, legally, or otherwise. The task-centred model does not suggest that this kind of social work is invalid, it merely makes certain distinctions clear. It is, after all, important to know whether the social worker is visiting the client because the client wants him or her to or because that is what the agency requires. The task-centred method should also help the social worker to distinguish more sharply between work which is aiming at change and the long-term surveillance and maintenance which may be required by clients with chronic problems. The purpose of making this distinction is that the latter kind of work may often be appropriately carried out by social work aides, community groups and neighbourhood networks of various kinds.

Nevertheless, many of those whose behaviour has brought them under the surveillance of social workers have problems for which they require help and to which the task-centred model would be appropriate. Many services would be better adapted to the clients' needs if those responsible for assessment paid more attention to the principles of task-centred casework. In short, most areas of welfare would benefit if aims were less global, methods less paternalistic and more scrupulous attention was paid to what the client wants and is capable of achieving.

Unfortunately, difficulties in employing the task-centred approach do not only arise from defects in social work training or attitudes. They also have to do with issues of power and resources, and with the expectations of others. The task-centred model requires the social worker to treat the client as an equal, when the client may have little control over the resources he or she requires, when social service procedures emphasise the role of the social worker in rationing, rather than enabling, and when referrers sometimes expect the social worker to act as a kind of 'nanny' or policeman, or a cross between the two.

Despite these difficulties, the method can be used, and with advantage. As one of us has already written (Goldberg, *et al.*, 1977):

Even within a social services agency which dispenses many services and undertakes long-term statutory and voluntary surveillance, the task-centred approach has much to offer. It stimulates clarity of thinking, more explicitness about aims and ways of achieving them, and more forward-planning of individual cases; it invites greater participation by the client, who is encouraged to accomplish as much as possible by his own efforts...The method discourages aimless 'visiting', unnecessary follow-ups, and a kind of vague responsiveness to any problems that might emerge.

REFERENCES: CONCLUSION

Goldberg, E. M., Walker, D., and Robinson, J. (1977), 'Exploring the task-centred casework method', *Social Work Today*, vol. 9, no. 2.' pp. 9–14.
Reid, W. J. (1978), *The Task-Centred System* (New York: Columbia University Press).

APPENDIX TO PART II

Worker Styles, Methods of Intervention and their Relationship to Outcome

One of the problems in any evaluation of social work is to establish the links between the workers' input and the outcomes. Reid and Shyne's work (1969) suggested two observations on this link: that spending more time over a longer period with the client did not lead to greater success, and that in time-limited casework the content of interviews with the client changed so that less time was spent on exploration and more on other activities. Other research (Reid, 1967; Mullen, 1969; Sinclair, 1971) has suggested that workers' characteristics are also important factors in the link between input and outcome.

The following four sections focus, therefore, on the relationship between worker, amount of input (number of interviews), type of input (method of intervention), and outcome. The important issues seem to be:

(1) Did some probation officers achieve more successful results than others, both in the number of cases closed (and followed-up) and on the outcome measures of task achievement and problem reduction?
(2) Was success associated with the number of interviews per case?
(3) Was success associated with the proportion of interviews spent working on the task?
(4) Was success associated with the methods of intervention used in the interviews?

Our definition of success requires that the following conditions be met: that an order is converted at six months and the client seen in a follow-up interview, and that high scores are reported for both problem reduction ('No longer present' or 'A lot better') and task achievement ('Complete' or 'Substantial').

As there are several ways in which clients could succeed or fail, we divided the sample (excluding two transferred cases) into five 'outcome groups':

Group A1: twenty-two one-year probation orders converted at six months and followed-up; with high scores for both problem reduction and task achievement – rated 'successes'.

Group A2: twenty-two one-year probation orders converted at six months and followed-up; with lower scores for problem reduction or task achievement – not rated 'successes'.

Group B: twenty one-year probation orders converted at six months but not followed-up.

Group X: seventeen one-year probation orders not converted at six months and continued on the initiative of magistrate, probation officer or client.

Group Y: seventeen one-year probation orders ending in breach, custodial sentence, or loss of contact.

OUTCOME AND WORKER

Did some workers achieve more success than others? Table B1, which shows the distribution of each worker's cases over the five outcome groups, suggests that this may be so. The proportion of 'successes' (cases in outcome group A1) is 22 per cent overall, but ranges from 44 per cent for officer A, to nil for officers H, J and K. (Workers are ranked in this table according to the proportion of successful cases they supervised.) Four of the ten officers achieved above-average

Table B1 *Probation Officers and Outcome Group*

| Probation Officer | Outcome group | | | | | |
	A1	A2	B	X	Y	Total
A	4	—	2	1	2	9
B	6	4	1	5	1	17
C	2	—	—	2	2	6
D	3	2	4	1	2	12
E	2	1	2	1	3	9
F	4	9	1	5	3	22
G	1	2	1	1	1	6
H	—	1	1	—	1	3
J	—	2	5	1	1	9
K	—	1	3	—	1	5
Total N	22	22	20	17	17	98

Notes: Where two or more officers were involved in a case, the officer who held most interviews with the client is considered to be the main worker for this analysis.
All cases where *a student* was the main worker are grouped together as one probation officer.

success rates, supervising fifteen of the twenty-two cases in outcome group A1, and these may tentatively be regarded as 'more successful' than the other six. We have already seen (Table 14.8, p. 152) that the cases of these four officers were less likely to be reconvicted of a standard list offence than were the cases of the other six, and that this overall difference in reconviction rates appears primarily attributable to the lower reconviction rate of younger first and second offenders supervised by officers A–D.

The number of cases supervised by the different officers in the project is too small for us to test the differences in success rates for statistical significance. Nevertheless, we believe that the differing rates of task-centred success and reconviction reflect a reality: that some workers achieve better results with the task-centred method than do others.

AMOUNT OF INPUT

The next question is whether success is related to the amount of input – the number of interviews per case. Table B2, setting out the mean number of interviews per case for each officer, shows a slight tendency for probation officers with higher success rates to have more interviews with their cases than do 'less successful' officers. (Figures in Tables B2 and B3 exclude the final interview.)

Table B2   *Mean Number of Interviews per Case*

Probation Officer	Mean no. of interviews per case
A	15·4
B	18·4
C	15·4
D	18·1
E	13·2
F	16·6
G	17·8
H	10·3
J	10·0
K	15·0
Total	16·0

It must be remembered, however, that the number of interviews in each case was not dependent solely on the progress made with task-centred casework. All the probation orders involved an element of surveillance which imposed certain constraints on the number and frequency of interviews. In addition, cases where the client absconded, reoffended, or failed to report to the probation officer typically had relatively few interviews.

The effects of this are set out in Table B3, which shows the mean number of interviews per case in each outcome group.

Table B3   *Mean Number of Interviews per Case in Five Outcome Groups*

Outcome group	Mean no. of interviews per case
A1	16·9
A2	17·5
B	14·2
X	21·0
Y	10·8
Total	16·0

The striking feature of this table is that the numbers of interviews in Groups A1 and A2 are very similar, suggesting that successful completion of the order rather than task achievement and problem reduction are associated with the number of interviews. Other variations (mainly in groups X and Y) are clearly related to the length of the case.

TYPE OF INTERVENTION

As already described, an attempt was made to collect information about the methods of intervention used by probation officers and to examine the relationship between these methods and outcome. To this end, the officers were asked to indicate, on the interview schedules to be completed after each interview, the proportion of time spent on each of the five activities described in Appendix A2 – exploration, structuring, encouragement, direction and enhancing awareness – and to state which was considered most important in that interview.

Such an approach had its problems, both methodological and practical. Probation officers classified their intervention methods from memory. As not all schedules were completed immediately after the interview, a further source of error was introduced; and for some interviews no schedule was completed or could be reconstructed. Recognition of these problems and discussions with the workers about the reliability of the data led to a decision to carry out a limited analysis only focusing primarily on the most important activity. Only ninety-two cases could be used in the analysis since too many schedules were missing in six cases. In all, 1,389 schedules* were analysed an average of 15·10 per case (we know from the case records that ninety-three interviews were unrecorded).

The first question we examined was whether the activity taking up most time in an interview was also the most important. Table B4 shows the results of this analysis.**

The activity most frequently mentioned as the longest was exploration (706 times), followed by encouragement with 409 mentions. The activity most frequently mentioned as the most important was encouragement (519 times), followed by enhancing awareness with 341 mentions. Overall, the same activity was recorded as most important and longest 968 times, a concordance rate of 56 per cent.

In over half (706) of the 1,389 interviews analysed 'exploration' was rated as the *longest* activity (or as one of the longest activities), but it was rated as the *most important* in fewer than a quarter of interviews overall, and in only 40 per cent of those where it had been rated as the longest. All the other activities were rated *most important* more frequently than they were rated *longest*: 'Encouragement', 'enhancing awareness' and 'structuring' were each rated as the most important activity in over 100 interviews where most time was spent on 'exploration'.

Next, we examined probation officers' individual ratings of the importance of each activity to see whether these pointed to any differences in style between officers. Table B5 summarises the results.

Caution is indicated in interpreting this table since the number of cases per officer is small. A further problem is that some officers rated two or more activities as equally important. The table indicates, however, that there are differences between workers in the importance they assigned to different activities.

No great differences were found between officers in the frequency with which they rated 'exploration' as their most important activity but, in contrast, there were considerable differences in the frequency with which officers rated each of the other four activities as most important.

The next question is whether these differences of 'style' as classified

---

* Excluding those for the final interview.
** In many interviews two or more activities were equally the longest or most important; in the 1,389 interviews, there were 1,738 mentions of activities as the most important or the longest in an interview (thus in Table B4 an interview where two activities were recorded as the longest and two as the most important could be counted four times).

Table B4 Longest and Most Important Activity (No. of interviews analysed = 1,389)

Most Important Activity	Longest Activity						
	Exploration	Structuring	Encouragement	Direction	Enhancing awareness	None	Total
Exploration	281	8	4	1	6	1	301
Structuring	106	150	33	6	14	4	313
Encouragement	146	41	274	24	27	7	519
Direction	62	31	45	112	13	1	264
Enhancing awareness	111	17	53	7	151	2	341
Total N	706	247	409	150	211	15	1,738

Note: Some interviews had more than one activity rated as longest or most important (or both).

Table B5 Probation Officers' Ratings of Most Important Activities

Probation Officer	No. of cases analysed	No. of interviews analysed N %	Activity Exploration N %	Structuring N %	Encouragement N %	Direction N %	Enhancing awareness N %
A	8	113 100	19 17	28 25	34 30	12 11	20 18
B	16	274 100	47 17	70 26	121 44	73 27	29 11
C	4	59 100	14 24	13 22	17 29	6 10	15 25
D	12	215 100	53 25	70 33	65 30	7 3	20 9
E	8	96 100	26 27	22 23	34 35	5 5-	39 41
F	22	345 100	67 19	31 9	82 24	65 19	119 34
G	6	106 100	22 21	10 9	50 47	16 15	8 8
H	4	60 100	16 27	10 17	19 32	4 7	11 18
J	9	90 100	19 21	16 18	23 26	24 27	13 14
K	3	31 100	7 22	8 26	9 29	1 3	6 19
Total	92	1,389 100	290 21	278 20	454 33	213 15	280 20

Note: In some interviews more than one activity was coded as 'most important'.

by the relative importance attributed to the five activities between officers are related to outcome.

OUTCOME AND THE IMPORTANCE OF ACTIVITIES

We have seen that there are differences between probation officers in terms of the importance they attribute to different types of activity; we therefore investigated whether there was any relationship between outcome and the relative importance attached to the five activities. Their distribution over the five outcome groups is shown in Table B6.

Only small differences were found in the frequencies with which 'exploration', 'structuring' and 'enhancing awareness' were rated as the most important activity in each outcome group, but a considerable difference was found in the frequency with which 'direction' was rated as the most important activity. 'Direction' was least often mentioned as the most important activity in cases in groups A1 (10 per cent) and B (9 per cent), and most often in cases in groups A2 and X. There seemed to be a tendency for officers to report use of 'direction' more often when clients were not making progress towards achieving tasks.

Conversely, there is a slight indication that 'encouragement' was rated as the most important activity more frequently in successful task-centred cases than in unsuccessful ones. 'Encouragement' was the most important activity in 39 per cent of cases in outcome group A1, 32 per cent in outcome groups A2 and B, 31 per cent in group X and 27 per cent in group Y. The results may indicate a tendency for officers to use 'encouragement' as a reinforcing agent more often when clients are making progress towards achieving tasks.

These apparent differences between outcome groups in the reported use of direction and encouragement seem to us to be worth noting, and to reflect real differences in probation officers' approaches to their clients (as opposed to different descriptions of essentially similar styles of intervention). We doubt that this association is a causal one in the sense that, for example, more emphasis on 'encouragement' would lead to a better chance of task-centred success, but suspect that this association illustrates probation officers' responses to achieving and non-achieving or conforming and non-conforming clients.

SUMMARY AND CONCLUSIONS

In answer to our four original questions we have found that:

(1)   Some probation officers had a higher percentage of successful outcomes among their clients than did others, although the differences in success rates could not be tested for statistical significance.

Table B6 Outcome and Importance of Activity

Outcome group	No. of cases analysed	No. of interviews analysed N %	Activity				
			Exploration N %	Structuring N %	Encouragement N %	Direction N %	Enhancing awareness N %
A1	19	311 100	71 23	63 20	120 39	32 10	61 20
A2	22	361 100	63 17	66 18	114 32	71 20	75 21
B	19	262 100	58 22	61 23	85 32	23 9	45 17
X	15	289 100	56 19	56 19	90 31	63 22	55 19
Y	17	166 100	42 25	32 19	45 27	24 14	44 27
Total	92	1,389 100	290 21	278 20	454 33	213 15	280 20

Note: In some interviews more than one activity was coded as 'most important'.

(2) There was a slight tendency for more successful officers to have more interviews with cases than less successful ones, but differences in the number of interviews per case in outcome groups appeared to be related to the length of contact.

(3) There is a tendency (see Chapter 14) for the most successful cases to contain a higher proportion of interviews in which some work on a task was carried out, in many 'failures' a considerable number of interviews also contained work on the task.

(4) There are some weak indications that success may be associated with the methods of intervention used in the interviews. But, as the emphasis on different methods varied somewhat between officers without showing any strong pattern in relation to success, it is unlikely that this association is simple or direct.

Thus, while this investigation gives us some grounds for believing that input and outcome are related, we have found no evidence that the association is either simple or obvious, and still less that there is a cause and effect relationship between the two.

APPENDIX TO PART III
RESEARCH INSTRUMENTS

————

BASELINE

(1) Patients' account of parasuicide
(2) Medical seriousness
(3) Present State Examination (PSE)
     (Wing, Cooper and Sartorius, 1974)
(4) Psychiatric data sheet
(5) Beck Depression Inventory (BDI)
     (Beck, Ward and Mendelson, 1961)
(6) Beck Suicidal Intent Scale (SIS)
     (Beck, Herman and Schuyler, 1974)
(7) Risk of repetition scale
     (Buglass and Horton, 1974)
(8) Social Problems Questionnaire
(9) Demographic data sheet

Social Work
(1) Task-centred casework record
(2) Final interview

Follow-Up
(1) Satisfaction with service questionnaire
(2) Beck Depression Inventory (see above)
(3) Social Problems Questionnaire (see above)
(4) General Practitioner services record
(5) Psychiatric services record
(6) Social services/probation services record

The instruments are available to inquirers at the Social Work Studies Department, University of Southampton.

INDEX